Meeting Jesus

To Randy,
with warm regards
in Christ,
Bill Brownson

MEETING
JESUS

Through the Good News in Mark

William C. Brownson

BAKER BOOK HOUSE
Grand Rapids, Michigan 49516

Published by Baker Books,
a division of Baker Book House Company
P.O. Box 6287, Grand Rapids, Michigan 49516-6287
ISBN 0-8010-1036-5
Printed in the United States of America

Unless otherwise noted, all Scripture references are taken from the Revised Standard Version of the Bible, copyright 1946, 1952, 1971, and 1973 by the Division of Christian Education of the National Council of the Churches of Christ in the United States of America. Other versions cited include the New International Version (NIV), King James Version (KJV), New King James Version (NKJV), and New Revised Standard Version (NRSV).

Contents

Preface

THIS BOOK IS ABOUT JESUS. It springs from the fast-moving, action-packed Gospel according to Mark. It focuses on what various contemporaries said about Jesus, on persons who encountered him and were changed, and on the heart of what he taught. It paints a vivid picture of the matchless one called Christ.

Those who have never heard of Jesus can learn to know and follow him through this witness. Those who have served him for years can be renewed and heartened in their labors as they once again see Jesus in the simple terms of the inexhaustible gospel.

Each chapter of this book was originally written as a radio message for listeners who have never known Jesus. All of the messages have now been broadcast on every continent and in a number of languages. As each radio message was given it included God's gracious invitation to repent and receive Jesus, to trust and follow him. Many listeners have responded.

This is a book for all who yearn to grasp the living center of the Christian message. It comes with questions for reflection and discussion at the end of each chapter. It goes out with prayer that through its use Jesus will be better known and served.

1

The Gospel of Jesus Christ

The beginning of the gospel of Jesus Christ, the Son of God.

[Mark 1:1]

IT WAS IN THE ROME OF THE CAESARS, when the infamous Nero was emperor, that it appeared—the first written gospel. This was a new form of popular literature. Nothing like it had ever been composed before.

We've all heard about epic poetry. In that connection, the name of Homer is the first that comes to mind. His Greek *Iliad* and *Odyssey* introduced the world to what we call the epic poem. It was the ancient Romans who first developed the form of literature called satire, a commentary in verse on some prevailing vice or folly. But it was a Jewish Christian named John Mark, also in Rome, who first produced about A.D. 65 a gospel. (There would be three other gospels named for their authors: Matthew, Luke, and John.)

Here are the first words that Mark wrote: "The beginning of the gospel of Jesus Christ, the Son of God." Think what that means: "the gospel of Jesus Christ."

The word itself, *gospel*, meaning good message or good news, was well known in the ancient Roman world. When a mighty ruler began his reign, or when a son was born in the royal house, this was called gospel, good tidings. An event that introduced something new to the world or a happening charged with special significance for the future was gospel. Our modern world has had an experience like that recently in the German city of Berlin. Suddenly, in November 1989, an event of enormous meaning for the whole world took place. The Berlin Wall came down! That for all of us was gospel, good news. It altered the human situation in Germany. It quickened joy and hope throughout the world.

When John Mark wrote this book that we call a gospel, he was celebrating something like that, something even more grand and world transforming. A new state of affairs for mankind had arrived because God's promises were being fulfilled and his salvation was at hand. John Mark's little nation of Israel had cherished this hope for centuries. Throughout her sacred Scriptures—what we call today the Old Testament—there throbbed a thrilling kind of expectation. The God whom Israel worshiped as Creator and Lord over all, the one who had entered into covenant with them at Mt. Sinai, had promised a great future for his people. His salvation was coming to the world. That would mean both rescue from danger and distress and a marvelous restoration. God would come to set his people free and give them new life. For John Mark and other Hebrew believers, God's coming as the gracious Deliverer was gospel, good news.

Who was the gospel about? Mark makes that plain in the very first sentence. It's about Jesus. Jesus was probably born during the year 4 B.C. He was born into a poor family in the Judean village of Bethlehem and spent his childhood years in the tiny Galilean town of Nazareth.

In some ways his life seems quite ordinary. It was relatively brief; he lived only about thirty-three years. He never traveled outside the borders of his own little country. He held no public office, commanded no armies, wrote no books. When he died, he possessed nothing but the clothes on his body. He never had advanced schooling and, apart from the Hebrew Scriptures, never read widely. Though he was immensely popular at one point in his career, he saw most of his followers turn away. Some of them eventually even clamored for his death. At the end he was rejected by his own nation and put to death by the Roman authorities. After going through the cruelest torture imaginable, he died a death reserved for the vilest criminals. He was crucified at the time of the Jewish Passover about A.D. 30.

Still, the gospel, as Mark relates it, is all about Jesus. We read a good deal in Mark about Jesus' teaching, though not as much as in the later gospels. In this swiftly moving drama, we also witness his mighty works, the expressions of remarkable power in his ministry. But most of all, strangely, we are told about his sufferings.

Someone has called Mark's Gospel "a passion narrative with an extended introduction." In other words, everything seems to lead up to the events surrounding Jesus' suffering, death, and resurrection. Almost one-half of the sixteen chapters of the book describe this final period of Jesus' ministry. Apparently, it is in his cross and resurrection victory that the gospel is most clearly seen. Here the ancient promises are fulfilled and the world-changing events occur.

One thing Mark wants to tell us about Jesus is that he is the Christ. *Christ* is the Greek word meaning "the anointed one." It corresponds to the Hebrew word *messiah* and describes someone chosen, set apart, and equipped by God for a mission. In the Old Testament, before someone began a special mission, he was anointed with oil. Kings were anointed as they began their reigns. Priests were anointed as they entered their religious service. Prophets were anointed to speak God's truth. This anointing with oil was a sign that God's Spirit was coming on these people, enduing them with gifts and power to fulfill God's mission.

But all those anointings were partial and temporary. The Old Testament witness pointed consistently forward to a great high priest, a prophet like Moses, the supreme king yet to come in David's line. When he came, the one in whom all the promises were to be fulfilled, he would be *the* anointed one, *the* Messiah, *the* Christ. Mark wants us to see that this long-awaited person is none other than Jesus.

Jesus didn't begin his ministry with a claim to be the Messiah. In fact, when people began to believe this about him, he urged them not to tell anyone. Apparently Jesus didn't want to encourage popular misconceptions about what kind of Messiah was coming, but he never denied that he was the Messiah, the Christ. And when one of his disciples, Simon Peter, blurted out in Caesarea Philippi, "You are the Christ," Jesus accepted his witness, acknowledging it as true. For the time being, though, he told his disciples "to tell no one about him."

At this point in their lives the disciples had a very limited understanding of what it meant that Jesus was the Christ. He had to teach them over and over again that suffering, rejection, and death lay ahead for him. He accepted their witness to himself but then helped them to understand more fully what that meant.

In largely Gentile Rome where Mark wrote his gospel it may not have seemed significant that Jesus was the Jewish Messiah, the Christ. What did they know about the Hebrew Scriptures? Of what interest were these ancient prophecies to the citizens of imperial Rome, the greatest power in the world? Maybe you feel as they did. You're not sure about this business of Jesus being the Christ. Even if it's true, you can't see that it has anything to do with your life. You aren't Jewish. You don't live in Palestine. What does Jesus have to do with you? In what sense are his life, death, and resurrection a gospel for you?

John Mark makes another claim in the opening words of his gospel. He says not only that Jesus is Israel's Messiah but also that he is God's Son.

To Mark, God was the majestic creator of the heavens and the earth, the one who preserves and rules over all that he has made. He was the God of Abraham, Isaac, and Jacob—the one who had entered into covenant with his people and bound himself with solemn promises. He was the holy Lord who loves what is right and hates what is evil. He was the God who had revealed his will to Israel in the Ten Commandments and his saving purpose through the words of his prophets. To Mark, God was the holy one, infinitely high above and separate from all the works of his hands. He was the Almighty, the Eternal, so exalted that he could look far down on the heavens and the earth.

Now for the truly staggering claim: According to Mark, this Jesus who was born in Bethlehem and died in Jerusalem has always been the Son of the Most High God. He has shared God's being from the beginning. He revealed in a full and final way God's nature and purpose. He is the everlasting, almighty God who became a human being like ourselves. John the Baptist bore witness to this fact by saying that Jesus is infinitely worthy. God the Father spoke from heaven at his baptism, "You are my beloved Son." The demons of hell recognize that Jesus is the Son of the Most High. And at the end of Mark's Gospel, it is a soldier—a Roman at that—who after watching Jesus die, says with trembling awe, "Truly, this man was the Son of God." That, for Mark, is the gospel.

This Gospel was not written as a biography of Jesus, although he is its central figure. It isn't designed as a history book, although it includes a wealth of historical data. The Gospel is a written compilation of what Jesus' apostles had been preaching throughout the Roman Empire for over thirty years. The aim of that preaching and of this Gospel was to create faith. When they had told their story and borne their witness, they would invite their hearers to respond. More than anything else in the world, they wanted them to believe in Jesus.

This Gospel of Christ is good news even before you hear about it and whether you believe it or not. Mark is announcing what God has done, how God's saving plan has broken into our history. He's telling how in the ministry, suffering, death, and rising of Jesus, God has done something new and wonderful that transforms the world. It's great good news for everyone that God so loved the world that he came in the person of his Son to dwell among us. It's good news that he went about doing good, healing and helping, forgiving and transforming people. It's supremely good news that in his death, he somehow suffered what we deserve, bearing our sins and dying in our place. And it is good news beyond imagining that on the third day God raised him from the dead and offers now to all who will believe in him, forgiveness and everlasting life.

But reading Mark's Gospel may be something like hearing read a deceased person's will. You hear what disposition he or she has made of the property involved and learn the names of the beneficiaries of the estate, but that probably seems dull and tedious unless you happen to hear your own name mentioned. Then you perk up your ears. Then the reading quickens interest because you know it's meant for you.

It's the same with the gospel of Jesus Christ. It becomes your good news in a vital, personal sense when you realize that it's meant for you. When you see Jesus' coming into the world as an event that makes everything different for you, when you name him as the Christ, the long-awaited Messiah of God, and when you worship him as the Son of the

Most High God, the Gospel according to Mark becomes the gospel according to you, the most wonderful news that you have ever heard. If you have never said it, you may want to say now someting like this: Yes, I see it. In Jesus of Nazareth, God has acted for the salvation of the world and to save me. Praise God! I now believe.

Study Questions

1. What does the word *gospel* mean?
2. How do you explain the concentration of the book on Jesus' suffering, death, and resurrection?
3. What is the significance of calling Jesus the Christ?
4. What difference does it make to you that Jesus is God's Son?
5. Why do you think Mark's gospel was written?

2

Speaking of Jesus: John the Baptist

<hr/>

After me comes he who is mightier than I, the thong of whose sandals I am not worthy to stoop down and untie. I have baptized you with water; but he will baptize you with the Holy Spirit.

[Mark 1:7–8]

IN THE GOSPEL ACCORDING TO MARK, we meet a number of people who give their assessment of who Jesus is. The first of these is John the Baptist. We know a good deal about John. He was born in about 5 B.C. of godly Jewish parents, both of whom were in the priestly line in Israel. He grew up in the hill country of Judea. The circumstances of his birth were unusual. When his father, Zechariah, was performing his priestly duties in the temple in Jerusalem, an angel appeared to him and promised that he, though of advanced age, would father a son. He was to name the boy John and was to bring him up as a Nazarite, like the Old Testament greats Samson and Samuel. Zechariah was told that John would be filled with the Holy Spirit from his birth and would prepare the people of Israel for the coming of the Lord.

The first thing of note about John in the Gospel according to Mark is that he was a man of the wilderness. He apparently spent his early years in seclusion out in the desert near his home, west of the Dead Sea. He lived simply—on the locusts he gathered in the wilderness and on wild honey. He began to be noticed by others in about A.D. 26. It was during one of Israel's sabbatical years when people had been relieved of labor in the fields and had leisure for other things. John began to preach in the wilderness by the Jordan River. He must have been a striking figure, clothed with camel's hair and wearing a leather girdle around his waist. Instantly he reminded people of the great Old Testament prophet Elijah, another man who had roamed the desert, scorning the luxury and corruption of the rich and powerful. John, like Elijah, came to his contemporaries out of nowhere, fresh from communion with the living God.

The people of God know about the wilderness from their history. It was there that God had guided and provided for them after their miraculous escape from Egypt. Prophets like Hosea, Amos, and Isaiah often spoke of that wilderness period as the time of Israel's true sonship to God. When they called the people in their generation to repent, they called them back to this beginning of God's history with his people. It was a call to return to the wilderness, to come back to God and the close relationship they had known with him there.

Their understanding of the wilderness was the reason the people of John's day found it so significant that he haunted the desert places and preached there. His message, like that of the prophets of old, was a clear, poignant, powerful call to repentance. He summoned the people back to God, to a new start in their relationship with him. He called them to recognize again their dependence on the Lord of heaven and earth, to exchange pride for humility, and to acknowledge their wanderings and confess their sins. They must flee from the wrath to come. Repent! repent! repent! was the burden of John's message.

John called the people to repent and be baptized. The people of Israel knew about water baptism. It was a rite used to receive proselytes into the community of faith. We have learned from recent archeological discoveries that water baptism was also used as the rite of initiation into some of the religious communities in Israel. John encouraged all of God's people to be baptized. John's insistence on baptism was a prophetic sign, so singular and striking to his generation that he became known simply as John the Baptist or John the Baptizer. What a spectacle he must have been, standing in the midst of the waters of the Jordan, baptizing people one after another as they confessed their sins!

This man made an enormous impression on his generation. Though he stayed in the wilderness and preached by the Jordan, people came to him from everywhere, not only country folk from the surrounding area of Judea but multitudes from Jerusalem also, including the religious leaders of his day. For almost 400 years no prophet had appeared in Israel, but the people who heard John the Baptizer knew that he came with an authentic word from God. He was the man of the hour. His bold preaching was the most exciting thing that had happened in Israel for a long time.

This gave his words about Jesus special significance. John was regarded, like no one in memory, as a man through whom the word of the Lord had come. He described himself in Old Testament words from Isaiah, Malachi, and Exodus as a "messenger" from God, "a voice crying in the wilderness." Everything about the Baptizer's ministry bore witness to a greater than human power. How did he attract people from villages and hamlets and crowded cities to come out to him in the desert? Whence the magnetism that drew people to his side and made them willing to accept baptism at his hand? Why the awe of him awakened in the hearts of learned religious teachers and powerful rulers? No one had shaken Jewish culture to its foundations as John had in his meteoric rise to distinction. But he discounts all that. Famous and influential though he became, John refused to call attention to himself. He saw himself as a witness, a finger pointing, a voice proclaiming someone else. "After me," thundered John, "comes he who is mightier than I." The man of whom he spoke was the son of his mother's cousin, Jesus, from little Nazareth.

John continued, "I am not worthy to stoop down and untie the thong of his sandals." That was a menial service. It was something that no student or disciple was expected to do, even for a revered rabbi. Only a slave would stoop down and untie someone's sandals. But John says, I'm not worthy to do that for the one who is coming after me. In other words, he is so vastly superior to me that it would be a great honor for me to perform for him the service of a slave.

Imagine the effect of that on his hearers. Everyone regarded John as a holy man. He lived above reproach, loving righteousness, hating evil, walking single-mindedly in the will of God. His contemporaries saw him as a moral and spiritual giant, but John refused to bask in their admiration or to cultivate a personal following. Look at Jesus, he said. He is supremely worthy.

The message was the same when John compared his work with that of the one who was to follow him. "I have baptized you with water; but he will baptize you with the Holy Spirit." John's work was in the natural order; Jesus would perform a work in the realm of the Spirit. John was doing what an ordinary man could do; Jesus' work would be miraculous, imbued with heavenly power. John could apply water to the body as an outward sign of God's cleansing; Jesus would cleanse peoples' hearts and make them new with the gift of God's Spirit.

So it was that John bore witness to Jesus' true identity. John, viewed by many as the greatest man of his generation, considered Jesus far greater than himself. John, the holiest of men, declares himself unworthy to kneel before Jesus. John, the agent of the Most High, points to the one in whom God had come to visit his people. John was the voice crying in the wilderness:

> Prepare the way of the Lord,
>   make straight in the desert a highway for our God.
> Every valley shall be lifted up,
>   and every mountain and hill be made low;
> the uneven ground shall become level,
>   and the rough places a plain.
>   [Isa. 40:3–4]

John was saying, Let there be in the midst of the wilderness, and more profoundly in the hearts of people, a way prepared, a highway for the King!

I believe that John was a true prophet of the Lord in the succession of Elijah, Isaiah, Jeremiah, and the rest. He spoke fearlessly the word of the Lord, affirming that Jesus is the incomparably mighty one, the uniquely worthy one, the one who gives the Holy Spirit, the Lord himself from heaven.

John, as God's messenger, had no choice but to relate the message. He had nothing to gain from it. In fact, this kind of preaching eventually led to his imprisonment and execution. He could have had the world at his feet, it seemed, but he gave it all away by pointing to someone else, a slightly younger man, a relative.

God's call to John must have been compelling. The word of the Lord must have been for him, as it was for Jeremiah, a "fire in his bones" so that he couldn't stop proclaiming it even if he had wanted to. And John must have believed passionately that Jesus was indeed Israel's promised Messiah, the everlasting Word made flesh, the Lord who would visit his people and bring salvation.

John had ventured his entire life on this conviction: In Jesus, God was about to do a new thing. In Jesus, the kingly rule of God was about to break into human history in an unprecedented way. John was standing on the threshold of the most momentous event in the history of the world: The God of Abraham, Isaac, and Jacob was coming to save and to rule. All the people needed to be prepared.

John proclaimed this faith and preached this word with one consuming end in view: to lead all those whom he addressed to repentance. There is no way to prepare the Lord's way, to open our hearts to his reign, apart from repentance. It's our sin that blocks the way, our rebellion that impedes his coming, our pride that leaves no room for him. So John calls all his hearers to repent. As the other gospel writers tell us, he makes that call explicit for particular groups of people. "Bear fruit that befits repentance," he said. Don't simply confess your sins and receive baptism but turn from them to God and begin a new life. If you have two coats, he says, then share with the person who has none. If you have food enough and to spare, give some to the hungry. If you're a tax collector, then collect no more than is right. No more heartless gouging of the poor, no more greed and extortion. If you're a soldier, he says, "rob no one by violence or by false accusation and be content with your wages."

We, too, must take John's words to heart. Whatever we have done that breaks God's law and grieves his heart, whatever destroys our integrity or wounds other people, we must hate. We must turn from it, for the Kingdom of God draws near. He comes in judgment and he comes in forgiveness.

Study Questions

1. How was John the Baptist like Elijah?
2. Why was John's witness to Jesus so impressive?
3. How would Jesus' work differ from John's?
4. How does the call to repent apply to your life today?

3

Speaking of Jesus: God the Father

◆

In those days Jesus came from Nazareth of Galilee and was baptized by John in the Jordan. And when he came up out of the water, immediately he saw the heavens opened and the Spirit descending upon him like a dove; and a voice came from heaven, "Thou art my beloved Son; with thee I am well pleased."

[Mark 1:9–11]

I BELONG TO A GROUP that meets about once a month to study a book that we all have read. Not long ago the book we considered was one that I had just written. As you can imagine, that gathering was an especially exciting one for me. The members of the group were going to talk about work that I had labored on for years. I especially valued their input because of the kind of people they are. They are intelligent and discerning and well equipped to evaluate literary content and style. More than that, they are good, upright people whose reactions and opinions I greatly respect. Best of all, they are good friends who know me and care about me. How eager I was that night to hear what they would say!

All of us, I suppose, appreciate reliable feedback about who we are and what we do. We like it especially when fine people like my friends tell us what they think. What if it were possible to know what God thinks about us? What if we could have his verdict, his evaluation, on our lives?

What if there could be some voice from heaven in which the Almighty would say, this is who you are and this is how I feel about you and the life you have lived. Feedback from the one who knows everything about you, who loves you most and best, and whose judgments are infinitely right and good would be the ultimate in feedback.

In the Gospel according to Mark, we learn that something like this actually happened to Jesus of Nazareth. We read these words from the first chapter of that Gospel, beginning at verse 9: "In those days Jesus came from Nazareth of Galilee and was baptized by John in the Jordan. And when he came up out of the water, immediately he saw the heavens opened and the Spirit descending upon him like a dove; and a voice came from heaven, 'Thou art my beloved Son; with thee I am well pleased.'" This was Almighty God's appraisal of Jesus.

Jesus was at the Jordan River when God spoke his approval. As we have noted, John the Baptizer had been drawing great crowds by his fervent preaching in which he called the people to repent, to turn toward God, and to receive water baptism at his hand. Water baptism was a sign of a changed heart accompanied by a confession of sins. A kind of religious awakening was going on there by the waters of the Jordan. Many were profoundly affected by it.

Now Jesus came to be baptized. What could that mean? John himself was puzzled and uneasy at the prospect. We learn in Matthew's Gospel that he said to Jesus, "I need to be baptized by you, and do you come to me?" (Matt. 3:14).

We can understand his feelings. John knew that Jesus was a blameless man. He had said earlier that he, John, was not worthy to stoop down and untie the thong of Jesus' sandals. John had been preaching to sinners. Jesus was not in that category. John was calling for repentance and confession, but in the presence of Jesus, the Baptizer knew that he himself needed to repent and confess. Do you mean it, Jesus? he might have said. Do you really want me to baptize you?

Here was Jesus' answer, "Let it be so now; for thus it is fitting for us to fulfil all righteousness" (Matt. 3:15). Jesus understood John's reluctance and accepted the reason for it, but he wasn't deterred. He wanted to be baptized. He knew it was profoundly appropriate—a fulfillment of God's holy will.

John had introduced Jesus as the one who would baptize with the Holy Spirit, cleanse people, and make them new with the gift of God's own Spirit. Now Jesus said it was fitting that he should be baptized with a sinner's baptism. The only way to understand this is to see it as a way for Jesus to identify with others. Jesus, though he had no sin of his own to confess, was expressing his oneness with sinful people. He was taking on himself what was theirs and committing himself to be their representative. By being baptized, he was acknowledging that God's judgment upon rebellious Israel was just but he was also identifying himself with the guilty people who needed pardon and release. In the waters of the Jordan, Jesus took on himself the responsibility for the sins and wrongs of others. His baptism meant a solidarity with the people, a complete commitment of himself to them.

One of the times in the Old Testament when the people of Israel had disobeyed God's commands and wandered away into idolatry, God was ready to let his judgment descend on them. God told Moses that he would begin all over again with him and his family, but Moses couldn't bear to have that happen. He interceded on behalf of his people, praying that they might be spared, but if that could not be, then he was ready to perish with them. Thus he identified himself with the people in their guilt and condemnation. Here is Jesus by the waters of the Jordan doing that in a far more profound way.

Mark says that when Jesus had been baptized and had come up out of the water, the heavens "opened." You might call this a kind of breakthrough from above. God was making direct contact with the earth; it was a heavenly visitation. It's interesting to notice that the same verb is used here as is used to describe what happened after Jesus' crucifixion when the veil in the temple at Jerusalem was torn in two from top to bottom. That was another heavenly rending. In both cases, God was acting to bring together heaven and earth. He was overcoming distance and initiating togetherness and reconciliation with mankind.

What could be seen at the Jordan River was a dove, fluttering down from heaven and alighting on Jesus. Proverbially, the dove is harmless, gentle, affectionate, often a symbol of peace. In this case, the descent of the dove was the visible expression of a reality that could not be seen.

God's own Spirit was coming on Jesus to equip him for his life's work. The one who, according to John, would later baptize others with the Spirit, was himself being so anointed. Jesus later quoted from the prophet Isaiah to that same effect, "The Spirit of the Lord is upon me, because he has anointed me to preach good news to the poor. He has sent me to proclaim release to the captives and recovering of sight to the blind" (Luke 4:18).

We aren't told that the crowds lining the Jordan River saw the descending dove, but it seems that at least John the Baptist did. Jesus surely did. This was powerful confirmation to him at the outset of his public ministry that he was indeed the Messiah, the one anointed by God for a great mission.

Then came the Father's word: "You are my beloved son; with you I am well pleased." We don't know whether or not anyone else heard this. The words seem addressed to Jesus, "*You* are my beloved son; with *you* I am well pleased." Perhaps they were meant for his ears alone and we only know about them because he later related them to his followers. For Jesus the message was unmistakably clear. God was confirming Jesus' inner conviction. God was powerfully underlining mysterious things that Jesus had been reading in the Hebrew Scriptures, in which God was speaking of him and to him, revealing his true identity. There were references to the suffering servant, the compassionate king, and the prophet like Moses. This son of Mary, born in a totally unprecedented way and living on earth as a genuine human being, was now declared to be Son of the Most High God, which meant that he shared God's being and came forth from his heart. That's the word from heaven; that's the word of the Father about Jesus: "You are my beloved Son."

Between the Father and his Son, there had always been a relationship with a bond of unity and perfect love. The man who came up from the waters of the Jordan had been from all eternity the object of his heavenly Father's special favor. Now God was saying something about Jesus' life as a human being. He had lived for some thirty years in the home of his parents. He had learned to work in Joseph's carpenter shop. As the Gospel writer puts it, he had "increased in wisdom and in stature, and in favor with God and man" (Luke 2:52). It was about this career on earth, this adventure in the art of living, that the Father said, "In you I am well pleased." God, looking down, liked what he saw.

When I read that, I think of another divine investigation recorded in the Old Testament in Psalm 14.

> The LORD looks down from heaven upon the children of men,
>> to see if there are any that act wisely,
>> that seek after God.
> They have all gone astray, they are all alike corrupt;
>> there is none that does good,
>> no, not one.
>
> [Ps. 14:2–3]

That's the way it was until Jesus walked the earth. But finally, there was one who did act wisely, who sought after God, and who did what was good. God could no longer say from heaven, "No, not one." Now he looked down from heaven on the human life of his Son and saw nothing that did not please him. This is what the Almighty had intended a human life to be like.

Maybe the word of approval had special reference to what had just happened, to Jesus' act of obedience in being baptized and his identification with the sinful people whom God longed to save. When Jesus took on himself the weight of our sins and set out on the road that was to lead to a cross, God said, "That's good!"

What does it mean for us, this word from heaven? It surely says to us that God has set his seal on Jesus. He would continue to do that all through our Lord's ministry, attesting to the truth of his claims again and again by works of power and compassion. He would do it supremely and finally after Jesus' crucifixion when he raised him from the dead on the third day. But all of that would simply confirm the word with which Jesus' ministry had begun. God has given us strong and moving reasons to believe that this Jesus is indeed the Son of God, the Savior of the world.

Later, God would declare from heaven how Jesus' identity should affect the way that all of his disciples live. On the mount where Jesus was transfigured and met with great saints of the past, God said in the afterglow, "This is my beloved Son . . . listen to him." God's assessment of Jesus should mean that we acknowledge him as our Lord and devote ourselves henceforth to hearing and heeding his word. That's the difference it should make that he is the Son of the Blessed and has lived a blameless life of obedience to God. He abundantly deserves our allegiance. Remember the Father's word about him, "You are my beloved Son; in you I am well pleased." Jesus comes, you might say, well recommended!

Study Questions

1. Why did Jesus submit to baptism? What was different about it for him?
2. What was the significance of the descending dove?
3. How do you think the words from heaven affected Jesus?
4. What response should they bring forth from us?

4

Speaking of Jesus: His Family

◆

Then Jesus entered a house, and again a crowd gathered, so that he and his disciples were not even able to eat. When his family heard about this, they went to take charge of him, for they said, "He is out of his mind."

[Mark 3:20–21 NIV]

WHAT DID JESUS' FAMILY MEMBERS have to say about him? That's an interesting question, isn't it? These are brothers and sisters who grew up in the same home and cousins or other relatives who knew him well. What did they think of his ministry? How did the things he said and did affect them?

These verses from Mark may surprise or shock you. It's the sort of thing you wouldn't expect to find in one of the Gospels. If I had been writing one of those books and had desired, as those writers did, to lead others to believe in Jesus, I wonder if I would have included this passage. It's too unsettling. It raises too many questions. But here it is in the Gospel according to Mark, one of the evidences that this is an authentic, reliable witness.

Why would Jesus' family members say, "He is out of his mind"? All we are told in this passage is that when Jesus was in a home (perhaps the one in Capernaum that belonged to Simon and Andrew), people thronged around him. The pressure was so great, the demands so many, that Jesus and his followers "were not even able to eat." That's the report Jesus' siblings and relatives heard.

They knew that his ministry was creating a sensation in Galilee: all these crowds, all these needy people, all these reports of miraculous healing and deliverance. That was exciting to his immediate family but also disturbing. What was he doing out there? This didn't seem like the Jesus they knew. There was so much publicity and controversy. They were disturbed because he sometimes didn't go along with their advice. Once before at a Jerusalem feast, his brothers had said to him, "Leave here and go to Judea, that your disciples may see the works you are doing" (John 7:3). But Jesus had responded, "My time has not yet come" (John 7:6). Once when his mother told him at the wedding in Cana of Galilee that there was no wine, he answered, "O woman, what have you to do with me? My hour has not yet come" (John 2:4). When people, even well-meaning people close to him, tried to remonstrate with him about going to Jerusalem, tried to rescue him or tell him what to do, he was notably unmoved. Did this show that he was out of his mind and beyond control? Or did it evidence control of a higher kind? Was Jesus listening to another voice, bowing to a supreme authority? That's what he had said, wasn't it? "My food is to do the will of him who sent me, and to accomplish his work" (John 4:34). "As the Father gave me commandment, even so I do" (John 14:31 KJV).

Now they were hearing that Jesus and his disciples were so beset by the crowds that they weren't even able to eat, and they became even more anxious. Jesus, apparently, was so caught up in this new movement, whatever it was, that he was forgetting about his basic needs. He wasn't taking care of himself. Surely, this wasn't normal. Jesus had never acted like that before. The whole situation appeared ominous to his loved ones and intervention seemed an urgent necessity. They were so concerned that they went out after him, intent on bringing him back home, even if they had to carry him off bodily. They feared, "He's out of his mind."

The word that his family members used to describe Jesus' condition is the root from which we get our word *ecstasy*, which means "a standing outside." Someone in ecstasy is so carried away, so transported, we say, as to be beyond reason and control. Jesus' family members feared that they couldn't talk sense to him any longer, that he wouldn't listen to reason and wouldn't let his activities be curbed.

There were other things in the life and ministry of Jesus that might have given people this impression. For one, there was a tremendous sense of intensity about him, a burning sense of mission. He talked about having to go to Jerusalem and how he must suffer there. He wouldn't let himself be dissuaded from that. He had a cup to drink, he said, a baptism with which to be baptized, and he was constrained until it should all be accomplished. He talked mysteriously about his destiny. That must have impressed some people as strange.

Then there was his urgent drive to minister—to do good. "[I] must work the works of him who sent me, while it is day," he said; "night comes, when no one can work" (John 9:4). He moved on from city to city preaching. He spent long, draining hours in ministry to all kinds of human need. In the course of his ministry, he visited the most despised people of his day. He ate with social outcasts. He even reached out to touch people who were unclean through leprosy. No one had ever done that kind of thing before. And so people reacted to him in the most extreme ways. Many of Israel's most respected citizens were scandalized by the way he acted. What was behind it? What kept driving Jesus on?

His zeal for God and the astonishing acceptance he showed toward scorned and rejected people were unusual, to say the least. It's interesting, though, that this sort of thing should be interpreted as insanity. We don't marvel at the fervor that people show in other pursuits, do we? Who calls someone caught up passionately in the pursuit of wealth unbalanced? When people are carried away in some amorous intrigue or when they throw themselves with abandon into a revolutionary cause, we don't tend to question their sanity, do we? Watch them as they go into the wildest contortions as performers. We admire such people. We see them as talented and shrewd. We don't call them crazy. Is Jesus out of his mind because he cares so much and because all his thoughts are centered in the Father's name and kingdom and will? Or is the very opposite true? Isn't the fear of the Lord the beginning of wisdom? Isn't having God in all our thoughts the highest kind of sanity?

Jesus didn't act according to conventional wisdom—that is certain. He wasn't like the ordinary religious teachers of his day. He didn't line up with the interests of any particular group in Israel. He repeatedly said things that made important people furious and acted in ways that left others plotting how to get rid of him.

He made stupendous claims about himself. "Before Abraham was, I am" (John 8:58). "All authority in heaven and on earth has been given to me" (Matt. 28:18). "Come to me, all who labor and are heavy laden, and I will give you rest" (Matt. 11:28). What man in his right mind would ever say things like that?

What does this tell us about these family members who said of Jesus, "He is out of his mind," and who determined to rescue him? On the positive side, it certainly demonstrates their concern. They cared about him. After all, he was one of their own, and they were apprehensive that he might be headed for trouble. They sensed danger in the circumstances they saw developing and they cared too much to ignore it and simply look the other way. In their eyes, Jesus needed help, and they felt a keen sense of responsibility for him. If they didn't go to him, if they didn't do what they could to bring him to his senses, who would? They were family.

Their intentions were good. They felt that if they could get him back home and have him under their care, he might be all right again. What could be better than rescuing someone you love from a bad situation? Let's give them due credit. They had caring hearts and the best intentions.

Still, it's obvious that they didn't understand. They showed no awareness of his vision, no appreciation of his heart for people. Though they had grown up with Jesus, it was evident that they didn't really know him. Imagine branding his zeal, his self-giving love, his passion to do God's will, as a kind of madness. True, it wasn't the same hostile charge that some of Jesus' enemies had made. They said that he was actually in league with the powers of evil. His loved ones didn't accuse Jesus of malice. On the contrary, they thought he was carrying benevolence and concern for others to an unhealthy extreme.

The family's most grievous error was that they didn't believe. They didn't take his claims about himself seriously. Having a merely human perspective on the situation, they were unable to see how powerfully God was at work in Jesus' life and ministry. On another occasion it's expressly said of his brothers that they did not believe in him. They seemed to dismiss what they couldn't fully understand about him and refused to trust even in the face of strong evidence. At one point Jesus had this to say about them: "A prophet is not without honor except in his own country and in his own house" (Matt. 13:57). How it must have wounded him that his family members would not follow him and even called him insane!

What do you think? Were these relatives right in their assessment? We can easily understand how they must have felt. There was no doubt that what was going on around Jesus was extraordinary. It had to be accounted for in some way. Either you had to say as the Pharisees did that he did all these things by Beelzebub, the prince of demons, or you had to say as others did that he was the Son of God. Some called him a troublemaker who led people astray. Try to imagine the kind of life and ministry that Jesus had that caused such strong, diverse reactions.

The reality of it was undeniable. He was doing amazing things. He was speaking as no man had ever spoken before. There had to be some way of accounting for all of this. Those who had known him as a child were unable to explain the transformation. They were troubled that he had become so different from them. The changes couldn't be explained by his background and upbringing. Was he indeed out of his mind? Was he living in a dream world? dangerously disconnected? Or was he more in touch with the real than anyone had ever been before as he walked in unclouded fellowship with God, his Father in heaven?

Mark doesn't stop to give us an answer. He simply writes down in the course of the narrative what various people said. He doesn't presume to tell us whether they were right or wrong, wise or foolish, righteous or wicked. In each case he lets us draw our own conclusions.

There's another important detail about Jesus' family members. A time came, after he had been crucified and raised from the dead on the third day, that they felt differently about him. Some of Jesus' brothers were in that group of believers who gathered in the upper room and experienced the marvelous outpouring of God's power on Pentecost. One of them, a brother named James, wrote a letter in which he spoke of Jesus as the "Lord of glory." He quoted Jesus frequently.

Somewhere along the line, he and the others had come to realize that what had seemed like foolishness in Jesus' teaching was really the wisdom of God and that the fiery zeal driving him on had been kindled in heaven. Some of the same family members who once were ready to institutionalize Jesus later came to worship him as Lord over all and to see his ministry as God's last, best word to the world. What a change of outlook!

Study Questions

1. Why might his family members have thought that Jesus was unbalanced?
2. What does this reveal about them—both positively and negatively?
3. Will living in God's way always strike the world as strange? Explain.
4. How would you account for the actions of Jesus? What was in his mind?

5

Speaking of Jesus: His Critics

◆

And the scribes who came down from Jerusalem said, "He is possessed by Beelzebul, and by the prince of demons he casts out the demons."

[Mark 3:22]

JESUS' FAMILY MEMBERS FEARED he was out of his mind. His enemies made a much more serious charge. They said he was not crazy but crafty, not deluded but demon-possessed! Let's try to understand that accusation, how Jesus responded to it, and what it all means for us today.

The scribes in this passage were apparently legal specialists. Their arrival in Galilee from Jerusalem suggests that by this time Jesus had caught the attention of the Sanhedrin, the ruling body of Israel's religious establishment. It's possible that the great Sanhedrin sent these scribes as official emissaries to examine Jesus' miracles and evaluate his ministry. If the decision proved unfavorable, Capernaum might have been declared a "seduced city," the prey of an apostate teacher. Such a verdict required, of course, a thorough investigation made on the spot by special envoys like these scribes. After a time of observation and consultation, they would make a public statement about their findings. This one was decidedly unflattering to Jesus.

The first indictment said that he was "possessed by Beelzebul." We don't know a great deal about the origin of that strange word, but it seems to have been a colloquial expression, a name local people gave in those days to the master strategist of evil, the wicked one, the devil. This arch-enemy of God at times gained possession of human beings through his agents who were called demons in the New Testament. Jesus, during the course of his ministry, encountered a number of people who were so possessed. Sometimes this possession affected the victim physically and produced certain ordinary diseases. One possessed boy is described as having a "deaf and dumb spirit" and exhibiting from time to time symptoms resembling those of epilepsy. Some have concluded from descriptions like this that at the time of Jesus' ministry people used demon possession as a way of accounting for physical and mental ills and their visible effects.

This doesn't take into account all the New Testament data about demons. At times they are heard to speak. They possess knowledge beyond that of human beings. They have a distinct individuality, not related to the one they are possessing. Jesus definitely recognized them as real, personal beings. He rebuked them on occasion and cast them out.

Now the scribes are saying that Jesus himself is demon possessed. This charge was designed, of course, to discredit Jesus and discourage his considerable following. If the people took this accusation seriously, they would want nothing to do with Jesus. As a man thought to be driven by demonic forces, he would be seen as unclean, unreliable, even dangerous.

The second part of the verdict was even more damaging. "By the prince of demons he casts out the demons." The crowds in Galilee had been marveling at the way Jesus could deliver people who were enslaved by evil powers. He was freeing them one after another from sin, possession, disease, and death. Now the scribes try to put that activity in a bad light. They give it a bizarre twist. Jesus is doing this, they claim, as the agent of the devil. In other words, a malignant power is at work in him. It only seems to be a good thing. Actually, in the view of the scribes, it is a kind of satanic conspiracy, a sinister deception. They are branding Jesus here as a kind of magician, an agent of hell who leads people astray by his tricks.

Sometimes Jesus ignored the vicious things that were said about him, but not this time. This was a charge too serious, too deadly, to let pass. Here's how he responded.

How can Satan cast out Satan? If a kingdom is divided against itself, that kingdom cannot stand. And if a house is divided against itself, that house will not be able to stand. And if Satan has risen up against himself and is divided, he cannot stand, but is coming to an end.

[Mark 3:23–26]

Jesus wanted his hearers to think through the scribes' accusation that he was casting out demons as the devil's agent. Does that really make sense? Would Satan want to drive out his own emissaries? Would he want to defeat his own plans? He may be monstrously evil, but no one has ever accused the devil of stupidity. The thought of Satan waging war against himself, opposing his own kingdom, pulling down his own house was too ridiculous to be considered seriously. Is it likely that the enemy of God and man would want to see people whole and forgiven, healthy and free, full of praise to God?

Then Jesus gave a different interpretation of what had happened. "But no one can enter a strong man's house," he said, "and plunder his goods, unless he first binds the strong man; then indeed he may plunder his house" (v. 27). The "strong man" that Jesus referred to here is Satan, prince of the kingdom of darkness. Jesus acknowledges both his existence and his power. Then he described his own ministry as an entering of the strong man's house and a plundering of his goods. Consistently, this is how Jesus spoke of what he had come to do. He had entered enemy-occupied territory. He had come into a world ravaged by the effects of sin and to a people who, by their disobedience and estrangement from God, had opened themselves to alien power. He knew the people around him were bound by sin and oppressed by Satan. By invading this present world system, Jesus had come right into the strong man's house with the express purpose of taking away his possessions. He had come to set Satan's captives free.

But would a strong man, a formidable enemy like Satan, let that happen? Surely, he wouldn't give up his captives willingly, but since someone stronger than he had come upon the scene, he had no choice. With Satan bound and his power neutralized, these deliverances could occur.

Jesus knew that he was stronger than the strong. His mission was to contest the dominion of evil powers at every point, subdue the devil, and destroy his works. The aim behind it all was that human beings, precious to God but preyed upon by Satan, might be released. Jesus knew that he was not Satan's agent but his adversary. Instead of serving the kingdom of darkness, he was overthrowing it. So far was he from being Satan's minion that he had mastered Satan altogether.

Now Jesus exposes the full seriousness of what the scribes have said.

> "Truly, I say to you, all sins will be forgiven the sons of men, and whatever blasphemies they utter; but whoever blasphemes against the Holy Spirit never has forgiveness, but is guilty of an eternal sin"—for they had said, "He has an unclean spirit."
>
> [Mark 3:28–30]

This passage has often been misunderstood, and the misunderstanding has brought much pain and distress to conscientious, struggling people. Jesus speaks here about what has been called the unpardonable sin: blasphemy against the Holy Spirit. It's crucially important that we understand what that is and what it is not. Remember the setting in which these words were spoken and why they were spoken. It was, as Jesus said, because of the accusation that the scribes had just made.

In a profound sense, their charge was not being made against Jesus himself. If the scribes or others had misjudged Jesus, if they had failed to see his glory, they could surely be forgiven for that. Many people have ignored Jesus, rejected him, even cursed him but have later repented and received forgiveness.

The source of Jesus' power over the demons was at issue here. Was it God's power or the devil's? from heaven or hell? Some kind of spiritual dynamic was at work but was it an unclean spirit of evil or the Holy Spirit of God? The scribes were looking on the same wonderful works of deliverance that the rest of the crowd had seen but were making the considered judgment that the source of them all was diabolical. Jesus called that blasphemy. He saw it as the most perilous attitude a human being can ever adopt. When, in the presence of overwhelming evidence, we insist on calling light darkness and good evil, we are in serious trouble.

What can we learn from this interchange? For one thing, whatever view we take of it, there can be no doubt that Jesus did marvelous things for afflicted and enslaved people freeing them from all kinds of miseries and evils. Even his worst enemies never denied that this was so. They disputed about his motives and about the source of his power, but they could never dismiss the reality of his works.

Also, it's interesting that they focus on the spirit or power that was at work in Jesus. That tells something about the way in which he approached his ministry. Jesus always claimed to be the agent of another. He insisted that everything he taught had been given him by his Father in heaven and that all of his works were the Father's works. He carried out his whole ministry by the leading and power of God's Spirit and never claimed to do anything by his personal virtue, power, or charisma. He presented himself always as God's Messiah, God's Anointed One, a man filled with God's Holy Spirit.

That brings into focus the great question confronting everyone who learns about Jesus. The question is: How do we account for his life and ministry? What is the strange dynamic at work? How do we explain him? What shall we say about him? According to Jesus, everything depends on the answer we give. The fact of what he did and continues to do for people is undeniable. He brings them forgiveness. He releases them from enslaving evils. He makes God real to them. He fills their hearts with joy. He gives them hope. They find in Jesus a new power to live and serve.

The scribes insisted that the source of Jesus' power was evil, that Jesus could not have come from God, and that the spirit inspiring him had to be unclean. Jesus gave them a solemn warning. Note that it was a warning, not a threat. He didn't say to them that they had already crossed the line, but he did say that if they continued in their stubborn rejection of the light, if they kept on calling good evil and God's Spirit a demon from hell, there could be no hope for them.

He spoke the warning, I believe, with a breaking and yearning heart. He didn't want people to shut their ears to the truth and turn their backs on God, dooming themselves. He wanted them—he wants us—to con-sider carefully his works and listen to his words. He wants us to realize that the one guiding and energizing him is none other than the maker of the heavens and earth, the holy Lord, the righteous Father, God him-self. He wants us to affirm today, each of us personally for ourselves, that Jesus is God's Son, moved by God's Spirit, our only Savior. The great question is: Who is Jesus? Is he the devil's mouthpiece or is he God's Messiah?

Study Questions

1. Why is the charge that is made against Jesus a serious one?
2. How does Jesus refute it?
3. How does this shed light on what is meant by "the unpardonable sin"?
4. In what sense are Jesus' words about blasphemy against the Holy Spirit a warning instead of a threat?

6

Speaking of Jesus: His Disciples

◆

On that day, when evening had come, he [Jesus] said to them, "Let us go across to the other side." And leaving the crowd, they took him with them in the boat, just as he was. And other boats were with him. And a great storm of wind arose, and the waves beat into the boat, so that the boat was already filling. But he was in the stern, asleep on the cushion; and they woke him and said to him, "Teacher, do you not care if we perish?" And he awoke and rebuked the wind, and said to the sea, "Peace! Be still!" And the wind ceased, and there was a great calm. He said to them, "Why are you afraid? Have you no faith?" And they were filled with awe, and said to one another, "Who then is this, that even wind and sea obey him?"

[Mark 4:35–41]

THIS IS ONE OF THE MOST REMARKABLE sea stories ever told. Notice the fascinating detail. Mention is made of "other boats." We read that this one was "already filling with water." Jesus' exact position is described: He was in the stern, sleeping with his head on a cushion. The disciples speak harshly to him in what sounds like a rebuke. Later they are described as utterly bewildered. The scene is so vivid that we may feel as though we are there in that swamped boat. And we can sense the awe behind the question, "Who then is this?"

It sounds like an eyewitness account with its awkward and embarrassing touches. Mark never seems disposed to add details like this on his own. He's writing, for the most part, from Simon Peter's reminiscences.

Master, don't you care that we are perishing? How many times has a plaintive, frightened question like that been hurled toward heaven? We're in big trouble, Lord. Aren't you going to do anything? Don't you care?

We wouldn't expect questions like these from Jesus' disciples. They had heard his call and trusted him enough to leave everything behind and become his followers. They had seen marvelous things: A leper had come to Jesus one day and had his flesh restored. A man with a paralyzed hand was commanded to do the impossible and did it. He stretched out that withered hand. Jesus had told a helpless cripple to pick up his pallet and go home, and the man had done just that. How that set the crowd buzzing! His disciples had begun to get the idea that Jesus of Nazareth could do just about anything. Then came the storm.

At the end of a long day of ministry, Jesus wanted to go across the lake. It seemed a perfect evening for a boat ride. The water was calm. The wind, as usual, had died down when the sun slipped behind the hills. Every now and then the Sea of Galilee could be whipped into a frenzy by a sudden storm. At times, high winds were known to sweep in through a southern cleft in the hills. But no one could remember anything like that happening at night. The men with Jesus scarcely gave the weather a thought.

Suddenly, the wind came up from the south, blowing steadily. This was more than a night breeze. The men, idle at the oars, bent again to their work. The lake was choppy now, the going difficult. Soon the voyagers were getting wet, first with spray and then with the crest of an occasional wave. As the wind began to gust fiercely, a huge breaker crashed down on them, drenching them all. The men in the center of the boat bailed frantically. By now even the seasoned fishermen were alarmed. The boat was filling rapidly, and still Jesus slept. Master, don't you care, they cried, that we're about to die?

That sounds harsh, but can you blame them? How could they show respect at a time like that? Their boat was about to go to the bottom of the lake. When anyone goes through something so stressful and it seems that the Lord is absent or asleep, it's hard not to get anxious.

Just then, amid the fury of the storm, Jesus got to his feet and shouted. It was loud enough for everyone in the boat to hear, even above the howling wind. "Hush, be still." What's this? they wondered. He's talking to the wind. He's giving orders to the storm. Just then the gale dropped. The waves fell back upon themselves. The scream of the tempest died away to a bare whisper. The men in the boat looked at each other and then stared off into the night. No one spoke.

Now Jesus had a question for them: "Why are you afraid? Have you no faith?" Why were they afraid? That's a strange thing to ask. The answer seems evident. A storm like that would terrify anyone, even a veteran seagoer. But the question goes deeper. It's not why did the waves frighten you? or why did the storm make you anxious? but it's why did you think you were forgotten? why did you doubt me?

We're not called to be super heroes, people of iron who never know what it is to be frightened. The oft-recurring phrase in the Bible, "Fear not," doesn't blame us for having failed. God wants us to lay aside our fears, not because they're not real or justified, but because of something even more real and significant. "Fear not," he says, "for I am with you, be not dismayed, for I am your God" (Isa. 41:10). If you were alone, left to your own resources, the circumstances would be dreadful indeed. But you're not alone.

What the disciples forgot in the boat that night was that Jesus was there with them, and he is the healer of the sick, master of the demons, and Lord of all life. They forgot that he had called them. He had led them to entrust their lives to his care and he had assumed responsibility for them. They thought that he didn't know because they saw him asleep. They thought that he didn't care because right up until the last moment, he did nothing to help them. Jesus challenged those doubts, "Why are you afraid? Have you no faith?" That last question is the really disturbing one. The disciples were believers, but this was the first emergency they had faced with Jesus. How they acted now revealed a good deal about them.

Crises test character. We never know how strongly rooted a tree is until winds of gale force begin to beat against it. We can never tell how powerful a muscle is until it has to work against stubborn resistance. For us who call ourselves believers, it's often the cruel pressures of life, the seemingly overwhelming difficulties, that bring to light the depth or shallowness, the strength or weakness, of our faith. What that night at sea made clear was that these men still had much to learn about trusting their master.

It was an ocean storm that later taught John Wesley that same lesson. Early in his ministry, he was sailing to the New World, hoping to do missionary work among the Indians there. A group of German believers was also on board. When a violent storm threatened all of their lives, these Moravians displayed amazing courage. While the tempest raged around them, they were cheerfully calm, sure of God's care over them and their families. Wesley realized to his chagrin that they had something he lacked. They had an assurance of faith that he was to find only years later when his heart was "strangely warmed." Many of us haven't yet been liberated from faithless fears and anxious mistrust. Maybe what we're going through right now points up our personal need along those lines.

But that doesn't mean that we are hypocrites or that we have never trusted Jesus at all. The Lord isn't accusing his disciples of apostasy. He isn't saying, see, you never knew me. Rather, he's asking them to take a fresh look at themselves. Whatever their convictions, they're acting as though they don't trust him.

These disciples, like many of us, were doubters, not unbelievers. Unbelief is a settled kind of disposition, a refusal to believe in spite of evidence. Doubt is different. Doubt is a sickness that afflicts real faith. Those who doubt want to believe but have difficulty doing so.

You may be battling with doubts like that. You've seen the Lord's hand at work before and you want to believe that he's with you now, but you're almost at the end of your rope and he doesn't seem to notice. Your faith seems to be slipping away. You may be struggling with cancer. You know God is with you and he has the power to heal, but the tumor keeps on growing, and he seems to do nothing about it. What painful, frustrated, sometimes bitter questions come boiling up in your mind! You may have lost your job after working twenty years in the same place. All your benefits and all your security for the future are gone. Sure, God's never going to leave you, but how is he helping you now? The bills keep coming. The problems mount, and you're just about to go under. Where is God in all of that? What good is it to believe in him?

For the disciples in the boat, who had similar questions, the answer was dramatic and sudden. At one moment they were about to abandon all hope and in the next they were saved. They were asking him if he really cared and then he was asking them if they really believed. Their complaints to their master, at least for the time being, were gone. They hardly dared look at him, but they whispered to one another, whoever can he be? Even the winds and waves do what he tells them.

That's the question we're driven again and again to ask. Confronted by the fact of Christ, the life he lived, the works he did, the words he spoke, and the mysterious way in which he affects peoples' lives even today, we shake our heads in wonder. We can't escape the insistent question, whoever can he be? He seems on the one hand totally human. There he is, a weary sleeper in a fishing boat at the end of a hard day. Moments later he is the storm king, giving orders to a mighty wind, and those elemental forces, which we can hardly predict let alone control, quiet down at his word like docile puppies. Who then can he be? It's one thing to give religious talks, even to make sick people feel better. The ingenious can always find ways of explaining those cures away. But when you scold hurricanes and get immediate results, you must be someone out of the ordinary. Jesus speaks to the wind and the sea as though he had them in his pocket. He treats the world as though it belonged to him. Can he really be the Lord of everything?

Maybe you're not convinced. It was impressive back then. Seeing him calm a storm would make anyone believe. But you've seen some storms he didn't stop, some ships go down, some 747s crash. Cancer has killed a lot of people, and many believers go to torture and death without God's intervention at all. What does it mean to you that God did something great on the other side of the world centuries ago? How do you know today that he cares about you and what happens to you?

This is how. We know something now that those men in the fishing boat didn't know. Since they rode out the storm that night, Jesus has gone to Jerusalem and given himself to suffer for our sins and die for us. He came from heaven not simply to startle people with the wonders he could do but to meet our greatest need and to make us right with God. He showed his love in the most powerful way imaginable by dying in our place. And now he's alive, victor over death, Lord of heaven and earth, Savior of the world.

He may not always bail you out of your troubles at the last minute as he did the disciples. He may let the waves swamp your boat while he seems to sleep through it all. That night on the Sea of Galilee still shows who he is, and that day on Golgotha proves for all time that he cares when we're about to perish. Trust him. Even though he doesn't still all your storms, you can be sure of this: He'll be with you in the midst of them and bring you to a safe harbor at last.

Study Questions

1. What are the details here that suggest an eyewitness account?
2. What experiences have you been through recently that seemed stormy?
3. What is the difference between unbelief and doubt?
4. How is the stilling of the tempest in a somewhat different category from Jesus' other miracles? What significance has that for you?

7

Speaking of Jesus: King Herod

◆

King Herod heard of it; for Jesus' name had become known. Some said, "John the baptizer has been raised from the dead; that is why these powers are at work in him." But others said, "It is Elijah." And others said, "It is a prophet, like one of the prophets of old." But when Herod heard of it he said, "John, whom I beheaded, has been raised."

[Mark 6:14–16]

"When Herod heard of it, he said, 'John, whom I beheaded, has been raised.'" That's how Herod Antipas explained the ministry of Jesus. This Herod, son of Herod the Great, was tetrarch of Galilee and Perea from the time of his father's death in 4 B.C. to A.D. 39. He had been ruling for more than thirty years when John the Baptist began his fiery preaching in the wilderness. Herod's encounter with John proved to be a fateful experience in his life.

Herod's direct contact with John began with his highly questionable marriage. He had taken as his wife Herodias, a woman who had formerly been married to his brother Philip. Very few people in those days would have dared to challenge a monarch's marital behavior, but John did. He told Herod to his face, "It is not lawful for you to have your brother's wife" (Mark 6:18). He did Herod the great kindness of telling him the truth about his life. For his trouble he was seized and thrown in prison.

Herod himself may not have been to blame for that. The one who most bitterly resented John the Baptist and his interference was the woman involved, Herodias.

Herod apparently feared John. This man of the wilderness, clothed in camel's hair, had a strange intensity about him. Herod knew that John was a righteous man and that what he had said was the truth. He sensed also that John was holy, separated to God for his purpose, and there was a deep uneasiness in the king lest John's words to him should be a divine message. He may have imprisoned the Baptist not so much to punish him as to keep him safe, because Herodias was the real enemy. She had a grudge against John and wanted to kill him. Finding no way to persuade her husband to cooperate in this, she decided to trick him and waited cunningly for the right moment.

Finally the day came when Herod held a birthday celebration. All his courtiers and officers were there, along with the leading citizens of Galilee. A high point in the program was the provocative dancing of Salome, Herodias's daughter. The king was captivated. Much wine had put him in a carefree, reckless mood, and he made a rash promise to give Salome anything she wanted—even half of his kingdom.

This was the opportunity Herodias had been looking for. When Salome conferred with her mother, "What shall I ask?" Herodias didn't hesitate for a moment. "The head of John the baptizer." That meant more to her, apparently, than half the kingdom. How could this boor from the wilderness have dared to criticize her marriage to the king? At last Herodias would have her revenge.

When Herod heard Salome's request, the color drained from his face. All the merriment was suddenly forgotten. The king, we read, was deeply grieved. Sadly, however, the unrest was not great enough to make him resist. He saw through it all now. He saw the malice and cleverness of Herodias and realized that she had duped and betrayed him, but his anger at her and his concern for John were not enough to make him swallow his pride. Because of all the people who had heard his foolish vow, he couldn't bring himself to back down. He gave the command to murder a blameless man.

Some time later Herod heard about the ministry of Jesus, about his mighty works and his arresting words. That's when he said, "John, whom I beheaded, has been raised." What was behind that reaction?

I hear in it, first of all, a deeply troubled conscience. Herod had not planned to kill John the Baptist. He had been manipulated to do something he knew was wrong. He was angry with himself about it, depressed, perhaps even fearful. Herod was a tyrant, but some kind of moral sense had apparently remained alive in him. He knew that John had been a good man, God's man. For no reason at all, except to save face, Herod had taken off his head.

Even for a Near Eastern monarch, to whom cruelty was commonplace, this must have been disturbing. Herod was haunted by memories of the just man he had murdered. When he heard reports of Jesus' ministry in the same locale and among the same people, Herod felt fresh twinges of guilt and fear. Could his nemesis have returned? Could John be back again, armed now with supernatural power? It was a chilling thought, even for a seasoned ruler like Herod.

But there must have been other resemblances too. Jesus and John, in some respects at least, preached the same message. John called people to repent because a greater one than he was at hand. Jesus preached repentance also because, as he said, "The kingdom of heaven has drawn near."

John had shown a remarkable fearlessness in telling Herod bluntly that the king had no right to marry his brother's wife. The same bold denunciation of evil seemed to be a hallmark of Jesus' ministry too. He called the leaders of his day "a brood of vipers." He spoke the truth, even when it involved serious personal risk.

Even more notable was the sense of divine destiny that both John and Jesus possessed. Both spoke of being sent. Both heralded a word from beyond. Both announced the breaking of God's kingdom into history. Both spoke with a note of divine authority. It's easy to see why Jesus reminded Herod of the innocent victim who had disturbed the king's dreams.

Then there were those reports that Jesus was able to make blind people see and the deaf and dumb hear and speak, that he restored cripples, freed demoniacs, even raised the dead to life again. John, of course, hadn't done things like that. But, who knows? If he came back from the dead, he might. That's what worried Herod. A man who had returned from the mysterious realm beyond could be expected to do amazing things.

Herod was in a way like the killer in Edgar Allen Poe's horror story *The Telltale Heart*. The murderer in that tale kept imagining that he heard the heart of his victim pounding louder and louder. Herod also nursed a superstition awakened by fear. Now, in the spirit and power of Jesus, he thought he heard John's heart beating again.

From our perspective centuries later, what can we say about King Herod's strange belief? Was he right in thinking that Jesus and John the Baptist were the same person? We know that the two men were not identical. In some respects, they were not even similar. Remember how Jesus contrasted his own ministry with that of John? "For John the Baptist has come eating no bread and drinking no wine; and you say, 'He has a demon.' The Son of man has come eating and drinking; and you say, 'Behold, a glutton and a drunkard, a friend of tax collectors and sinners!'" (Luke 7:33–34). The lifestyle of the two men was evidently different. John was a kind of recluse from the wilderness; Jesus, a man who loved being with the people. John never drank wine or attended celebrations, but Jesus was often sitting at table with others and sharing their feasts. It's interesting that Jesus compared John to Elijah rather than to himself. Jesus was not John the Baptist back from the dead. Rather, John was like Elijah—a man of the wilderness, a critic of kings, a preacher of repentance. Jesus actually said of the Baptist on one occasion, "If you are willing to accept it, he is Elijah who is to come" (Matt. 11:14).

In another sense, Herod was not so far from the truth when he identified Jesus with John. John pointed to Jesus not only in his preaching but in his career. He was hated and opposed for speaking God's truth fearlessly. He was arrested by the authorities even though he had committed no crime. After being conspired against by the cunning and the cruel, he was cut off in his prime and unjustly put to death. John truly fulfilled the word of Jesus, "It is enough for the disciple that he be as his master, and the servant as his lord" (Matt. 10:25 KJV). John walked the path of obedience and rejection, of suffering and death. Jesus walked a similar path but as our representative, our Savior.

What Herod had mistakenly assumed about John became reality in the case of Jesus. Herod feared that John the Baptist had come back from the dead. Jesus actually did come back from the dead. Herod's fear that God might avenge John by bringing him back to life was in a sense prophetic. That mighty work of God to turn the tables and reverse the human verdict became a reality of history in the resurrection of Jesus Christ. Death could not hold him.

Herod was afraid that John the Baptist back from the dead would possess heavenly power. He would be able to do unheard-of things, the king feared. In that way, he was again an unwitting prophet of what God would do in the raising of his Son. Jesus risen from the dead is mighty to save. The powers of the age to come are abundantly at work in and through the risen Lord. He poured out his Spirit on his followers so that they were able to do the works that he had done and, as he said, even mightier works. The work of the Holy Spirit was precisely to bring the powers of the coming age to God's people so that they could become the agents of his mighty works.

In dealing with John and with Jesus, Herod was fighting against a kingdom that could not be defeated. He was discovering that while prophets can be slain, the truth they proclaim lives on. Tyrants can kill the witnesses, but they cannot destroy the witness. The blood of the martyrs becomes again and again the seed of the church. Nothing can stop the power of God's gracious rule in Christ. Jesus builds his church, as he said he would, and the gates of hell cannot prevail against it.

So Herod's instinct was sound when he saw in Jesus of Nazareth something that reminded him of John the Baptist. The same truth was proclaimed by both, the same kingdom announced. The same God—the God of Abraham, Isaac, and Jacob, the God and Father of our Lord Jesus Christ—was at work in both, and no power on earth or in hell could finally defeat either one.

Why do you suppose Mark included these strange words of Herod in his Gospel? Remember his purpose. Above everything else, Mark wants to bear testimony to Jesus as the Christ, the Son of God. In doing that, he brings forward various witnesses. Herod doesn't really intend to be one, but what he says is telling. It shows us something about his guilty fears; it helps us see how much he stood in awe of John the Baptist as a holy man of God; and it bears an indirect yet convincing witness to the mighty works that Jesus did. For Herod, the only way to explain the ministry of Jesus was by appeal to supernatural power. It must be someone come from another world, he seems to say, to do the things that Jesus is doing. Herod was mistaken, of course, to conclude that this was John the Baptist come back from the dead, but he was right in recognizing that in Jesus, heaven had indeed come down to earth. The life of the age to come was breaking into history, and the man of Galilee really was the Lord of life and death.

Mark's purpose in calling forward these witnesses to relate what they had to say about Jesus is to bring his readers and hearers to a personal decision of faith. He wants us to see how God's power is at work in Jesus and how God's kingdom is coming in him. He wants us to believe that Jesus is indeed the Messiah of Israel, the Son of God, the Savior of the world.

Study Questions

1. What evidence is there that Herod respected John the Baptist?
2. Why would he view Jesus as John come back from the dead?
3. How was he wrong? How was he on target?
4. What significance does Herod's witness have for us?

8

Speaking of Jesus: Simon Peter

◆

And he asked them, "But who do you say that I am?" Peter answered
him, "You are the Christ."

[Mark 8:29]

WHO IS JESUS CHRIST? That's a strange question to ask about a person.
Do we raise it about any other historical figure? Has anyone wrestled lately,
for example, with the question, who is Julius Caesar? Or have you ever
been asked, who is Plato? or who is Michelangelo? or who is Napoleon?
Yet year after year significant books are published that probe the question, who is Jesus? Why, after all these years, is that still a live issue? Why
does the question of Jesus' identity still spark interest and stir up controversy? We often talk about this first-century person as though he were a
contemporary. Perhaps we sense that a great deal hangs on the answer we
give to the question, who is Jesus? Of this we can be sure, the answer we
give will determine the attitude we take towards him.

Is he only a memory from the distant past? a respected religious leader,
perhaps? Or is he the Lord of all? The decision is weighty because choosing the last option may cost you your life. At the very least, it will cost
you the right to run it in your own way.

Right at the start of Jesus' ministry the question began to be raised.
The Gospel according to Mark sketches for us what happened. People

were impressed from the outset with the power of Jesus' words. They shook their heads and whispered to each other, "What is this? A new teaching! With authority he commands even the unclean spirits, and they obey him" (Mark 1:27). They couldn't understand it. Sometimes they were incensed at the claims he made for himself. On one occasion when he pronounced the word of forgiveness to a crippled man, the authorities complained angrily, "Why does this man speak thus? It is blasphemy. Who can forgive sins but God only?" (Luke 5:21).

Even his disciples were astounded when they saw him quiet the raging storm. They began to ask each other, "Who then is this, that even wind and sea obey him?" (Mark 4:41). The people from his own hometown asked, "Where did this man get all this? What is the wisdom given to him? What mighty works are wrought by his hands!" (Mark 6:2). The things he did, the words he spoke, the majesty of his bearing puzzled the people, awed them, and raised troubling questions in their minds. Who could he be?

Then came a turning point in Jesus' ministry. We read about it in the Gospel according to Mark, chapter 8, at verse 27: "Jesus went on with his disciples, to the villages of Caesarea Philippi." There, amid its rounded hills and clear springs, he raised the question himself, "Who do men say that I am?" That is, what's the popular impression of me? He was asking, when people get together in the marketplace, when they witness a healing, when they hear what is taught and later talk it over among themselves, what do they say?

"Some," they answered, "say that you are John the Baptist restored to life; others say that you are Elijah come back again; and still others class you as one of the prophets." Those were illustrious names. John, for example, had been a popular hero, a man of immense influence. Some were saying that his fearless mission was now being perpetuated in Jesus. To call Jesus Elijah was an even higher tribute. That man of faith and fire was remembered by the masses as the greatest of the prophets. Never before or since had God's power been so evident in a human life as in that of Elijah the Tishbite. Everyone else, it seemed, even if they didn't see him as John or Elijah, at least acknowledged that Jesus was in the prophetic tradition. They saw him a man with a divine commission, sent to proclaim the word and will of God to his people.

The disciples probably expected Jesus to be pleased at their report. These were high commendations. For what other man in Israel could such exalted claims have been made? But Jesus seemed unimpressed. He wasn't content to be thought of as another John, a contemporary prophet, or even a new Elijah. Those men, great as they were, had all been forerunners, announcers of great things that were to come.

Jesus knew that his coming was not a promise only but a fulfillment, not a mere announcement of something wonderful to come, but its actual arrival. And so he pressed the point and made the question personal for his followers, "But who do you say that I am?"

This was different. Before, there had been the relaxed atmosphere of a classroom as they told him the talk they were hearing. They were dealing at the academic armchair level as they discussed the various views expressed about Jesus. Now the query was far more direct and personal. Now they had to expose their own convictions. They were hardly ready for that. They hadn't been told what the right answer was, so that they could repeat it with confidence. Jesus was probing. What do you think of me? What am I to you?

And that's the way it comes to us whenever it's a personal question. We can't answer with a learned discourse, reciting all the possible views. We can't hide in a neutral crowd. It isn't what our parents say or our pastor or the people in our church. It's a personal question, and each one must respond to the one who raises it. Yes, that's all very well that you're familiar with the options, Jesus seems to say, but when you add it all up, where do you come out? Speak for yourself. In the original Bible language, the pronoun *you* receives special emphasis. It's as though Jesus had said, you, who do you say that I am?

As often happened, the one who spoke for the group of disciples was Simon Peter. His answer was brief but electric with excitement. "You are the Christ." A hush must have fallen over the group. This went far beyond what the crowds were saying. It set Jesus apart from the prophets, even the grandest of them. It marked him as the one for whom every prophet, Israel herself, and all the world had long been waiting. Prophets and priests, heroes and kings had been God's anointed ones before, but always foreshadowing the one to come. In their day the final word had not yet been spoken. The ultimate sacrifice had yet to be offered. The long-awaited king was still unborn. There loomed in Israel's hope a mighty figure in whom all these partial fulfillments were to be gathered up and consummated. Peter was saying, Jesus, you are the one we've been waiting for, the anointed one. You have come in God's name to save and to rule. You are the Lord!

That was the answer Jesus wanted to hear. He didn't want it spread around at that time, however, so he urged his disciples to tell no one. He had no desire to encourage the various mistaken notions about what it meant to be the Messiah, but he sought to hear from his disciples where they stood. Were they still as confused and uncertain as the multitudes—still classing him with giants of the past—or had they glimpsed something of his divine glory? Now that they had declared themselves, they were ready for the further things he had to say to them, hard things, grimly forbidding.

"He began to teach them," writes Mark, "that the Son of man must suffer many things, and be rejected by the elders and the chief priests and the scribes, and be killed, and after three days rise again" (Mark 8:31). There was much in all of this that they couldn't comprehend. Peter, the man who had made that magnificent confession, now completely missed the point. He began to chide his master for these words about suffering. It seemed impossible to Peter that such gloomy days could be ahead. Yet in spite of his dullness and arrogance, he and all the others in that apostolic band had grasped the heart of the mystery. They knew who Jesus was.

When Christians proclaim the Good News of Jesus Christ, they aren't simply talking about someone. Jesus is not merely the central subject of what they say. He is the real speaker as well. The resurrection means that Jesus is alive. He isn't confined to the history books or to some prominent shelf in a cathedral. He confronts people and speaks to them today. It is he who keeps alive his church, in spite of all her weaknesses, failings, and even treacheries. It's he who summons men and women to be his witnesses and sends them to herald his name. It is he who addresses all of us now, asking anyone who hears his word that inescapable question: You there, who do you say that I am?

Let's suppose for a moment that you say what the crowds said in his day. You're a prophet, a great teacher, a shining example of faith. That sounds fine, but what difference will that make in your life? How much have others who could be described in that way affected you? If you class Jesus with other men of religious genius, you can select what you like of his teaching. You can put it together with what other sages have said and form you own religious philosophy, but that drains away any unique significance of Jesus' life. It won't make a great deal of difference to you.

And what about his death? That may impress you, even move you. You may think about it as the noblest example of martyrdom the world has witnessed, but that view will leave you with no great sense of personal indebtedness to him. Limited ideas of who Jesus is tend to cloud the meaning of his ministry and obscure the preciousness of his death.

The issue is this: Does Jesus Christ belong in a list? Is he only one—perhaps the best—among many? Is he, notwithstanding the claim of the Christian church, after all just another good man? Or is his appearance in the world unique? Does his coming represent not merely a word and a mission from God but God himself coming in person? Is what he did not merely interesting but decisive for the whole human race? Is the death he died not simply a sad occurrence but God's action to save his people from their sins? And does he live on today not simply as a hallowed memory but as master of everything, ruler of history, Lord of glory?

No one can compel belief in another. It would be foolish and offensive for anyone to make such an attempt. Even if it succeeded, the results would not be real faith. Those who believe can raise the question, point to the evidence, bear their witness, and highlight the importance of the issue. The rest is up to the hearer.

Because I believe that Jesus is the Christ, my faith can have a sure and final resting place in him. I know that what Jesus says, God says; what Jesus does, God does; how Jesus feels about human beings shows me unfailingly the heart of God.

Since he is truly a man, Jesus could die a death like mine, but since he is the illimitable God, he could also die for me, bearing away my sin and guilt. And his dying convinces me, as nothing else could, that I am wonderfully loved by the Lord of the universe.

Because Jesus is the Christ, I owe him the worship, honor, gratitude, and obedience that every human being owes to the Creator. And he, as the ever living, risen Lord, is with me through all my days. He gives me a mission to fulfill in a cause that cannot finally fail. And he is coming one day, judge of the living and the dead, to welcome all his people home. Now, if Jesus is not the Christ, all of this is just a wistful dream. But if he is the Christ, then there is nothing so wonderful in all the world to know and to say as this: You are the Christ! Jesus is Lord!

Study Questions

1. What is unique about the question, "Who is Jesus?"
2. What do we learn about Jesus from the answers his contemporaries were giving?
3. When did you first grapple with this question?
4. What is the significance of the question? How much depends on the answer we give?

9

Speaking of Jesus: Pontius Pilate

And he answered them, "Do you want me to release for you the King of the Jews?"

And the inscription of the charge against him read, "The King of the Jews."

[Mark 15:9, 26]

PONTIUS PILATE WAS NOT A MAN that should be remembered. He was a ruler of sorts, but never on a grand scale. He was a kind of middle management official in the vast structure of the first-century Roman Empire. His title was procurator of Judea. That made him the head man—but over a modest domain. He was Rome's governor in a troublesome out-of-the-way province, a post that few would have coveted. There was nothing in his political career that marked him for greatness or lasting renown.

There was certainly nothing memorable about his character. Historians of that time tell us that Pilate as a ruler was uncommonly obstinate and insensitive. He did not hesitate to do things that he knew would offend his subjects deeply. For example, the Jews under his jurisdiction had long held that images of the Roman emperor were abominable, but Pilate had his troops carry ensigns into Jerusalem bearing those very images.

He was also merciless. Annoyed with some Galileans who had been offering sacrifices in Jerusalem, Pilate had them killed, mingling their own blood with that of the sacrifices they had brought.

If you consider how a man's life ends, there is nothing that would make you think highly of Pontius Pilate. His cruelties were so barbarous that, in response to appeals from his subjects, Rome relieved him of his command. Banished to the south of France, he died in shame and seclusion by his own hand. Why then would you and I remember Pontius Pilate? For only one reason: the role he played in executing Jesus of Nazareth.

In the ancient statement of Christian belief, called the Apostles' Creed, there are only three people mentioned: Jesus Christ, the Virgin Mary, and Pontius Pilate.

> I believe in God the Father Almighty, Maker of heaven and earth; and in Jesus Christ his only Son our Lord; who was conceived by the Holy Ghost, born of the Virgin Mary, suffered under Pontius Pilate . . .

Isn't that remarkable? Here are Jesus, his godly mother, and Pilate! Wherever Christians rise to confess their faith, this unworthy Roman official is spoken of by name. Why?

The Christian gospel has a unique relationship to history. It is not simply a body of doctrines to believe and a code of ethics to follow, although belief and practice are tremendously important to Christians. The gospel of Jesus Christ is primarily and basically concerned with events. According to the Holy Scriptures, certain things have happened in history on which our hope and salvation depend. God became man in the birth of Jesus. He lived among us and went about doing good and preaching good news. He suffered and died in Jerusalem for our sins and rose again from the dead. Those tremendous events constitute the heart of the Christian faith.

The Apostles' Creed is a recitation of these great happenings and others. The phrase "suffered under Pontius Pilate" serves to anchor the Christian faith in the history of this world. It testifies that God's work for our salvation happened at a specific time and place under a particular political regime, headed by a human leader named Pontius Pilate.

In the fifteenth chapter of Mark's gospel, the procurator of Judea refers to Jesus of Nazareth on four different occasions as "the King of the Jews."

First, he asked him the direct question, "Are you the King of the Jews?" When the issue came up about one prisoner to be released at Passover time, Pilate asked the crowd, "Do you want me to release for you the King of the Jews?" Then, when they demanded the criminal named Barabbas instead, Pilate said, "What shall I do with the man whom you call the King of the Jews?" Finally, when the crowds clamored for Jesus' crucifixion, Pilate consented. He had these words inscribed atop the cross: "The King of the Jews."

We don't know exactly what that term meant to Pilate or whether he believed it to be accurate. Israel's religious authorities had presented to him this charge against Jesus. They wanted Pilate to believe that Jesus had made this as a political claim. Under Roman rule, no Jewish court had the power of life and death. Only a Roman official could decree an execution. If his enemies then wanted to get rid of Jesus, they had to persuade Pilate that he was a threat to imperial Rome. They accused him of having claimed royal power and of setting himself up as a rival to Caesar. On that basis Pilate would have to condemn him to death as a revolutionary, a dangerous enemy of the state.

Pilate wasn't sure about this. He knew that the leaders in Jerusalem feared Jesus, envied him, and hated him. He resented their attempt to manipulate him into condemning Jesus. Yet he knew that if Jesus had no defense against this serious charge, execution was inevitable. So he asked the prisoner directly, "Are you the King of the Jews?" In other words, is their accusation true? Did you make this claim?

We sense a note of incredulity in his question. The very idea seemed ridiculous to Pilate. Jesus had no arms, no body guards, no fighting men. No reports of violence or intrigue had been made about him. He seemed harmless, almost pathetically so. Pilate probably expected Jesus to deny the accusation. But the answer came back, "You have said so." That seemed puzzling, cryptic, neither an admission nor a denial. Then the religious authorities present accused him of all kinds of crimes, but when Pilate wanted Jesus to respond to these charges, he said nothing. Not a word. Only that original, mysterious, "You have said so."

The whole experience left Pilate shaking his head. He didn't know what to make of this. He had never had a prisoner before him like Jesus.

He marveled at the way he listened to all the damning accusations against him but gave no answer. Jesus' silence made Pilate more uncomfortable than ever. Why were these leaders so intent on killing Jesus? And why didn't he say anything in his own defense? Didn't the man realize that silence would seal his doom?

The procurator looked for a way out. It was his custom at the Passover feast to release to the people one prisoner whom they selected. When they called for this privilege, Pilate suggested Jesus. If he expected some popular support to surface for the Galilean, he was quickly disappointed. They roared instead for Barabbas, a man who clearly had been a revolutionary, who had even taken lives in an armed uprising.

Well, what about Jesus, then? Pilate wanted to know. "What shall I do with the man whom you call the King of the Jews?" They screamed, "Crucify him." When Pilate asked why, no reason was given. Only another cry for blood.

Pilate was shrewd enough to know that, politically, he had no options left. Serious charges had been made and no defense offered. The crowd didn't want Jesus free—he seemed to have no advocates at all. What could Pilate do? He suspected that Jesus was innocent, but here was an opportunity to placate an unruly crowd with little risk. He did the expedient thing. He declared Jesus guilty, had him whipped, and gave him over to the executioners.

Pilate wasn't through with these obnoxious subjects of his. He was smarting at the way they had pressured him, forced him into a corner. He thought of a way to get even. He had an inscription written and affixed to Jesus' cross. It proclaimed for all to see, in Hebrew, Latin, and Greek, "The King of the Jews."

Pilate knew that this would make the leaders furious. Technically, there was reason for such an inscription. It simply recorded the charge made against Jesus. But it was mainly an insult to the people. It said, in effect, all right, you rebellious subjects, this is your king. Here is what we think of him—and of you. Here's what we do to anyone who dares challenge our rule.

It wasn't only Pilate who used this title for Jesus. When the Jewish chief priests and scribes were mocking the crucified one, they jeered, "He saved others; he cannot save himself. Let the Christ, the King of Israel, come down now from the cross. . . ."

They knew, of course, that Jesus had never made a bid for political power. They used the title for Pilate's benefit, but it had significance for them, as well. Jesus had spoken of himself as the son of David, the anointed of God, Israel's Messiah, but he wasn't the Messiah they were looking for, and they hated him for the threat he was to them and to their leadership. If they didn't stop him, he might soon ruin everything. His views were too controversial and the things he did too disturbing. He was altogether too popular with the masses. Now at last, they had him where they wanted him. "Let's see some miracles now," they mocked, "if you really are the king of Israel."

Even the soldiers who guarded Jesus exploited the idea. The charges against him seemed like a huge joke. How could this helpless prisoner be a king? Since they had the task of flogging him and getting him ready for crucifixion, they had the opportunity to make some sport out of him. They threw around him a purple robe—mock royalty—and made a crown of thorns for his head. Then they cried out, in a laughing pretense of allegiance, "Hail, King of the Jews."

For these soldiers, the political claim they supposed he made was ridiculous and the religious pretensions were meaningless. He was nobody, a nothing, to them. They could pretend to be his loyal followers, but they had no intention of serving him. If he were a king at all, he was certainly not theirs. Their job was simply to get rid of him and forget about it.

Pilate, the high priests and scribes, the common foot soldiers, and those who inscribed the placard on the cross all called Jesus the king of the Jews. But none of them, as far as we know, really believed that he was. He certainly was not the kind of king they had in mind. His kingdom was not of this world. His servants, even the most loyal of them, did not fight in his defense. When he was accused, he made no indignant denials. When he was mocked, there was no answering contempt, and when cruelly tortured, no oaths, no threats. Only this: "Father, forgive them."

For Pilate, under Caesar's rule, the thought of another king was trea-sonous and dangerous. The rulers of Israel didn't want Jesus as their king for he had challenged their authority and called them to repentance. And the soldiers surely wanted no condemned prisoner as their sovereign.

Pilate was no prophet, but when he called Jesus the king of the Jews he spoke better than he knew. Even though the chief priests and scribes failed to recognize it, Jesus was and is Israel's Messiah, their king. He was crucified, but he rose from the dead to reign as King of Kings, Lord of all the Caesars, Lord of everyone. He is the Almighty come in person to redeem us and reign over us. He's worthy today of your allegiance and mine and waits for us to say, in the words of a hymn, "King of my life I crown Thee now, thine shall the glory be!"

Study Questions

1. Why is it so remarkable that Pilate is mentioned in the Apostles' Creed? How do you account for that?
2. Why was the issue of Jesus' kingship a dangerous one for Pilate?
3. How would you assess Pilate's character? Explain your answer.
4. How is Jesus a different kind of king?

10

Speaking of Jesus: A Roman Soldier

---◆---

And when the centurion, who stood facing him, saw that he thus
breathed his last, he said, "Truly this man was the Son of God!"
[Mark 15:39]

IT'S INCREDIBLE THAT THE CLEAREST, most powerful witness in all of
Mark's Gospel to who Jesus is should come from the lips of his chief exe-
cutioner!

We don't know the man's name, only that he was a Roman centurion—an officer in command of about a hundred soldiers—and that he
superintended the crucifixion on Golgotha that day. It was his responsibility to see that the execution was carried out efficiently and without
interference, so he had carefully monitored all the actions of his soldiers
and watched the crowd for troublesome onlookers.

He must have looked the other way inside the palace when some of
his men made fun of Jesus by robing him in purple, crowning him with
a circlet of thorns, and offering him mock worship. They also slapped
him and spat on him. This was not part of the regular procedure, but
apparently the centurion did nothing to stop it. He may have reasoned
that this victim deserved it because of his outrageous claims, and perhaps he thought his soldiers needed a diversion from such grim duties.

It was probably by the centurion's order that Simon the Cyrene was
commandeered to carry Jesus' cross up to the place of execution. It was

the centurion who gave instructions as to where the hole should be dug for the vertical beam and it was he who supervised the nailing of Jesus' hands to the crossbar. He later arranged for his prisoner to be offered the wine mingled with myrrh—a kind of sedative to dull the pain—but Jesus refused it. Perhaps this officer had the clearest, closest view of the condemned man's dying agonies, and he watched it all, with mounting interest.

Crucifixion is an ingenious, horrible form of punishment, one of the most shockingly cruel tortures ever devised. Even in a Roman world accustomed to violence and gore, the very thought of this spectacle made people shudder. The victim hung in unrelieved agony for hours, and sometimes days. We can only imagine how most condemned criminals subjected to this kind of torment must have reacted.

With piercing cries of rage and pain, many victims would curse their executioners, calling down maledictions also on those who watched them suffer. There were vileness, blasphemy, dire threats, and hateful fumings. While enduring the worst punishment imaginable, all of a man's anger, bitterness, and hostility would come pouring out. The wretched victim on a cross could, and often did, shout unspeakable things.

The centurion was a veteran soldier. Probably he had engineered many crucifixions. He must have become callous to human suffering, but for him, there was something about this crucifixion that was strikingly and movingly different. It was so moving that he was compelled to say, "Truly this man was the Son of God!"

Perhaps in part it was what he *didn't* see and hear as he stood beneath Jesus' cross. On either side of him the men being crucified railed against the crowd. They even joined in berating and taunting Jesus. But Jesus, the man on the center cross, was different. Even when his enemies jeered at him, laughed at his sufferings, shouted their contempt, and dared him to save himself, he held his peace. No one could detect the slightest bitterness in him. Without complaining or condemning, he endured it all. When he finally spoke, it was not to his tormentors but to God: "My God, my God, why have you forsaken me?" He was quoting the ancient Scriptures, calling God his God, and struggling to understand why he was forsaken, but he never once showed toward his worst enemies anything but patient, suffering love.

This caused the centurion to wonder. Despite all the brutal mockery of the soldiers, all the scorn and hatred of his enemies, all the shame and pain heaped on him, he never answered in kind. He never let their malice cause him to shout at them in anger.

It wasn't that he was afraid or struck dumb with terror. Jesus could still speak, quite plainly. And he surely wasn't immune to the pain. His cry, "My God, my God, why have you forsaken me?" gave a poignant glimpse into the depths of his suffering. He was conscious, strangely calm, clearly self-controlled. What was his secret?

In the moment before Jesus' death something happened that appears to have convinced the watching centurion. Just before he breathed his last, Jesus uttered a loud cry. This was not the way it usually happened. In most instances, victims of crucifixion weakened gradually, drifted into unconsciousness, and died a lingering death. Jesus died with a shout. He spoke with force, with triumph. It appeared as though Jesus had decided when it was time to die. He committed himself into God's hands and consciously breathed his life away. When he observed this, the awestruck soldier declared, "Truly this man was the Son of God!"

We don't know what the Roman officer was saying about Jesus when he called him the Son of God. We can't be sure how much the soldier knew about the God of Israel, the God of Abraham, Isaac, and Jacob, or if he knew that Jesus claimed to be the unique Son of God.

By "Son of God" the centurion may have meant a kind of divine man or a deified hero who was accepting humiliation and death as an act of obedience to some divine mandate. It's clear that the centurion knew that he was in the presence of someone supernatural, and his declaration implies that he sensed in Jesus, the Almighty come among men. In this outcry he expressed his admiration, wonder, even worship.

Mark, the author of this Gospel, had an important reason for including this confession. He's writing for people who live in Rome and wants to bring to their attention the fact that the man who made this great confession, at the very moment in which Jesus gave up his life, was a citizen of Rome, a soldier in the imperial army. A representative of the

Gentile world saw in Jesus during his crucifixion something wonderfully godlike.

In this Gospel Mark introduces many witnesses to Jesus, but many of them didn't realize fully what they were saying. They were like Jesus' disciples after he calmed the storm when they wondered, "Who then is this, that even wind and sea obey him?" Herod thought Jesus must be John the Baptist come back from the dead. Peter called him the Christ but only partly understood what that meant. Pilate unwittingly, almost perversely, testified again and again that Jesus was the king of the Jews. All of them, this centurion included, spoke better than they knew. The partial witness of each one points to the marvelous fullness that believers find in Jesus. Taken all together, they testify powerfully to Jesus as the Messiah, the Christ, the Son of the living God.

Isn't it marvelous and fitting that someone there at the cross perceived the truth about Jesus and proclaimed it? It was not his disciples or followers who did that but a Roman soldier. In all that darkness and gloom, there was one testimony to hope and victory. In his death Jesus won the Roman centurion who had presided over his judicial murder. It was a sign of the way in which he would yet topple the throne of the Caesars and bring the Roman Empire to the foot of his cross. It was a token of wonderful things to come, of the great multitudes who would yet come to believe.

The centurion's witness was true except for the tense of the verb he used. He said, "Truly this man *was* the Son of God." The centurion thought it was all over for Jesus, but we know something that he didn't know. That incomparably moving spectacle on Golgotha wasn't the end. On the third day Jesus was raised from death. He came forth from the tomb and appeared to his followers. We see now that sin and death could not destroy him, that the grave could not hold him, that the one who died is forever alive. Whatever could be said about Jesus' divine glory in the moment of his death can be said with new joy and new confidence now. Full-orbed Christian faith proclaims it in the present tense: He *is* the Son of God. Jesus is Lord.

In fact, as the apostle Paul has expressed it, this victory over death is the most powerful of all testimonies to who Jesus is. The resurrection is

God's mighty word about the Lord's identity. As Paul writes, Jesus is "designated Son of God in power according to the Spirit of holiness by his resurrection from the dead" (Rom. 1:4). By Jesus' resurrection God heralded the same message to all the world that he had declared from heaven at Jesus' baptism: "You are my beloved Son." By raising Jesus from the dead, God accepted all his work, endorsed all his claims, and said in the most powerful way imaginable, this is my beloved Son. Through the miracle of resurrection, God has the last word about who Jesus is. And that last word confirms the witness of this nameless Roman who looked at the dying Jesus and said, "Truly this man was the Son of God!"

In the springtime when Christians remember Christ's death and resurrection, we stand in grateful memory where the centurion stood. We look with him toward that lonely sufferer on the cross, marveling at his patient love. Unlike the Roman soldier, we know that it was for us he died that we might be forgiven and find true life. We know that his suffering and dying was for our sins. We know that he has conquered death and lives now, mighty to save all who trust in him. With each fresh reminder of his death, we can say with even greater depths of wonder, truly this is the Son of God. Jesus, you are my Lord. You are Lord of all.

My prayer is that you will consider carefully and thoughtfully, the crucified Jesus. Consider how terribly he suffered, how he bore hatred and scorn without reviling or threatening, how he committed himself to his Father, having fully accomplished our salvation. Then join with Jewish disciples and Roman soldiers, with those from every land and nation, from every tribe and tongue, with a multitude no one can number and call him the Son of God!

Study Questions

1. Trace what you imagine the Roman centurion's involvement to be in the events surrounding Jesus' crucifixion.
2. Why do you think the centurion said that Jesus was the Son of God?
3. What might this have meant to him?
4. What does it mean to you that Jesus is God's Son?

11

Speaking of Jesus: An Angel

◆

And when the Sabbath was past, Mary Magdalene, and Mary the
mother of James, and Salome, bought spices, so that they might go
and anoint him [Jesus]. And very early on the first day of the week
they went to the tomb when the sun had risen. And they were saying to one another, "Who will roll away the stone for us from the
door of the tomb?" And looking up, they saw that the stone was
rolled back; for it was very large. And entering the tomb, they saw
a young man sitting on the right side, dressed in a white robe; and
they were amazed. And he said to them, "Do not be amazed; you
seek Jesus of Nazareth, who was crucified. He has risen, he is not
here; see the place where they laid him. But go, tell his disciples
and Peter that he is going before you to Galilee; there you will see
him, as he told you."

[Mark 16:1–7]

THE TESTIMONY THAT FIRST EASTER MORNING, the day Jesus rose from
the dead, is that of an angel. He appeared to the devoted women, and
all we are told about him is that he was young and clothed in white.
Matthew says that his appearance was "like lightning," Luke that his
apparel was "dazzling." The features were human, the language familiar,
but there was something extraordinary about this messenger. He spoke
with a strangely other-worldly style. Those who saw and heard him were

sure that the vision and the report had been angelic. This was a messenger from the Lord of Hosts.

In effect, the angel said three things about Jesus to the women and the disciples: He's alive, he's in command, and he has a mission for you.

The women arriving at daybreak and the disciples, when they came a bit later, saw an empty tomb. They knew where the body of Jesus had been buried. The idea that they could have been confused about the location seems highly improbable. Jesus had been the light of their lives, their leader, the one whom they trusted and loved. Is it conceivable that what had been done with his body had escaped their notice? They knew where they were going when they started out early that morning carrying spices to anoint his body.

The empty tomb by itself did not assure the women that Jesus had been raised from death. All the tomb could say was, his body isn't here. Some have said that his body was stolen by his enemies, but if his enemies wanted to have it as evidence that he was truly dead, then surely they would have brought forth that proof when word began to circulate that he was alive.

Perhaps the disciples carried it away, we are told. That seems plausible. If they planned to spread the news of a resurrection, then they would have had to hide Jesus' dead body. If they had done that, however, could they have later preached with such confidence and joy that he was alive? Are people willing to risk, suffer, and gladly die for what they know to be a lie? It doesn't seem likely.

There were no human witnesses to the resurrection event. No soldier, no disciple, no passerby saw the stone move or Jesus emerge from his tomb. Later many would testify that they had seen him alive, but none could tell just when or how the original miracle had occurred.

So the empty tomb raised the possibility that Jesus had conquered death, and it gave his followers something to wonder about, but its cold silence could give them no certainty. The absence of his body did not prove that he was gloriously alive.

The first word about Jesus' resurrection came from God through his messenger. That's the literal meaning of the word *angel*. His report, though brief, was highly specific. It left no room for doubt about the per-

son involved: "Jesus of Nazareth," said the angel, the one "who was crucified. He has risen, he is not here; see the place where they laid him."
It was evident to those who entered the tomb that he was not there.
They could see the empty shelf in the sepulcher where his body had been
lying. They could do that without angelic help. But the angel's words
were crucial—the overwhelmingly joyous report, "He is risen," or "He
has been raised."

That latter way of saying it is more precise because it uses the passive
verb. The resurrection is something that happened to Jesus. God raised
him from the dead. It's something only the Almighty could have done
and to which only he could bear reliable testimony. God did it and God
told us about it through his appointed messenger. "Don't be amazed," he
said. Don't be alarmed, upset, worried, or afraid. Jesus, the one who was
crucified, is now alive!

The disciples were utterly devastated by what they had been through.
The arrest of Jesus, his trial, the hatred heaped upon him, the shame and
suffering he bore, and his execution had all but destroyed them. They
had believed that their destiny and that of the whole world was in the
hand of the one they called Rabbi, even Lord. They had ventured on his
promises, risen to obey his commands, but the events of the past week
seemed to make a mockery of all that.

Jesus had seemed totally helpless. When they came to arrest him, he
offered no resistance. When they falsely accused him, he had nothing
to say in his defense. When they treated him with scorn, slapped and
spat on him, nothing happened. No angelic hosts came to his defense.
No sword of divine judgment struck down his tormentors. The grisly
spectacle went on and on until finally, forsaken and in darkness, he
breathed his last.

What could these brokenhearted disciples say after that? Two of them
discussed it while walking on the Emmaeus Road: He "was a prophet
mighty in deed and word before God and all the people . . . our chief
priests and rulers delivered him up to be condemned to death, and crucified him. But we had hoped that he was the one to redeem Israel" (Luke
24:19–21). They had hoped that he was the one. But what hope could
they have now? Jesus, the one to whom they had looked as Savior and

Master, had been defeated and destroyed. Where were his power, authority, and kingdom now?

The angel's message to the women had a second theme. It implied that Jesus was in command. Later the Lord himself would say that. "All authority in heaven and on earth has been given to me" (Matt. 28:18). The startled women heard Jesus' command through his ambassador to go and tell his disciples and Peter that all of them were to make their way to Galilee. It was a command like the one they had heard when Jesus first called them from their fishing boats, the tax collector's booth, and under a fig tree: "Follow me."

All of this happened just as Jesus had said it would. On the Mount of Olives, just after the Last Supper, Jesus had warned his followers, "You will all fall away; for it is written, 'I will strike the shepherd, and the sheep will be scattered.' But after I am raised up, I will go before you to Galilee" (Mark 14:27–28). And so it was. All the disciples forsook him and fled. The Shepherd had been struck down and the sheep dispersed. The Lord had been crucified, and his followers melted away into the crowd and went into hiding. Now the Good Shepherd had been raised up and was leading his own to a rendezvous in Galilee, just as he had said he would.

The angel's word meant don't be afraid; he is still in command. He's still your King, your guide, and he's still keeping his promises. He hasn't been taken by surprise. He hasn't been victimized or vanquished. He's still on the throne and he's saying, "Go, tell the disciples and Peter."

That leads us to the last great theme of the angel's word: It seemed to say, he has a mission for you. Can you imagine how the disciples must have felt after the crucifixion? It was not only the loss of their leader that crushed them, not only having to witness their dearest friend subjected to such torture, not only the cruel smashing of their hopes, but beyond all that, what a wound it was to their self-esteem! They had been his trusted followers, but in the hour of his great need they had feared for their own safety and run away. They hadn't even spoken in his defense, hadn't raised their voices in protest when the crowd screamed for him to be crucified, hadn't dared to be identified with him when he hung on the cross. He had warned them about their weakness, but they had promised to be faithful. What waves of self-reproach must have swept over them in those hours after he died! How could they lift up their heads now? How could they live with themselves any longer?

It's striking that the command was to "tell the disciples and Peter." Peter is singled out, but apparently it wasn't because he, as the leader of the apostles, should have the honor of hearing the message first. Then the word would have been "Peter and the disciples." Peter is singled out by name, but he's mentioned last.

On that night of warning when Jesus told his followers that they would all fall away, Peter protested vehemently. He declared, "Even though they all fall away, I will not" (Mark 14:29). Jesus said to him, "Truly, I say to you, this very night, before the cock crows twice, you will deny me three times" (v. 30). Peter was insistent, "If I must die with you, I will not deny you" (v. 31).

We can scarcely doubt that Peter meant that at the time. At the time, his intentions were good. He wanted to be loyal to Jesus and stay by him to the end, but he had no idea how weak and vulnerable he really was. He couldn't imagine any kind of circumstance in which he, Peter, would not be valiant for the sake of his Lord. He was committed enough and courageous enough to face anything without flinching. He could envision the others going down, but he never would.

In the time of crisis, however, Peter proved no more brave or loyal than the rest. In fact, he failed more grievously and shamefully than any of the others because he repeatedly denied with oaths and curses that he ever knew Jesus. If the rest of the disciples felt guilty and self-condemned afterwards, what must the inner misery have been for Peter? He must have wondered if he could ever trust his own promises after that.

By specifying, "Tell Peter," the Lord was assuring Peter that he had not been disqualified. The Lord was still counting on him and wanted to see him in Galilee.

In Matthew's Gospel we are told what happened when that meeting took place on a mountain somewhere in Galilee. Jesus gave his disciples and Peter what is called the Great Commission: "Go . . . and make disciples of all nations." In other words, Jesus had a mission for them, even after they had failed him so miserably. If they felt insufficient and unworthy, as they surely did, he had a promise for them too, "Lo, I am with you always, to the close of the age." By his Spirit, he would walk with them, go on before them, and fill them with his own life and power.

The angel's message to the women is the message for us today. Jesus is alive, he's in command, and he has a mission for us. We may have been doubters, we may have failed him in a crisis as all the disciples did, we may have denied ever knowing him, like Peter, but the resurrection makes everything new. There's forgiveness, there's hope, there's power now for our lives and witness to him.

That's what the angel was saying. That's what the Gospel according to Mark is echoing. That's what prophets and apostles, saints and martyrs, the church in every age and place, are declaring: Jesus is Messiah and Lord of all because Jesus is alive.

Study Questions

1. What is the significance of the first herald of Jesus' resurrection being an angel?
2. What explanations might account for the empty tomb? Evaluate them.
3. What made Jesus seem helpless during his trial and crucifixion? What made him seem in charge after the resurrection?
4. What was the significance of Jesus' special instruction to tell Peter?

12

Encountering Jesus: Satan

———◆———

And he was in the wilderness forty days, tempted by Satan; and he was with the wild beasts; and the angels ministered to him.

[Mark 1:13]

IN THE GOSPEL ACCORDING TO MARK, we read of a number of people who encountered Jesus during his public ministry. Strikingly, the first one to meet him after his baptism in the river Jordan was Satan.

The literal meaning of *Satan* is "adversary." Satan is the "adversary" or the "enemy" and appears frequently on the pages of the Old Testament as one opposed to God and his people, seeking to destroy the relationship between them. Satan is an accuser of God to Adam and Eve, and of Job and Joshua to God. He is malicious and destructive but ultimately subject to God's control, requiring divine permission to carry out his evil designs.

Satan has great power, however, and extraordinary cunning. He is a master of deception and rules over a kingdom of evil, with underlings who carry out his plans. Gaining entrance and power wherever people turn away from God, he is the prince of this world, an unseen ruler, from whose control human beings are totally unable to free themselves.

Mark mentions expressly that Jesus is led by the Holy Spirit into encountering this adversary. The Spirit of God comes upon him with special fullness at his baptism and directs him toward the wilderness. The Spirit makes it clear to him that accepting his vocation as servant of the Lord leads directly to this encounter with the evil one, and Jesus, as the obedient Son, follows God's leading. Some of the translations read "the Spirit immediately drove him out into the wilderness." The verb pictures a forceful act, but not one that Jesus in any way resists. He is under a sense of inner constraint, knowing that this encounter must take place if he is to fulfill his mission. He is "driven," indeed, but by his own sense of divine destiny.

In those days, the desert or the wilderness was often associated with the demonic. Jesus goes there, not because it is conducive to meditation and prayer, but because he is marching to confront the enemy. While others must avoid temptation as much as possible, Jesus must seek it out. He must go on the offensive and enter enemy-occupied territory, taking the battle to the foe.

According to the New Testament records, it was precisely to overcome the kingdom of Satan and to set people free from his bondage that the Son of God became man. In his first letter John wrote, "For this purpose the Son of God was manifested, that he might destroy the works of the devil" (1 John 3:8 KJV). The Gospel is the record of that dramatic conflict.

This, for Mark, sets the tone for his entire Gospel. Mark sees all the aspects of Jesus' ministry as so many assaults on this kingdom of evil. He casts out demons by his sovereign word, releasing the crazed and the bound. Evil spirits are compelled to recognize his authority and obey his command. These exorcisms are done by the power of the Spirit, by the finger of God, as Jesus puts it. They testify that in Jesus God's saving rule is breaking into history, setting Satan's captives free.

Jesus heals those who are afflicted by all kinds of illness. Even death must yield up its victims when he calls them to rise. In Jesus' ministry, the kingdom of darkness is being shaken to its foundations.

Whereas Satan accuses sinners before God, bent on their destruction, Jesus identifies himself with these sinful people, seeking to save the lost. Now the Lord of life is about to face the prince of death. The light is invading the realm of darkness. What will happen?

The wilderness encounter we read about here in Mark's Gospel is like round one of a boxing match or the first period of an athletic contest.

Jesus goes there, we read, to be "tempted by Satan." The word translated "tempt" here means "to test" or "to prove" a person. Sometimes, in the Old Testament God tests men, as God tested Abraham, for example; sometimes men put God to the test. In each case the idea is, crudely put, let's see what he will do, how he will react in this crisis situation. Let's find out what he's made of, what his real character is.

With Satan, however, testing is something different. The aim is not to ascertain something or to give a person opportunity to display his mettle. Satan's objective is thoroughly malicious. He wants to decisively defeat his victims. In the wilderness, he wants to incite Jesus toward evil. He wants to lead him to sin. Everything he suggests is calculated to do harm. Everything he offers is poisoned bait. The "test" here is not a search for truth, but a determined effort to deceive and destroy.

Unlike Matthew and Luke, Mark does not describe the temptations in detail, but his language suggests that the temptations went on during all forty days. We get a glimpse later on in the Gospel of what they must have been like.

It's interesting to note that in each of the three temptations described by Matthew and Luke, Satan attempts to turn Jesus away from the path of obedience so that he cannot accomplish his saving mission. The evil one tempted Jesus to turn the stones into bread. For Jesus, though he was hungry, that would have been a self-chosen way out of difficulty, an easy road, a quick fix, an alternative to utter dependence on God. The next temptation was to cast himself down from the highest point of the temple, trusting that God would cause his angels to bear him up. For Jesus to leap from the pinnacle of the temple and alight unharmed would have been a dazzling way to attract disciples. That would have won them quickly and painlessly, but that was not the way that God intended them to be won. Again, the evil one, as he shows Jesus all the kingdoms of the world, says, "All these I will give you, if you will fall down and worship me" (Matt. 4:9). To worship Satan was a certain way to win the world without the cross. You can do everything, Jesus, Satan seemed to whisper, if you'll only compromise a little bit, if you'll only give up this madness of obeying God all the way to death.

But Jesus wouldn't, and he didn't. He refused to give in to the tempter in the wilderness. He would not abandon the way of obedience. And the angels came to refresh him after the ordeal.

There were other times when Jesus had to resist the temptation to stray from God's chosen way. When Jesus asked the disciples, "Who do you say that I am?" Peter responded "You are the Christ." Speaking for all the rest of Jesus' followers, he made the great confession. Then Jesus began to teach them that the Son of man "must suffer many things from the elders and chief priests and scribes, and be killed, and on the third day be raised" (Matt. 16:21). This is when Peter began to rebuke his Master, to call his words into question, to assure him that these tragic events would never come to pass.

The reaction of the Lord was swift and startling. "Get behind me, Satan! . . . for you are not on the side of God, but of men" (v. 23). Imagine that! He called his disciple and friend Satan. What could he mean by that?

Jesus was not identifying Peter with the adversary nor accusing him of being the devil in disguise, but he was certainly rejecting out of hand Peter's counsel. It did not express the wisdom of God but rather a short-sighted piece of human prudence, and because Peter was not accepting the Word of God through Jesus but opposing it, he was becoming the unwitting spokesman for Satan. Jesus wanted to wake his disciple up to that reality and to shake him from the foolish confidence that he, Peter, knew better than his Master.

What a sobering reminder for us! I may be, as Peter was, a genuine disciple of Jesus. I may believe that he is Israel's promised Messiah and God's unique Son. I may see myself as a loyal disciple and believe that my intentions are the best in the world, but when I call into question God's revealed Word, when I protest against the "hard sayings" of Jesus, I become the tempter's mouthpiece. When I insist on looking at things from a human point of view, setting aside God's counsel, I cannot offer others good advice. It is more likely that I am the devil's dupe, putting a stumbling block in their way.

What did Jesus recognize here that put him instantly on guard? What was the telltale sign that Satan was really behind Peter's well-meaning counsel? It was the suggestion that Jesus should take an easier road.

He had been speaking of what lay ahead for him. He faced a way of sorrow and pain, of shame and rejection. The rulers of his own people would judge Jesus unfit to live and have him executed. But, Jesus said, it has to be so. The Son of man "must" endure these things. That "must" was not a submission to a blind fate, but to the Father's will, his mysterious saving purpose. It had been foretold in the Holy Scriptures that the Servant of the Lord must suffer on behalf of others. He must be wounded for their transgressions, bruised for their iniquities. He must bear their griefs and carry their sorrows. The Almighty would lay on him the iniquity of us all. Only so could the Father's loving plan be accomplished and his banished ones be brought home.

For Peter to say, "No, Lord!" was more than impertinence, worse than gross misunderstanding. It was an effort to turn Jesus away from the path of obedience, to have him abandon his saving mission. It was Satan's strategy in a nutshell: anything but the cross. Jesus would not be turned aside by Peter's remonstrances. He kept right on going, enduring Gethsemane's bitter cup and the agonies on Golgotha. Nothing would stop him from seeing it through. And God vindicated him when he raised him from the dead on Easter.

Now Jesus is risen and reigning in glory unimaginable. He is Savior of the world, King of Kings, Lord of Lords. But it all began with that lonely struggle in the wilderness where he had the courage to meet the tempter on his own ground and say for all of us, "No!"

Study Questions

1. What do we know from Scripture about Satan's character, purpose, and power?
2. Why would the Spirit lead Jesus into a situation of temptation, since we are warned to avoid such?
3. What was the common thread in all the temptations that Jesus endured?
4. How was the encounter with Satan decisive?

13

Encountering Jesus: A Man with an Unclean Spirit

---◆---

And they went into Capernaum; and immediately on the Sabbath he entered the synagogue and taught. And they were astonished at his teaching, for he taught them as one who had authority, and not as the scribes. And immediately there was in their synagogue a man with an unclean spirit; and he cried out, "What have you to do with us, Jesus of Nazareth? Have you come to destroy us? I know who you are, the Holy One of God." But Jesus rebuked him, saying, "Be silent, and come out of him!" And the unclean spirit, convulsing him and crying with a loud voice, came out of him. And they were all amazed, so that they questioned among themselves, saying, "What is this? A new teaching! With authority he commands even the unclean spirits, and they obey him."

[Mark 1:21–27]

ONE DAY IN THE SYNAGOGUE at Capernaum, Jesus met a man with an unclean spirit. The keynote in this encounter was clearly authority. It was on the Sabbath day and Jesus had been invited to teach in the local synagogue. His teaching was scarcely what the people had expected. It was of a different order and they were stunned by it. It had the unmistakable ring of authority.

The teaching of Jewish rabbis in those days was largely based on tradition. The appeal was to doctrine handed down from the past. Rabbi Hillel said this. Rabbi Shammai said that. Their followers made these additions. And the greater number of scholars have taken this position. All this was instructive but highly predictable, sound, and safe.

Jesus, on the other hand, seemed to represent another strand in Jewish teaching, the prophetic. Prophets did not make their appeal to revered scholars. Theirs was the authority of a direct commission from God. They were not echoing the past but rather heralding God's message for the here and now. It was not a matter of comparing sources or counting votes. This was the word of the Lord and didn't invite discussion but claimed total obedience.

That's the way Jesus taught—with authority and not as the scribes. In his Sermon on the Mount he said, "You have heard that it was said to the men of old," thus and so. Jesus continued, "But I say to you . . ." He was clearly claiming in that way an authority beyond that of the rabbis. He spoke as one with an absolute right to proclaim the pronouncements and commandments of God.

His words in the synagogue that day had electrifying power. We read that the people were astonished, amazed, because they had never heard anyone speak like this. When Jesus encountered people, this reaction of amazement was common. The Gospel writer Mark calls attention to it again and again. He shatters our common stereotype of "gentle Jesus, meek and mild." Apparently what the real Jesus said shocked people. What he did sometimes startled them. At times the effect of his presence was frightening, almost overpowering. People were frequently awed by Jesus and never more than when he spoke with his compelling authority.

One of the people who heard him on this particular occasion is described by Mark as "a man with an unclean spirit." This was a description frequently used by Jewish rabbis to refer to the phenomenon called "demon possession." A man with an unclean spirit was a driven and dehumanized person. Somehow the demon was able to usurp the personality and so damage and disable it that the demon could speak through the victim.

To any reader of the New Testament it's evident that the realm of the demonic is taken seriously there. Satan is not a mythical figure to Jesus and the apostles, but a real, malignant adversary. Demons are personal spirits subject to Satan, seeking entrance to the lives of people, sometimes through physical infirmity, sometimes through traumatic experiences, sometimes through a sinful pattern of behavior.

In the New Testament, physical illness and demon possession were not viewed as identical. Through his compassion and power, Jesus healed many sick people by a word, by a touch, even through the hem of his garment. Exorcisms were quite different. The afflicted person sometimes had the symptoms of a disease, but his or her deliverance involved a personal encounter between Jesus and the demons. He would rebuke them. They would respond. He would command them to flee. To make a person whole in such situations required a power struggle and the word of authoritative command.

Are demons and evil spirits merely figments of a wild imagination or did they exist, and do they still oppress and afflict people today? It is often argued that what is called demon possession in the Bible is simply a primitive way of explaining certain kinds of diseases. These people, we're told, were really epileptics or manic depressives or schizophrenics. Today we understand those conditions and have no need for the quaint, bizarre conceptions of a bygone age.

But does our understanding of brain chemistry and neural discharges really dispel the mystery in such diseases? The more I learn about schizophrenia, for example, the less sure I am that anyone understands this strange and tragic affliction. Doubtless there's a physical component in it that can be treated by medication. It has a psychological element, for which counseling can in some cases be helpful. I believe there is also a spiritual dimension in which faith and prayer may produce remarkable effects.

The questions of demon possession cannot be resolved by scientific investigation. We can and do examine the symptoms of disease, we can analyze the behaviors of driven people, we can even know a good deal about the onset of such diseases, but whether or not demonic activity is involved cannot possibly be determined by what we call the scientific method.

That shouldn't trouble or surprise us, especially when we realize that science is incapable in a similar way of either proving or disproving the existence of God. Christians believe in God the Father Almighty, Maker of heaven and earth, not because this has been demonstrated in a laboratory or proved in an experiment. They believe that God has revealed himself in the history of his people Israel, in the Scriptures of the Old and New Testaments, and supremely in Jesus Christ. Responding in faith to that revelation, they then see many evidences in the world around them and in their own experience that confirm this conviction. But in no way do they claim scientific proof.

As one prominent New Testament scholar has pointed out, the evidence in the Bible for the existence of Satan and evil spirits is of the same character as that for the existence of God. Christians believe accordingly that Satan is a real adversary, that he has emissaries called demons and that at times he works through human sinfulness and weakness to hold people in bondage. They believe that he is a tempter, a deceiver, and a destroyer, working behind the scenes in human history, opposing God, and seeking to blight the human beings made in God's image. Believers believe these things on the basis of the clear witness of Scripture.

They also see evidence in history and in human life that seems to confirm these views and bear out this explanation of reality. They see evidences of evil and destructiveness in human relations, for example, that seem to go beyond the failings and frailties of the people involved. Is there a better explanation for the malignancy behind Nazism, blood feuds, and apartheid? Are there more satisfying ways to understand the depth of evil in the abuse of children, the torture of prisoners, and the systematic practice of genocide?

Christians do not insist that belief in the demonic is the only way to account for these ugly things in human experience. They simply maintain that this awareness does at least as much justice to the available evidence as any alternative explanation does.

In the situation Mark describes, the demon speaking through the man in the synagogue challenges Jesus, "What have you to do with us, Jesus of Nazareth? Have you come to destroy us? I know who you are, the Holy

One of God." The demon is asking, why do you interfere with us? It was almost as if it said, mind your own business, Jesus!

In the second question—"Have you come to destroy us?"—we sense fear and defiance mingled. The foreboding of the demon comes from recognizing Jesus' identity. Destruction of evil spirits was something expected on the great final day of the Lord. Was it going to happen now, before the time?

When the voice says, "I know who you are, the Holy One of God," the demon is not necessarily calling Jesus the Messiah of Israel. It's rather speaking of Jesus as someone from beyond this world who belongs to God and comes from God.

It's significant that Mark would record an encounter like this in his Gospel, and its unusual character points to the Gospel's authenticity. It's hard to imagine anyone in the early church inventing the idea of demons who call Jesus "the Holy One of God." Relating this story would hardly persuade people to believe that Jesus is God's Son. It would more likely give occasion for mockery or even the charge that Jesus was indeed in league with the demons.

These and other confessions we read about in the Gospel are not testimonies extorted from demons against their will. They're rather desperate attempts to get control of Jesus or render him harmless. In that time it was believed that if you used the correct name of a person you could gain some kind of mastery over him.

Jesus rebuked the unclean spirit, saying, "Be silent, and come out of him!" Why did Jesus silence the demon? This was in accord with the whole purpose and manner of his incarnation and his ministry. His coming was always veiled. To let the demons' assertion go unrebuked would compromise God's gentle, subdued way of revealing himself. Jesus did not want anyone, let alone the powers of evil, advertising who he was.

The demon departed, we read, but not without struggle. There was a loud outcry. The possessed man was thrown into convulsions. But then it was over. He was free at last. The people were more profoundly amazed than when they first heard Jesus. "What is this?" they asked. "A new teaching! With authority he commands even the unclean spirits, and they obey him."

For Jesus and the early church these exorcisms were signs of the coming of God's kingdom, signs of the royal, redeeming power of Jesus. They were an integral and important part of his work. We cannot really understand his ministry from a New Testament perspective without them. The fact that some modern people would not classify these afflictions as demon possession does not in any way alter the fact that Jesus delivered many who suffered in this way. His word of command freed them completely. There were other exorcists in those days. They customarily identified themselves with some divine name and often used spells, incantations, and magic. The striking thing about Jesus was that he exorcised by word alone. People had no frame of reference into which they could fit this kind of sovereign authority. A word from Jesus was invested with power for which there were no parallels in their experience. In its authority over people, this teaching was qualitatively new. No wonder they were alarmed.

Study Questions

1. Just what is authority? As you understand it, how does authority differ from power?
2. What do we learn from Mark's teaching about unclean spirits?
3. On what basis can we determine whether or not demons and angels actually exist? What lines of investigation will not help?
4. How are Jesus' exorcisms signs of the kingdom?

14

Encountering Jesus: A Leper

◆

And a leper came to him beseeching him, and kneeling said to him,
"If you will, you can make me clean." Moved with pity, he stretched
out his hand and touched him, and said to him, "I will; be clean."
And immediately the leprosy left him, and he was made clean.

[Mark 1:40–42]

"UNCLEAN, UNCLEAN!" That was the leper's pathetic cry when he
came near a human habitation, or when some passerby would venture
too close. It was a confession, "I have a dreadful, contagious disease. By
the authority of the priests in Israel, I have been declared an outcast."
It was also a warning, "Don't come near me. I'm a menace. I'm defiled.
Contact with me would be disastrous for you. Stay away!"

Imagine the life to which lepers were consigned in such a culture.
They were banished from all normal human interchange, living in iso-
lation and rejection, under an enormous social stigma. Even their own
children ran from them as though from deadly serpents. There was no
neighborhood within the city walls in which they were free to live. Any
house they entered would afterward be condemned. Anything they
touched became defiled. Even their breath was seen as dangerous. Each
leper had to place his hand over his upper lip as he cried "unclean." The
law required lepers to wear torn clothes and let the hair of their head

hang loose. All these measures were designed to guarantee that no healthy person would unwittingly contract defilement. It's difficult to conceive of a situation that could be more demeaning, more destructive to personhood.

There was one relief from this total banishment. Lepers were allowed within Jewish synagogues. They had to be separated by a screen from the rest of the worshiping congregation, but they could be present in the community of the faithful. Even here the reminder of their separateness, their exclusion from ordinary human fellowship, must have been exquisitely painful.

I haven't even mentioned the miseries of the disease itself. We aren't certain exactly what the ailment was of the man described in Mark's Gospel as "a leper." Experts who have examined the biblical data in the Book of Leviticus feel certain that the biblical term "leprosy" describes a wide variety of chronic skin problems, one of which may have been Hansen's disease, also known as leprosy. Whatever the exact symptoms, the disease of this man who came to Jesus was clearly disfiguring and debilitating. He was wretched in almost every sense of the word, exposed to sufferings and indignities we can scarcely comprehend.

We don't know exactly what led him to approach Jesus. He must have identified himself in the customary way: "Unclean!" He must have stood at an appropriate distance from Jesus, but there was a boldness in his request, perhaps born of desperation. He must have seen Jesus' mighty works of compassion and healing or at least heard the news of what he was doing. Into the blank despair of his life had come some hint of hope and faith. He pleaded with Jesus. He fell on his knees. "If you will, you can make me clean."

This was his confession of faith. He was sure that Jesus could make him well. He wasn't asking for what an Israelite priest could do, that is, declare him ritually clean. He knew that Jesus was not a priest and he was painfully aware that the marks of the disease were on his body. No, this man wanted an outright miracle. He was asking for something unheard of, undreamed of, and he believed that Jesus could do it.

But would he? Was Jesus willing to do this great thing? Probably the man knew of no other leper whom Jesus had cleansed. Would Jesus feel that such an act was appropriate? Would he care enough? Or were lepers perhaps beyond the pale of his concern?

Here, I suppose, is a kind of self-doubt with which many of us wrestle. We have no doubt about God's power to do wonderful things for us. What we sometimes question is his willingness. For the leper, perhaps there was the haunting fear that his affliction was a kind of divine judgment. Perhaps it marked him out as an especially grievous sinner. Would Jesus, the great prophet, the one who spoke from God, be willing to lift this divine curse? Or would he consider the curse fitting and just?

Maybe your appeals to the Lord for mercy have been shot through with the same anguished questioning. You wonder if you are worthy to ask for what you need or if your past failures and wanderings have put you beyond the reach of help. Maybe you feel unworthy to ask or expect the righteous God to lift some heavy burden from your life. And so your plea, like that of the leper, is one both of assurance and of questioning, of faith and of doubt. You know that Jesus could help you if he would. But there's the catch. So you say, too, struggling with those tense uncertainties, "If you will, you can help me."

Whatever doubts the leper might have had were quickly dispelled. "Moved with pity, [Jesus] stretched out his hand and touched him, and said to him, 'I will; be clean.' And immediately the leprosy left him, and he was made clean."

Jesus was moved with pity. The Greek word that is translated "pity" is a powerful term referring to the visceral organs. This was a heart-wrenching kind of concern. Jesus could not have cared more than he did. This was not mild emotion, not gentle sympathy, but what someone has called "a veritable pain of love."

And then Jesus did what the man could not possibly have expected. Jesus moved in the leper's direction, stretched out his hand, and touched him. We aren't told if anyone else saw that. Any onlookers would surely have been shocked. Everyone in Israel knew that the last thing in the world anyone should do was to touch a leper. That was to run the risk of a dreadful disease and invite ostracism and rejection. It was to violate the clear command of the law. But Jesus did it, and we get the feeling that he didn't especially care who was watching. That was the measure of his compassion. He cared so much, the need struck his heart as so urgent, that he didn't hesitate to break the regulations of the ceremonial law. He was constrained by a powerful, healing love.

It wasn't that Jesus had no respect for the law. After the healing, he urged the man to follow the requirements of the law and show himself to the priest and make an offering for his cleansing as Moses had commanded. Jesus knew also the underlying purpose of the law, that it was a gift and always for our good. He knew the Father whose loving will was behind it. Touching the leper simply revealed his consciousness of being the Father's Son. He didn't have the slightest fear of contamination. He knew that a cleansing power was going forth from him that no disease could withstand.

Then Jesus said, "I will; be clean." It was like saying to a blind man, "See!" or to a deaf man, "Hear!" or to someone who has just died, "Live!" It was a word with absolute power, accomplishing the very thing spoken. It sounds like those majestic commands we read in the first chapter of Genesis. "God said, 'Let there be light'; and there was light."

Jesus showed himself both able and willing to meet this man's need. That should encourage us. The God revealed in Jesus is on our side. He wants the best for us. He wants our healing, our wholeness, our salvation. He wants it so much that he comes to us in our need, making himself accessible to the most despised of human outcasts. The way in which he accomplished this leper's deliverance is a sign and parable of his ways with mankind. God doesn't stay remote from us, aloof in the heavens. Isn't that wonderful? He comes down and shares our humanity in Jesus of Nazareth. He doesn't shrink from the worst, most repellent things about us. He's not put off by our defilement. He reaches out to touch us.

The Gospel goes even deeper than that. Jesus identifies himself with us even in our sins. He stooped under the burden of them, bore them for us, and died to put them away. In the most profound sense imaginable, Jesus reaches out toward us in our need. He says to us when we hardly dare to believe or expect it, I want this for you. Be cleansed. Go your way. Your faith has made you whole.

And in that way Jesus the Savior becomes also a model for us. Where the love of Christ reigns in the hearts of people, there's a willingness to reach across all kinds of barriers to touch people in the depths of their need. That's what sends a Mother Teresa out into the streets of Calcutta to find the dying poor and give them comfort. The nurses and doctors who minister to victims of AIDS make us think of the Lord's own loving touch.

Now for the sequel to this miraculous healing.

> And he sternly charged him, and sent him away at once, and said to him, "See that you say nothing to any one; but go, show yourself to the priest, and offer for your cleansing what Moses commanded, for a proof to the people." But he went out and began to talk freely about it, and to spread the news, so that Jesus could no longer openly enter a town, but was out in the country; and people came to him from every quarter.
>
> [Mark 1:43–45]

Let's try to understand this. There's a note of sternness in these words of Jesus. Having healed the leper with marvelous compassion, Jesus now speaks with urgency, almost severity, about what the man must do. First, he is not to speak about this to anyone. Why? This is part of the reserve with which Jesus continually seems to have worked. He did not want his miraculous healings to be advertised. He didn't want to encourage misguided conceptions about his messiahship. He didn't want any public stir about the things he did.

In the case of the leper, this was not a prohibition for all time, but there were things Jesus wanted him to do first. He was to follow the prescriptions of the law, showing himself to a priest and bringing the required offerings, so that then he could be pronounced clean and could resume his place in normal society.

Strangely, the healed man paid no attention whatever to these instructions. As far as we know, he did not visit a priest to follow the procedure Jesus had outlined. Instead, he began to do the very thing he had been forbidden to do. He talked freely about what had happened and spread the news of who had done it.

Clearly the man felt that he knew best what ought to be done. Jesus had performed a wonderful miracle. The healed man must have thought to himself, shouldn't everyone know about it? Wasn't he paying tribute in this way to the one who had made him well?

His excited sharing of the news brought a strong reaction, but instead of enhancing the ministry of Jesus, it seemed rather to cause difficulty. Jesus could no longer openly enter a town because of the widespread excitement over what he had done.

Whatever he may have learned from his healing, the man did not learn submission to Jesus' authority. That's a sobering thought, isn't it? The fact that Jesus Christ has loved us, touched us, and healed us doesn't make our obedience to him automatic. It's possible for us to accept his gifts and forget his commands. We may think that we know better than he how his cause can best be advanced in the world. But if we want to honor the Lord and serve his kingdom, we need more than the faith that he can heal us. We need also a trusting commitment to his lordship. That means obeying Christ, even when it cuts across our own inclinations. Paul writes in one of his letters about "receiving the grace of God in vain." Oh, may that never happen to you or to me! When Jesus touches us with his marvelous love and healing power, may we be among those who rise up to obey.

Study Questions

1. Describe the wretched plight of a leper in the days when Jesus was on earth. Are there any parallels of that today?
2. What was extraordinary about the fact that Jesus touched this man? What lessons are in that for us?
3. What are some of the common substitutes we offer for plain obedience to Christ?

15

Encountering Jesus: A Paralytic

◆

And when he returned to Capernaum after some days, it was reported that he was at home. And many were gathered together, so that there was no longer room for them, not even about the door; and he was preaching the word to them. And they came, bringing to him a paralytic carried by four men. And when they could not get near him because of the crowd, they removed the roof above him; and when they had made an opening, they let down the pallet on which the paralytic lay. And when Jesus saw their faith, he said to the paralytic, "My son, your sins are forgiven." Now some of the scribes were sitting there, questioning in their hearts, "Why does this man speak thus? It is blasphemy! Who can forgive sins but God alone?" And immediately Jesus, perceiving in his spirit that they thus questioned within themselves, said to them, "Why do you question thus in your hearts? Which is easier, to say to the paralytic, 'Your sins are forgiven,' or to say, 'Rise, take up your pallet and walk'? But that you may know that the Son of man has authority on earth to forgive sins"—he said to the paralytic—"I say to you, rise, take up your pallet and go home." And he rose, and immediately took up the pallet and went out before them all; so that they were all amazed and glorified God, saying, "We never saw anything like this!"

[Mark 2:1–12]

WHAT IS THE DEEPEST NEED of every human being, the greatest miracle God ever performs, and the most precious gift we can receive? I can sum that up in one lovely word: forgiveness.

When Jesus was teaching in someone's house in Capernaum (it may have been the home of Simon Peter and his brother Andrew), word got around and a large crowd assembled. Inside the house people lined the walls, sat on every piece of furniture and hunched together on the floor. Many more were outside the door, peering in for a glimpse of Jesus, straining to catch his words. As others walked by, they inquired about what was happening and then lingered on the fringes of the crowd. All were pressing toward that open doorway.

Had you been standing there, you would have witnessed something quite remarkable. Down the street came four strapping fellows carrying a sick man on an improvised stretcher. They had heard of Jesus' healing powers and had come from some distance seeking help for their paralyzed friend. Weary and perspiring, they neared the home where Jesus was and tried to edge their way to the door. It was impossible. There wasn't room for a small child to wriggle through that mass of people, much less four men with a heavy burden. After repeated efforts, they were baffled and frustrated. All this way for nothing!

What was to be done? They looked again at their lame friend's pleading eyes and knew they couldn't give up. There must be a way! Just then one of the four noticed the steps by the side of the house leading up to the roof. After a hurried conference, the four picked up the pallet again and maneuvered around the crowd to the stairway. Moments later they were on the roof. What good is this? murmured one. No doorways up here, not even a window. Well, we'll make one! retorted the leader. And with that he began tearing away at the dried mud and heavy straw that made up the roof.

Inside the house, Simon and Andrew must have looked up with alarm. They had heard the footsteps above them, the thumping and scraping, but now debris was falling on their heads. To their astonishment, they suddenly saw an opening appear in the roof. Sunlight came streaming in. As they began to shout in protest, the opening grew larger and a pallet was lowered into the room. The men on the roof were exultant. Mission accomplished! They had gotten their man to where Jesus was.

By now the bewildered paralytic was being borne up by a dozen strong arms in the center of the room. I can imagine the owners of the house being furious at the disturbance, not to mention the damages, and Jesus looking up toward that shambles of a roof, throwing back his head and laughing. Moments later the whole house may have been shaking with mirth. But then the room grew suddenly quiet as Jesus moved toward the man on the stretcher. "Son," he said, "your sins are forgiven."

What a strange thing to say! The men watching from the roof were taken aback. Doesn't he know that this man can't walk? We want a miracle here. We want to see our friend on his feet again. He needs healing. He needs strength, not a sermon!

Why did Jesus say what he did? Why did he talk about sin and forgiveness? Couldn't he see what the man's real need was? Didn't he realize that he was paralyzed? Yes, but apparently he perceived that there was a more profound need. Sometimes it seems to us that nothing could be more important than our health. Whatever will keep us alive and well—good food, water to drink, exercise, shelter from the elements, and healing when we're sick or afflicted—that surely must be our prime concern. None of these gifts, however, can prolong our life and vigor indefinitely. And there's a reason for that.

If we had eyes to see it, we would know that behind our physical ailments, our bodily weakness and decay, is a more serious affliction. We human beings are estranged from God. In our stubborn rebellion, in our insistence on having our way, we have turned our back on the one who made us. We have forfeited his fellowship. We have lost our true life. Now everything about us is touched by the spell of death. All our illnesses, all our infirmities, all our aging speaks to us of the sober fact that we must die. And that is not a natural, normal situation for people made in God's image. Something has gone radically wrong.

At certain times in our lives, we all feel acutely this need for physical healing, but what we suffer from then is not the root of our problem. It's only a symptom. What we cry out for, all of us, sometimes without knowing it, is to be whole within, to be restored at the center of our being, to be at peace again with God. And that happens when God forgives us.

There were some in the crowd that day who were deeply offended at what Jesus said. They were the scribes, men schooled in the Jewish law.

They saw themselves as the official guardians of the faith. When they heard Jesus say, "Son, your sins are forgiven," they were outraged. What was this man? A charlatan, a fake? Was he trying to conceal his helplessness to heal by talking instead about forgiveness? In any case, for him to speak in that way seemed like blasphemy to the scribes. Every human being should recognize, they felt, that only the God of heaven and earth can forgive. Only one of God's special representatives could ever pronounce absolution, as Nathan once did to David, "Your sin is forgiven." But who was this unschooled Galilean? Jesus, they fumed, how dare you assume as your own a divine right? How can you claim to do what only God does?

Moments later, they were to see that Jesus' word about forgiveness was not a dodge. He wasn't skirting the obvious need for physical healing. He met that need. Jesus said to the helpless form before him, "Rise, take up your pallet and go home." And to the amazement of everyone in the house, the man did. He got up, shouldered his mattress, and pushed his way out the door.

The crowd was in a tumult, praising God. "We never saw anything like this!" Extraordinary as the healing miracle was, to Jesus it was secondary. Before he restored the paralytic, he had flung this question in the face of the scribes: "Which is easier, to say to the paralytic, 'Your sins are forgiven,' or to say, 'Rise, take up your pallet and walk'?" Some were doubtless thinking, these words about forgiveness sound impressive, but talk is cheap. How can anyone be sure about this? How can anyone check it out? It's easy to speak of a divine transaction that no one can verify. But a healing, now that would be really something! It would take the power of the Almighty to make this man well.

Jesus implies by his question that the physical miracle is by far the easier of the two. He catches the scribes in their own words: "Who can forgive sins but God alone?" It's a far greater miracle for God to do that for a man than to make him walk again. To Jesus, the healing is simply a pointer to the ultimate gift. "That you may know," he says first, "that the Son of man has authority on earth to forgive sins." There is no doubt that what Jesus did was an act of beautiful compassion, and certainly it was a manifestation of divine power. Above all, it was a sign that God's forgiveness was coming to people on earth through Jesus.

It isn't difficult for God to heal the sick and restore the afflicted. He does it every day, sometimes through doctors and medicines, often in ways we don't fully understand. When he came to the world in the person of Jesus, he could banish the most deadly plague with a word or open blind eyes with a touch. Talk about healing the sick—he could call people out of their graves to live again!

To offer forgiveness took infinitely more. For that, God needed to come among us and share our humanity. For that, he had to take on himself the whole weight of our guilt and rebellion. He had to suffer and be forsaken in our stead. He had to die on a cross for our sins. That's how difficult, how costly it was for the Almighty God to forgive sins.

What a dreadfully serious thing then our guilt and sin must be to God! The just Judge could not condone it. The Holy One could not wink it away. No power in heaven or earth could make things right except God himself, who would bear it out of his great love for us. That's why you and I can be forgiven.

If forgiveness is our deepest need and God's grandest miracle, there's nothing in all the world we ought to seek more eagerly, both for ourselves and for others. Think of how those four men in Capernaum sought healing for their friend. They were willing to spend time and toil to transport him to Jesus, and when nothing else would help, they were ready to defy convention and even risk a lawsuit to get this paralyzed man into the Lord' presence. Bold, resourceful, utterly determined, these men simply would not be denied. We, too, seek healing that way for ourselves and those we love. We'll go any distance, suffer any inconvenience, incur any expense if there's even a hope that we or our dear ones can be made well again. Other values fade into the background then. Nothing else seems to matter much.

Forgiveness is something to be coveted even more. How ardently do you seek that for yourself? To what length will you go so that someone else can receive God's forgiveness? Actually, of course, there's no great thing that any of us can do to gain this blessing. The great thing has already been done. We need what those men had in Capernaum long ago—the faith to believe that Jesus Christ can meet the need. Then we won't rest satisfied until we and others we know and love can come into his presence. It was trust in Jesus that led to the healing miracle. "When Jesus saw their faith," Mark says, "he said to the paralytic, 'My son, your sins are forgiven.'" Isn't that remarkable? Faith still opens the way for marvelous things, faith in the one who died on a cross and rose again and who lives today as Lord over all.

Remember this, he is very near to you today. You can go to him freely. No crowds will block the way and shut you out from his presence. You don't have to go through some ritual to find him. He, the loving, living Lord, is already looking for you. Wherever his word is being spoken, wherever his love is being proclaimed, Jesus is there. And if you turn to him and confess your deepest need, he will do for you his most wonderful miracle. He will give to you, as he gave to that paralytic, his very best gift: forgiveness of your sins.

Study Questions

1. What impresses you about the efforts of these four friends?
2. How would you defend the claim that our greatest need is for forgiveness?
3. Which of the two miracles is easier? Explain your answer.
4. What does this passage suggest about the possibilities of trusting the Lord on behalf of others?

16

Encountering Jesus: A Man with a Withered Hand

---◆---

Again he entered the synagogue, and a man was there who had a
withered hand. And they watched him, to see whether he would
heal him on the sabbath, so that they might accuse him. And he
said to the man who had the withered hand, "Come here." And he
said to them, "Is it lawful on the sabbath to do good or to do harm,
to save life or to kill?" But they were silent. And he looked around
at them with anger, grieved at their hardness of heart, and said to
the man, "Stretch out your hand." He stretched it out, and his hand
was restored.

[Mark 3:1–5]

THIS MEETING OF JESUS with a man in the Capernaum synagogue tugs
at my emotions with special power. We don't know anything about this
afflicted man except that he had a withered hand, and that's the point
of contact that triggers all the feeling for the Brownson family. Our son
Billy was stricken with encephalitis when he was almost seven. It was
one of those rare cases when the measles virus attacks the brain lining.
Billy's fever shot up to 107 and 108 degrees. He went into convulsions
and then a coma. When he finally regained consciousness about forty-

eight hours later, he had suffered considerable brain injury. Among the effects of that, as time wore on, was a paralyzed right arm and a withered hand. I'll never forget the moment when a compassionate doctor was checking Billy over after his hospitalization, examining especially that right arm. After a number of tests, with evident anguish, the doctor dropped Billy's hand and looked away. It's a sad thing, a heartbreaking thing, when a young boy loses the use of a strong right arm.

So our family can sense a little bit of what it was like for that man in the synagogue long ago and how excited he must have felt when Jesus noticed him, how ecstatic when the miracle happened.

First, Jesus issued here a kind of challenge. The atmosphere in the synagogue was tense because some there were watching Jesus with narrow, suspicious eyes. He had gained quite a reputation for healing afflicted people, which was all well and good, but the day when Jesus noticed the man with the withered hand happened to be the sabbath, the day set aside for worship. His enemies were wishing that he would do something for this afflicted man because then they could bring serious charges against him. Everyone knew that you weren't supposed to work on the sabbath day. So they sat there, watching intently, eagerly, to see what would happen.

They weren't disappointed. Jesus spoke directly to the man with the useless arm, "Come here," or literally, "Rise in the midst." He wanted the man to stand forth with his need, to go public, as we say. There would be no attempt here to hide what was being done. Quite to the contrary. Jesus wanted the man front and center so that everyone would know just what was going on. That was part of the challenge to his accusers.

Next came a searching question. Jesus looked right at his critics and said, "Is it lawful on the sabbath to do good or to do harm, to save life or to kill?" What, Jesus was asking, does the sabbath commandment mean? For what purpose was it instituted? And especially, what does it mean to keep it? What kind of conduct is appropriate, what sort of motivation should guide us on the sabbath day? Should we do good or should we do evil? Should we save life or should we destroy it?

In part, this was a question as to whether or not Jesus should heal the man on this occasion. Would it be better to heal him or better to leave him in the grip of his handicap? better to restore life and vigor to that arm of his or better to leave it useless? To this they might have objected as a ruler of the synagogue did on another occasion, "There are six days on which work ought to be done. Come on those days and be healed and not on the sabbath day." The scribes conceded that if it were a life-and-death matter, healing could be done in spite of the sabbath restrictions, but only in cases of dire emergency. Otherwise the healer and those he sought to help should wait.

There was more to Jesus' challenge. He knew what was in the hearts of his enemies, and he wanted to confront them directly with what they were seeking to do. What about their conduct on the sabbath day? What about their motives? Jesus wanted to do a man good on this sabbath day, but they were intent on doing Jesus harm. He wanted to impart life. They schemed how to take it away. Which, he was asking them, is real sabbath keeping? Which is what the God of the sabbath is looking for in his people?

In response to his question, Jesus' enemies had nothing to say. Perhaps they were stunned by this direct challenge, perhaps confused, afraid, or cunning. They would play a waiting game. Why get into a controversy that might see them losing face? They could afford to hold their peace. The next move was up to Jesus. No one spoke.

This is one of those occasions in the Gospels when we are allowed to see just what Jesus was feeling. This has the unmistakable ring of an eyewitness account. We can almost hear Peter telling Mark about it. As Jesus looked around at the men who refused to answer his question, he was evidently incensed. Nothing made him as angry as human heartlessness. These were professedly religious people who called themselves the defenders of God's law, but for them there seemed to be no connection between pleasing God and treating others humanely. Their piety had no heart to it. It had become a monstrous thing in which allegiance to God seemed to go hand in hand with malice toward human beings. The would-be worshipers were men with murderous intent. That was intolerable to Jesus. His eyes blazed as he looked at them.

But that wasn't all. He was also "grieved," we read, "at their hardness of heart." Anger, yes, but also heartbreak. To see people stubborn in their

hostility, resisting appeals to conscience, repressing all human sympathy, was unspeakably sad to Jesus.

Doesn't that picture God's reaction to the evil in your life and mine?
All rebellion against his commands and all refusal to live a life of love
anger him, but they also grieve him. Jesus, weeping over wayward
Jerusalem, is a revelation of the heart of God. "O Jerusalem, Jerusalem
. . . how often would I have gathered your children together as a hen
gathers her brood under her wings, and you would not!" (Matt. 23:37).
You were not willing. Is anything more profoundly tragic than that?

Stronger than Jesus' anger or even his grief was his healing love for
this needy man. In that moment so charged with tension, he gave a startling command, "Stretch out your hand." Have you ever watched a
person with a withered hand? The fingers usually are curled in upon
themselves, the hand usually smaller than a normal one, the wrist bent.
The fingers can usually be pressed inward to some degree, the fist semi-
clenched, but the voluntary extension of the fingers, stretching out the
hand, if it's anything like our Billy's was, is humanly impossible. Jesus
was calling the man in the synagogue to do something of which he was
totally incapable.

That may seem like the cruelest kind of mockery. It's like telling a
deaf man to hear or a blind man to see or even a corpse to live. It seems
to be the crudest insensitivity, the worst heartlessness, unless along with
the command is given some power to respond. That's what happened
here. At the call of Jesus, this man did what he otherwise could never
have done. As he sought to stretch out that useless, withered hand, it
was suddenly restored. It became as well and strong as his other one. At
the word of Jesus, he did the impossible.

I often think about that in my work as a preacher of the gospel. I tell
people about Jesus Christ, crucified and risen for them, and how God
offers to them forgiveness and a new life if they will believe in Christ. I
invite them then to repent, to turn away from sin, and to turn toward
God, receiving Christ with a trusting heart. The problem with that is
that according to the Scriptures, we're all sinners and we're all spiritually dead. Spiritually dead people simply don't respond to God. They
don't turn toward him. They don't open their hearts to his love. So what

good does it do to preach the gospel to them and then say, "Repent and believe in Christ"?

Well, here's the secret. When the gospel of Jesus Christ is preached, it's not only the preacher who speaks—weak, human, inadequate, as all of us are—but it's also the risen Christ himself who speaks. Didn't he say that to his followers, "He who hears you hears me"? When he speaks through the gospel and issues the call, "Repent and believe," these spiritually dead people somehow wake up and live. At his word, they do something that they could never do in their own strength or by their own virtue. They turn toward God and embrace his promise in Jesus Christ. At his mighty call, it's as though they rise from the dead to live for him.

The response of the Pharisees who were watching Jesus is recorded in Mark 3:6. "The Pharisees went out, and immediately held counsel with the Herodians against him, how to destroy him." They were confirmed in their purpose. They had seen enough now. They were more determined than ever to do away with Jesus. Here's the frightening thing about being confronted with the truth and refusing to listen. Here's the terrifying thing about seeing God's love in action and steeling your heart against it. You don't just stay the same then. You become more deceived and darkened than you were before. You wind up more entrenched in your evil way, more callous, more cruel than ever. This was what tore Jesus up with grief. He saw that happening to people before his eyes. It's the saddest thing in the world when human beings reject the light, the life, the redeeming love held out to them in Jesus Christ. Resisted truth always hardens the heart, and hearts that refuse to be broken soon lose all their humanity.

Here's another consequence of all this—a blessed one. In what we've been considering today, the encounter between Jesus and the man with a withered hand, we have a most thrilling revelation. We see Jesus—God come to us in a human life—as one who is willing to risk everything for our sakes. Even though he knew he would incur hostility and have the leaders of his nation plotting to destroy him, he would not turn aside from his mission of mercy. He was determined to heal this man no matter what it cost. He had the courage of an unspeakable love.

That is the gospel. "God so loved the world that he gave his only begotten Son." Jesus so loved us that he wouldn't let anything stop him from going all the way to a cross so that we could be whole, so that we could have life. He risked all, gave all, suffered all for our sakes. And now he's alive forever to be our Savior.

We must ask ourselves what the consequences of all of that are for us. What difference will it make for us that Jesus Christ loved us so bravely and so well? For my part, I will receive his gift of salvation with a trusting heart. I want to offer myself to him in gratitude. I want to live for him until my last breath.

Study Questions

1. What were the issues in this situation that were even more vital to Jesus than sabbath-keeping?
2. What revelations are found here about Jesus' feelings? What do we learn from them?
3. What significance do you see in Jesus' command that the man do something of which he was incapable?
4. What sobering truth is suggested to us in the response of Jesus' enemies?

17

Encountering Jesus: A Sick Woman

◆

She had heard the reports about Jesus, and came up behind him in the crowd and touched his garment. For she said, "If I touch even his garments, I shall be made well."

[Mark 5:27–28]

THERE SHE WAS on the fringes of the crowd, a frail woman, with the color drained from her face. She asked a bystander what was going on. They say it's Jesus of Nazareth, came the answer. He's gone to heal Jairus's daughter. It's Jesus? the woman asked. She was all ears now. Everyone had heard about this man from Nazareth, the way he spoke with such conviction, the way he cared about people so intensely. Most of all, everyone in Galilee knew about the astonishing things Jesus had done. People were saying he could even raise the dead. And now he was actually in her town, walking down her street. Could that be? Maybe someone like this Jesus could even help her.

She had been suffering for twelve years, this lady, with a recurring hemorrhage. She had tried all the usual remedies without success. Every doctor around had heard about her case, but some of their treatments had made her condition even worse. Fear and sadness had etched deep lines in her face. Her life was literally ebbing away and she knew it. She had spent all her money in search of a cure, and now hope was exhausted, too. She had almost resigned herself to this wasting illness.

Now, it seemed, help had come her way. Somewhere out in that noisy crowd was a man who could make her well—if only she could reach him! It wouldn't take much. People said he could heal with a word or a wave of his hand. God was in this Jesus. Power went forth from him. Maybe all she'd have to do would be to touch his robe.

Heart pounding, she groped her way ahead. She moved this way and that, straining for some sight of Jesus. As she edged farther into the street, she was caught up in a surging mass of people. She was pushed, jostled, sometimes almost lifted off her feet. It began to seem hopeless. Struggle as she would, there were still hundreds nearer than she. She groaned at her frailty and helplessness. Doggedly, she kept inching her way until suddenly the pressure eased and she was able to dart through a rift in the crowd. She could see him now right beside Jairus, the worried father. If she could slip between the two big fellows right behind him, she might be close enough. Then came her chance. Leaning forward, almost swept under by those behind her, she reached out to grasp the hem of his robe. Just as quickly, she released her grip again. There was no need to cling. The incredible had already happened. She knew that she had been healed.

Just then Jesus stopped and turned around. "Who touched my garments?" he asked. "And his disciples said to him, 'You see the crowd pressing around you and yet you say, "Who touched me?"'" (Mark 5:31). Jesus didn't seem to hear them. He kept looking around at the crowd. A few feet behind him the woman lowered her eyes, half wishing she could disappear. She had never expected this. Healing was all she had wanted. She would have been happy to go quietly on her way, but Jesus knew that someone had touched him. How did he know? Was he angry? Would he rebuke her since she was a woman who was ritually unclean, and had dared to reach out and touch him? Suddenly her new joy turned to fear. She felt trapped, desperate.

But there was no escaping. Jesus was determined to know who it was. Finally, she got up the courage to speak. It was I, Master. Falling at his feet, she told him all about her illness, her long, weary years of disappointment, and then what had just happened. She waited, hardly daring to look up, not knowing what to expect. "Daughter," came a strong, gentle voice from above her, "your faith has made you well; go in peace, and be healed of your disease." His words confirmed what she had felt. She was well again.

Why do you suppose Mark and the other Gospel writers have related this event? As a human interest story? It is certainly that. As a sign of Jesus' power? Surely. A pointer perhaps to the mystery of his person? Yes, but more even than that. The encounters of such people with Jesus tell us something about ourselves. The miracles are signs of what he came to do for us. All the sick, with their varied afflictions, speak to our need to be made completely whole. The blind man, for example, reminds us of our insensitivity to God, the deaf one of our dullness to his voice. The leper with his uncleanness represents our tainted character. Lazarus in a grave is our lack of response to God, our lifelessness apart from him. Seen in that way, the story of this woman is not simply an isolated happening from the past. It becomes your story and mine. All of us suffer a profound sickness of the soul. We, in our wandering and estrangement, have a need beyond any human power to help.

Many of us have tried various would-be healers. Let me picture, with a little imagination, some that you may have visited. First, there's the one we'll call Dr. Relax. You go to his pleasant, comfortable office and proceed to tell him your symptoms. "Doctor, I'm afraid something is terribly wrong. I seem to be in the grip of habits I can't break. I keep doing things of which I'm ashamed. I seem to go on hurting people around me, even betraying those who trust me most. I lack any sense of purpose. I'm troubled by deep feelings of guilt, and I'm desperately afraid—afraid of death. Can you help me?" Dr. Relax smiles benignly. "Now, now, you're not really ill. The problem is imaginary. All you need is a change of outlook. There's nothing really wrong with you. Forget those morbid thoughts and enjoy yourself." So you go away mildly reassured but unchanged. The symptoms remain.

Some time later when things are no better, you go to visit a second physician. We'll call him Dr. Reform. He listens to your report and nods with understanding. "Yes, I can see that you have a problem, but you mustn't take it too seriously. A little extra effort on your part can take care of everything quite nicely. It's time for you to turn over a new leaf. Decide that you're going to be a better person. If you will start today in earnest to do the very best you can, you'll find that this troubling condition of yours will clear up in time." That sounds plausible. It's a bracing word and stirs you to some new resolutions. But somehow, as time goes on, you aren't able to follow through. You begin to feel like a man with shin splints who has been urged to go running to make his condition better.

With growing distress, you seek out still another physician. Surely this one will take your condition seriously. His name is Dr. Religion. "Yes," he agrees, "you have a serious problem. It's obvious that you need a spiritual dimension to your life. Everyone needs some kind of faith, some religious orientation, to be really well. It doesn't matter, of course, which faith you choose. Your sincerity is what really matters. Believe in something with all your heart and you will improve remarkably."

That sounds promising, so you take a few classes in meditation and a correspondence course in world religions. But you have your doubts. Can it really be true, you wonder, that believing in just anything can make your life better? Isn't believing a bit like swallowing? The results depend on what you swallowed—spinach or strychnine, applesauce or arsenic.

You may be feeling about your soul's condition much as the woman did about her physical illness. You've tried a host of remedies, some of them quite expensive. The real need hasn't been met. You don't feel like a whole person yet. The advice you've gotten all sounded good at the time, but it hasn't changed your life. You've found that the treatments were all external, and they haven't made you well inside or brought you peace. You've just about given up hope that there is a cure for your condition. Remember the woman and her despair and what happened in her life. She believed that Jesus could help her. It's not for nothing, you know, that they call him the Great Physician. There are no cases too hard for him. He can deal with moral sickness. He can cleanse a guilty conscience. He can change a selfish heart. In fact, he specializes in forgiving sins and transforming people on the inside.

Jesus, in perfect, radiant health, came to a world full of sickness, where everyone he met was in the process of dying from a dreadful disease. He saw that. It moved him. It broke his heart. God's plan was that he would take our sickness on himself—gather up all the disease germs of our race and receive them into his own body. He would become the bearer of all our evils and moral wrongs and go down to death in our place. Possessing the only antidote, he has risen from the dead, and now as the risen Lord he has new power to heal, restore, and change us all. That, dear friends, is the gospel truth. The apostle Paul wrote, "[God] made him [that is, Jesus] to be sin who knew no sin, so that in him we might become the righteousness of God" (2 Cor. 5:21). Jesus bore our sicknesses, our sorrows, our sins, so that we can be completely whole through him.

The woman's story has another lesson for us. There was a vast crowd pressing around Jesus on that day and hundreds must have touched him, but Jesus responded only to the woman's touch, and it was she who was healed. In the midst of all the pressure and commotion, he turned and said, "Who touched me?" Her touch must have been different. Evidently it's possible to be around Jesus, to be within reach of him and yet not receive all that he has to give. Only those who know their need and reach out to him in trust experience the transforming miracle. It's only a living faith that truly touches Jesus Christ.

You may belong to a Christian fellowship, a congregation of believers. You may know a good deal about the Bible. On a number of occasions you may have heard the gospel preached or taught. You've been near Jesus Christ and interested in him, perhaps as that crowd was. The curiosity of the masses, however, is not the same as the touch of faith. It's when Christ and your personal faith come together, when you open your life to him and reach out to him, that his saving power is conveyed to you. When you meet him and your faith takes hold of him, you will know that he has made you a new, completely whole person.

When you receive the healing gift of his salvation, don't try to slip away quietly, like the woman did, as though nothing had happened. He wants you to acknowledge to him and to the world what great things the Lord has done for you. Let the world around you know that Jesus of Nazareth is ready to heal anyone who reaches out to him in faith.

Study Questions

1. This woman believed that if she touched Jesus' garments, she would be healed. What do you think about her faith? What seems inadequate about it? What about it should be a pattern for us?
2. What experience have you had with would-be "doctors" of the soul?
3. How does this act of touching point to the central reality of the gospel—union with Christ?

18

Encountering Jesus: A Madman

◆

They came to the other side of the sea, to the country of the Gerasenes. And when he had come out of the boat, there met him out of the tombs a man with an unclean spirit, who lived among the tombs; and no one could bind him any more, even with a chain; for he had often been bound with fetters and chains, but the chains he wrenched apart, and the fetters he broke in pieces; and no one had the strength to subdue him. Night and day among the tombs and on the mountains he was always crying out, and bruising himself with stones. And when he saw Jesus from afar, he ran and worshiped him; and crying out with a loud voice, he said, "What have you to do with me, Jesus, Son of the Most High God? I adjure you by God, do not torment me." For he had said to him, "Come out of the man, you unclean spirit!" And Jesus asked him, "What is your name?" He replied, "My name is Legion; for we are many." And he begged him eagerly not to send them out of the country. Now a great herd of swine was feeding there on the hillside; and they begged him, "Send us to the swine, let us enter them." So he gave them leave. And the unclean spirits came out, and entered the swine; and the herd, numbering about two thousand, rushed down the steep bank into the sea, and were drowned in the sea.

The herdsmen fled, and told it in the city and in the country. And people came to see what it was that had happened. And they came to Jesus, and saw the demoniac sitting there, clothed and in his right mind, the man who had had the legion; and they were afraid. And those who had seen it told what had happened to the demoniac and to the swine. And they began to beg Jesus to depart from their neighborhood. And as he was getting into the boat, the man who had been possessed with demons begged him that he might be with him. But he refused, and said to him, "Go home to your friends, and tell them how much the Lord has done for you, and how he has had mercy on you." And he went away and began to proclaim in the Decapolis how much Jesus had done for him; and all men marveled.

[Mark 5:1–20]

OF ALL THE ENCOUNTERS Jesus had with people, this was surely the strangest of all. Think of yourself as a bystander nearly 2,000 years ago in the land of the Gerasenes on the eastern shore of the Sea of Galilee. A fishing boat has just put into shore, and several men are making their way up the rugged slope from the lake. High on the forbidding hillside a lone figure watches. On his wrist is a battered manacle dangling a short length of chain. His body is gaunt but powerful, mottled with scars and open sores. His wide eyes betray mingled terror and cunning; his hair flies in wild disarray. Suddenly he screams at the top of his voice and begins vaulting from rock to rock on his way down to meet the new arrivals.

The leader of the group waits calmly. The crazed man is running at full tilt, and several of the men move up warily to protect their leader from attack, but then the madman stops abruptly and prostrates himself. "What have you to do with me, Jesus, Son of the Most High God? I adjure you by God, do not torment me."

As you watch, a kind of conversation develops. Jesus seems completely at ease. The kneeling figure continues to plead and shout. You see him pointing now to a herd of swine feeding on the next slope. Jesus speaks a word of command. Suddenly there's a commotion among the pigs. You watch with amazement as they thrash about in a frenzy and rush headlong toward the cliff's edge. In a matter of seconds, all have plunged into the sea to drown. The herdsmen stare in disbelief and then race back to their village.

Meanwhile, the man with the wrist iron has calmed down notice-ably. The visitors have found him clothes and he sits, conversing qui-etly. From time to time one of them puts an arm around his shoulder. He smiles warmly. You can scarcely believe the transformation you have just witnessed.

Moments later, the herdsmen return with a number of their fellow citizens. Catching sight of the group seated below, they hesitate for a moment and then begin a cautious approach. They stare with astonish-ment at the man with the borrowed clothes. He greets them reassuringly. Still visibly stunned, they whisper nervously to each other. Finally, one who seems to be a community spokesman motions to Jesus. He wants to talk.

As they step apart, the man from the city seems to be pleading. He wrings his hands, shakes his head, points insistently out across the sea. Jesus nods and then returns to his followers. They talk among themselves and then walk slowly back to their boat. The changed man goes with them, but when they reach the water's edge, you notice that Jesus turns and speaks with him. It's evident that the man wants to go along, but Jesus is shaking his head. A parting follows, prolonged and affectionate. Now you see this former wild man striding confidently up the hill, hur-rying to join his countrymen. The men on the shore soon clamber into the boat and start in the direction from which they had come.

What does it all mean? A maniac who can't be restrained kneels to worship a stranger. Moments later, hundreds of swine go berserk, and the wild man returns to his senses. The citizens of the land, instead of rejoic-ing, ask Jesus and his friends to leave. And the man himself, pleading to sail with them, is told to go back home. What a story!

Much here is puzzling, but some things are plain. For one, we learn how much it meant to Jesus to free one human being from the powers of evil. Jesus journeyed across the Sea of Galilee through the fury of a midnight storm to find this man. As far as we can see, there was no other objective for the voyage. Jesus came to heal this one man who was hor-ribly driven by demonic forces. His daily existence was sheer tragedy.

Uncontrollably violent, he was a menace both to himself and his community. In fits of awesome strength, he could tear apart the strongest chains and fetters. His dwelling place was among the tombs. His self-torment was a kind of living death. Evil powers had so captivated this wild man as to inhabit him and speak through him, overwhelming his personhood.

Jesus took those malignant powers very seriously. He knew them and was known by them. He had come to destroy this satanic kingdom and to set its captives free. His hour to vanquish it totally, to spoil the principalities and powers, had not yet come, but he would save the man and let the malicious spirits go their way. The fury that the demons flung against the swine expressed their deepest design against the man. They were set to destroy God's good creation, especially the one made in his image. Why they should be released on a herd of animals we cannot tell, but of this we can be sure: Jesus Christ the Lord saw one demented human life as more significant than thousands of animals—more precious than a small fortune in pork.

In his eyes each of us has that same value though we are unruly, scarred, and lost. For each one of us he came from glory to find us and share our humanness. He counted us as of more value than all else and gave his own life to set us free. If you had been the only one, the only wandering sinner, the only lost son or daughter, he would have come to die for you.

How our values differ from his! Those worried, small-hearted Gerasenes resemble us a bit, don't they? Here was the most marvelous thing that had happened in the history of their community. One of their own people, tormented and abandoned, had been completely restored. What a miracle of God's grace! How could anyone begin to repay such a wonderful act of power and love?

The people of the city did not rejoice. Instead, the miracle frightened them. Perhaps, too, they were upset about the swine. Two thousand pigs were lost in this bizarre incident. What effect would that have on the economy of the region? That loss may have prevented the people from sharing in heaven's celebration over a transformed man.

How like them we sometimes are! Jesus' teachings are supremely attractive to us—at a distance—but let his transforming power come too close to home and disturb the status quo in which we live and we are uneasy. Let's not go overboard about this Christianity business, we caution. After all, we don't want to be fanatics. Caring for the poor and deprived is all very well, but if it's going to cost much money, we'd like to take a second look at those programs. There's a lot of corruption and waste, you know, and probably the ones getting help don't really deserve it anyway!

Our economic security is often the sacred cow, which not even the Lord is allowed to threaten. Sometimes it's more comfortable and convenient not to have Jesus around. That's the chilling thing our world said to him when he came, no room in the inn for you. "He was in the world," writes John, "and the world was made by him, and the world knew him not. He came unto his own, and his own received him not" (John 1:10–11 KJV). He doesn't force himself on us. When we ask him to leave, he goes, but he doesn't give up on us. He sends his ambassadors to us and leaves in our midst those who can best reach us with his gospel. That's what he did for those people by the lake who rejected him. He left the man who was delivered of the demons as his ambassador. "Go home to your friends, and tell them how much the Lord has done for you, and how he has had mercy on you." The man did that. Mark writes, "He went away and began to proclaim in the Decapolis how much Jesus had done for him; and all men marveled." That's Jesus' strategy. He makes walking miracles out of marred people and then sends them to tell the world what he has done for them.

Sometimes the Lord sends his witnesses to distant lands but usually their mission is closer to home, to friends and people they know best. Who could possibly reach the Gerasenes like that man who came back from the tombs? His witness may have reached to distant countries, but he would touch most profoundly those who had already known him for years.

Before Pentecost, Jesus told his followers that they would be his witnesses to the uttermost parts of the earth. Before that, however, they would witness in Jerusalem, Judea, and Samaria—right where they were. And that's true for us too. If the transforming power of Jesus Christ has made your life new, if he has breathed into your heart his quickening

Spirit, don't look first for distant challenges and worldwide enterprises. Begin where you are. Let your light shine where God has put you. Seek out those who have known you and to whom the change in your life will be most evident. Be the Lord's witness to them. His challenge to you is "Go home to your friends, and tell them how much the Lord has done for you."

Study Questions

1. What do we learn here about the value Jesus placed on human life?
2. How do you explain the reaction of the townspeople?
3. What is revealed about the Lord's strategy for spreading the word when he tells the man to go home and tell his friends what happened?

19

Encountering Jesus: A Dead Girl

♦

Taking her by the hand he said to her, "Talitha cumi"; which means, "Little girl, I say to you, arise." And immediately the girl got up and walked (she was twelve years of age), and they were immediately overcome with amazement.

[Mark 5:41–42]

THIS WAS AN UNUSUAL MEETING, to say the least. When Jesus first met this young girl, she had just died. It was a meeting of the living and the dead—and the effects were astonishing. This event, with the circumstances that led up to it, is presented in the Gospel as a kind of drama in four acts. Faith in the love and power of Jesus is the master theme. First we see faith expressed, then challenged, then laughed at, and then vindicated.

In the first act, we meet a distinguished gentleman named Jairus. An important man in his community, he was president of the local synagogue—the lay official responsible for supervising the building and the arrangement for the synagogue services.

Jairus belonged to a class in Israel that was somewhat opposed to change and cautiously suspicious of new religious movements. Perhaps, in his professional capacity, he had greeted the news of Jesus' remarkable ministry in Galilee with some reserve, even resistance. Now his daughter was gravely ill, and remembering the reports of Jesus' healing miracles, Jairus sought him out. Forgetting his lofty position and caring nothing for appearances, he went straight to the man from Galilee in the midst of a crowd and fell down at his feet. That must have startled everyone. Jairus, president of the synagogue, fine robes and all, on his face in the dust before Jesus! "My little daughter is at the point of death," he anguished. "Come and lay your hands on her, so that she may be made well, and live" (Mark 5:23).

This is faith, beautifully and simply expressed. Jairus, overwhelmed with a sense of urgent need, came personally and directly to Jesus of Nazareth. He humbled himself in the Master's presence. He asked earnestly for help, expressing as he did a strong confidence in Jesus' power. He believed that if Jesus would come to his house and lay hands on his daughter she would recover. He trusted that Jesus could make the difference between death and life.

To that impassioned appeal, the Lord responded immediately, and without a word, he set out with Jairus for his house. Here was a faith Jesus delighted to honor.

It was as he was making his way to Jairus's house that the woman who needed healing touched his robe. As Jesus took time with the woman, Jairus must have agonized at the delay. His daughter was hanging between life and death and every moment was precious. There was absolutely no time to lose.

As Jesus was saying to the woman, "Your faith has made you well; go in peace, and be healed of your disease," messengers came from the president's house. For Jairus, the news was crushing. His worst fears were confirmed. The report was blunt and unmistakably clear: "Your daughter is dead." It was over. She had breathed her last. There was nothing to do now but make arrangements for a funeral.

The servants knew why Jairus had urgently come to Jesus, but it was too late now. "Why trouble the Teacher any further?" they asked. In effect they were saying Jesus has other needs to attend to and other people to help. Why bring him to a place of sorrow where nothing more can be done?

Overhearing what the servants said, Jesus turned to Jairus, "Do not fear," he urged, "only believe." That must have seemed strange counsel to a man who had just been told of his daughter's death. Don't be afraid? Jesus had heard the news as well as Jairus. The girl was gone. The light of Jairus's life had been extinguished. What could it mean for him to be told, "Don't be afraid"?

Fear and faith are being contrasted here. "Don't be afraid," Jesus said, "only believe." Believing is the alternative, the other way of dealing with the news. It's the opposite of fear. It's the antidote.

This contrast is often expressed in the Scriptures. The psalmist says, "When I am afraid, I put my trust in thee" (Ps. 56:3). When I'm threatened by fear, I reach out in faith. When I'm trembling, I trust. Fear means that I'm worried, insecure, anxious about the future. What will happen now? How can I deal with what's ahead? This doctor's report? This termination notice? This court hearing?

Faith means that I refuse to focus on circumstances and uncertainties. Instead, I look to the Lord, sure of his goodness to me, sure of his sufficiency for every need, sure that he will be faithful to his word of promise.

When Jesus said to Jairus, "only believe," he was reminding the president of the appeal that he had already made and the help that Jesus had undertaken to give. In light of the announcement, he needed only to believe. There could be no doubt about the eventual outcome, even though reports and circumstances seemed to indicate otherwise.

The call to trust is in the present tense. In New Testament language that indicates a continuing action. Jesus is acknowledging that Jairus has begun in faith. He's calling now for a steady believing. Jairus is to hold on in faith, not to lose heart, not to give up. He's to cling with tenacious conviction to the assurance that his daughter's well-being is in Jesus' hands. That's how to respond when faith is challenged, when circumstances seem to call it into question.

When Jesus, his disciples, and Jairus arrive at the house they find that the mourners have already gathered. Doubtless, some were his relatives and neighbors. Some may have been professionals called in to create an appropriate atmosphere. At any rate, the scene Jesus meets when he arrives is one of wild, unrestrained grieving. People are in a frenzy, wailing and screaming. That sort of thing was not uncommon in that culture.

When Jesus entered he quieted everyone down. Then he asked them, "Why do you make a tumult and weep?" Or, as another translation puts it, "Why this crying and commotion?" "The child is not dead but sleeping." There's no reason for this lamentation, he implies. This is no tragedy, no time for bitter tears. The girl you are wailing about is only asleep!

What did Jesus mean? Is he making an expert diagnosis without even having seen the girl? Does he really mean that she is only in a deep sleep from which she will soon revive? That is not likely since there would be no point to this narrative, no reason for Mark's including it, if Jesus had only prevented a comatose girl from being buried alive. All the evidence we have suggests that the girl had actually died. In what sense could Jesus say that she was only asleep?

No matter what the appearances are, no one really dies for whom the Lord intends life. In his mind, his heart, his purpose, she is alive. Soon that would become apparent in her revived body and clear to everyone around her, but at this point, the mourners need to take his word for it against all evidence. They are unwilling to do that. Suddenly, uproariously, they laugh him to scorn.

Try to picture the scene. What a shocking reversal! In a moment, these people who have been carrying on with the most extravagant grieving suddenly shift gears and burst out laughing. That may show their shock, nervousness, or tension at hearing something utterly unexpected, or it may mean that their grieving had been little more than a performance. In any case, it represents an outright rejection of what Jesus said. The laughter is blatant and derisive. It's the taunt of unbelief, a settled unwillingness to take Jesus' word seriously.

The last act of the drama shows how faith is dramatically vindicated. Jesus takes control of the situation. All the mourners and laughers are put out of the room, perhaps out of the house. As he's about to enter the girl's room, he takes only her father and mother and the three disciples whom he has chosen to be with him—Peter, James, and John. None of the people who just mocked his words will witness the miracle. Only those most vitally concerned—the parents, and the inner circle of his most trusted followers—will be there. There won't be even a hint of public display.

The little group gathers by the girl's bedside. Jesus takes her hand and speaks to her, "Talitha cumi." For some reason, the disciples wanted the exact words that he spoke in his native tongue to be recorded. His words were a command, "Little girl, I say to you, arise." At that moment, she opened her eyes, got up from the bed, and walked. It was the most amazing thing that anyone in that room had ever seen. Jesus' call had literally, before their eyes, raised a dead girl to life again. For a few moments, no one moved, no one spoke. The wonder of it stunned them all. Then, of course, the reunion and a flood of joy and tears.

Before anyone left the room, Jesus gave them clear, repeated instruction. First, no one beyond the circle of those who absolutely needed to know should hear about this. There would be no publicity, no general announcement. Second, the little girl was to be given food. What a down-to-earth, homely touch! It could only have come from an eyewitness. Doubtless, this was one of Peter's vivid reminiscences. Jesus the Lord, having brought a dead girl back to life again, reminds her parents that she needs some nourishment.

Two things in this drama stand out for me. One is the extraordinary reserve that Jesus showed. In the most painstaking way, he tried to keep his miraculous works from being widely known. There was disclosure to this intimate circle but a shunning of any notoriety. He would do the deed, express the love, but capitalize on it to draw a huge following, never. I'm struck also by what this narrative tells us of Jesus' attitude toward death. He's against it. He isn't daunted by it. He overcomes it. At his words, even the grim reaper has to give up its victims. This is true for each of us who have trusted in Jesus. The last enemy, death, is overcome. No grave can hold back the boy or girl, the man or woman, to whom Jesus says, "Arise!"

Study Questions

1. What are the elements of vital faith that can be seen in Jairus?
2. How are faith and fear related? Try to illustrate from your experience.
3. Can you explain why the mourners suddenly became laughers?
4. What do we learn here about Jesus' attitude toward death?

20

Encountering Jesus: A Concerned Mother

And from there he arose and went away to the region of Tyre and Sidon. And he entered a house, and would not have any one know it; yet he could not be hid. But immediately a woman, whose little daughter was possessed by an unclean spirit, heard of him, and came and fell down at his feet. Now the woman was a Greek, a Syrophoenician by birth. And she begged him to cast the demon out of her daughter. And he said to her, "Let the children first be fed, for it is not right to take the children's bread and throw it to the dogs." But she answered him, "Yes, Lord; yet even the dogs under the table eat the children's crumbs." And he said to her, "For this saying you may go your way; the demon has left your daughter." And she went home, and found the child lying in bed, and the demon gone.

[Mark 7:24–30]

WE AREN'T TOLD WHY Jesus went to the region of Tyre and Sidon, but it must have been to rest. He never seemed to hold public meetings in such non-Jewish areas. He usually passed through them only on the way to another place. On this occasion, however, he went to a home to stay for a while—and didn't want anyone to know where he was. Perhaps he was exhausted from the utter self-spending of his work. Perhaps he wanted some undisturbed time to better teach his disciples or to reflect on the scope and direction of his ministry. Maybe he just needed time to be quiet.

It's good to be reminded that Jesus sought such retreats and that he urged his followers to take them, to go apart and rest a while. In our well-intentioned zeal to do his will and accomplish his work, we may sometimes forget that and find ourselves frazzled and fretful. All of us need to unstring the bow at times, to get away, to take a break, and we shouldn't despise or be ashamed of that human need.

In this case, however, privacy proved impossible. Jesus' fame had crossed the borders of Israel. No sooner had he settled in the retreat house when people came looking for him. First in line was a Gentile mother from Phoenicia, a part of Syria. She had never seen Jesus but had heard of his power to cast out demons—and her own daughter was terribly possessed. We don't know what the daughter's symptoms were, but her mother was frantic. She had found no help of any kind for this girl and had probably cried herself to sleep over her many nights. The moment she heard that Jesus was in the area, she made her way to the house where he was. As soon as she saw him, she fell down at his feet, imploring him to free her daughter from this dreadful affliction.

This woman was like many others who came to Jesus under the pressure of a great need. She was so concerned for the daughter she loved that she was ready to go anywhere, do anything, to see her well again. And she somehow had become convinced that Jesus would help. That's faith. When you sense a deep need, come with it to Jesus, and humble yourself before him, appealing for his help, that's faith. When you do it for others, you're not only a believer, you're also an intercessor. Like this mother, you're pleading on behalf of another.

Jesus' response to the mother's plea is jarring. It's not what we would have expected. "Let the children first be fed," he said, "for it is not right to take the children's bread and throw it to the dogs."

Who are "the children" here who must first be fed and to whom the bread belongs? By "the children" Jesus meant Israel, God's chosen people. Though every human being has been created by God, though all peoples are his handiwork, the descendants of Abraham, Isaac, and Jacob are in a special sense his covenant children. In the mystery of his electing love, he chose them to be his special people. God's loving plans took in the whole world, but they began with little Israel. The message was always for the Jew first.

Why Israel? That's a question for which no one has an answer. God's people learned well that it was not because of any virtue or worthiness on their part, not because they were more numerous or more attractive than others. If anything, the opposite was often true. At its best Israel always viewed this choice with a kind of adoring wonder.

Evangelist Billy Graham was asked once why God chose to use him to bring the good news to so many people in our generation. Dr. Graham had no idea. "When we are finally with the Lord," he replied, "that's one of the first things I'm going to ask him."

If by "children" the Lord means Israel, who are "the dogs"? They must be the rest of mankind, the Gentiles, the nations. Sometimes Jewish zealots were known to describe Gentiles as dogs, the kind that prowl in the streets, the wild and ravenous sort. That usage was decidedly uncomplimentary.

Jesus doesn't use the word in that sense. The dogs to which he refers are household pets who sit under the table waiting for morsels to drop. It's not flattering, but there's nothing of hostility or contempt in it. There may even be a hint of affection, the feeling that almost everyone has for puppies.

In response to this woman's impassioned appeal, Jesus says, "Let the children be fed first." He's pointing to Israel's priority in God's plans. Jesus as Messiah is ever obedient to the Father's will. He is not a freelancer but a servant. He is dedicated to his mission to Israel right up to his death. The needs of his own people are, therefore, always paramount in his mind. They have to be fed first.

He carries the image further. "It's not right to take the children's bread and throw it to the dogs." For Jesus to conduct a mission to the Gentiles at this point would have been swerving from the path of obedience. It was not fitting that he should, for the sake of Gentiles, curtail his appointed ministry to Israel. Jesus had all he could do in his preaching, teaching, and healing ministry to the chosen people.

That's instructive for us. No one of us can do everything or be everywhere. We have to labor at a certain task, among a particular group of people. Who, in God's plan, are the people who come first for you? Your family? Your neighbors? Your fellow workers? A special circle of friends? Whatever else you do, don't neglect them. Spreading ourselves too widely can imperil our primary call. We have to establish clear priorities as to where we will invest our time and energies and whose needs we will concentrate on meeting. For Jesus, during his earthly ministry, that issue was crystal clear. The focus was Israel, and especially that little band within Israel whom he had chosen as his disciples.

Jesus says, "Let the children be fed *first*." He doesn't rule out a ministry to Gentiles. We know that others would later be included in God's gracious plan. So, along with a response that otherwise seems a bit harsh and insensitive, Jesus adds a glimmer of hope.

Surprisingly, the woman is not angry or resentful against this one who is supposed to be a healer and yet so heartlessly turns her down. She does not despair or turn away silently, crushed in spirit. She says, "Yes, Lord; yet even the dogs under the table eat the children's crumbs."

A number of things impress me here. First, she says, "Yes, Lord." She agrees with Jesus and speaks to him with the utmost respect. Further, she shows that she has been listening carefully. She takes the Lord's own metaphor and makes use of it. "Even the dogs under the table eat the children's crumbs." This woman recognizes Jesus' priorities. She agrees with them. She's not asking for primary consideration. She doesn't want to interrupt anything. All she wants is a crumb. Don't give me the children's bread, she says in effect, just let me have what's left over. Whatever the children don't eat, don't need, don't even want, whatever falls unnoticed off the table, let that be for me.

How could she have affirmed in a more beautiful way the truth of the Lord's words or better renewed her own appeal? She's content with the humble role assigned to her. Let her be one of the puppies, looking up eagerly for some tiny morsel from the feast. This woman believes that the Lord's bounty is abundant and overflowing. Even a crumb from his banquet table will be more than enough, so great is his sufficiency, so marvelous his power. She's like that other woman who felt that she could be healed just by touching the hem of Jesus' garment. In him there is measureless abundance. What faith in the Lord's grace emerges here! This mother believes his mercy to be vast, even though his priorities are right and good. Still he will help her, for his compassion knows no bounds.

This woman is a true suppliant, a model seeker. She has no plea but her need. She has nothing to commend her to Jesus, nothing to offer in response to his gift. All she presents is a heartbreaking concern, appealing simply and only to his loving will. She looks to his large-heartedness, the overflow of his kindness. How great is her faith! She seems to realize with a joyful heart who Jesus is. She ascribes to him power without limit. She keeps on appealing to him in spite of opposition and discouragement and will not swerve from the conviction that in Jesus she will find help. She is sure that behind his seeming indifference and rejection he really does care and he really will help. And she is right!

The Lord answers, "For this saying you may go your way; the demon has left your daughter." For this saying, yes, and for the remarkable faith it expressed. Jesus made a promise that her daughter would be healed. No, not a promise, because the thing had already happened. It was really a pronouncement of what had come to pass, by his sheer sovereign will. The demon had been banished. The girl was released and restored.

Believing what had been told her (and, I'm sure, celebrating all the way), the mother went home. She found that her daughter was herself again, free at last. What joy!

What happened here? Did Jesus abandon his priorities for the sake of this Gentile woman? Did he turn aside from his primary mission simply because of her cleverness and persistence? I don't think so. Jesus did not mean to exclude or discourage her but rather to stir her heart, to awaken faith. She saw the Lord's intention and sensed the invitation hidden in his words. She knew that the deepest reality about Jesus was grace and that stronger than anything else in him was a passion to heal and to save. Faith, more than anything else, was what Jesus wanted to see in people.

The heart of God can also be touched by our appeals of love and prayers of faith. If you are burdened and are praying earnestly and urgently for the Lord's help, don't lose heart. There may be delays. There may be times when he seems stern or insensitive. You may be tempted to doubt that he really cares at all, but don't give up. Keep doing what the Tzeltal Indians of Mexico translate as *believing*, "holding on to God with your heart." When you hold fast to his love and faithfulness and come to God through Jesus and appeal to him, you won't be finally disappointed. This is Paul's logic: "He who did not spare his own Son but gave him up for us all, will he not also give us all things with him?" (Rom. 8:32). In other words, if he cared enough to give his own Son, will he withhold from us any good gift? No matter how unpromising it seems, keep on asking, seeking, knocking. It won't be for nothing. Sometime, somewhere, you'll discover as this woman did that the love of God is "broader than the measure of man's mind, and the heart of the Eternal is most wonderfully kind."[†]

Study Questions

1. Why did Jesus need to retreat? How could you benefit from similar retreats?
2. What are the marks of genuine faith in this mother's behavior?
3. How do you explain Jesus' seemingly insensitive response to her?
4. In what areas of your life do you need persistent faith and prayer?

[†] From Frederick William Faber, "There's a Wideness in God's Mercy."

21

Encountering Jesus: A Boy with Seizures

———— ◆ ————

And when they came to the disciples, they saw a great crowd about them, and scribes arguing with them. And immediately all the crowd, when they saw him, were greatly amazed, and ran up to him and greeted him. And he asked them, "What are you discussing with them?" And one of the crowd answered him, "Teacher, I brought my son to you, for he has a dumb spirit; and wherever it seizes him, it dashes him down; and he foams and grinds his teeth and becomes rigid; and I asked your disciples to cast it out, and they were not able." And he answered them, "O faithless generation, how long am I to be with you? How long am I to bear with you? Bring him to me." And they brought the boy to him; and when the spirit saw him, immediately it convulsed the boy, and he fell on the ground and rolled about, foaming at the mouth. And Jesus asked his father, "How long has he had this?" And he said, "From childhood. And it has often cast him into the fire and into the water, to destroy him; but if you can do anything, have pity on us and help us." And Jesus said to him, "If you can! All things are possible to him who believes." Immediately the father of the child cried out and said, "I believe; help my unbelief!" And when Jesus saw that a

crowd came running together, he rebuked the unclean spirit, saying to it, "You dumb and deaf spirit, I command you, come out of
him, and never enter him again." And after crying out and convulsing him terribly, it came out, and the boy was like a corpse; so
that most of them said, "He is dead." But Jesus took him by the hand
and lifted him up, and he arose. And when he had entered the
house, his disciples asked him privately, "Why could we not cast it
out?" And he said to them, "This kind cannot be driven out by anything but prayer."

[Mark 9:14–29]

IF YOU HAD BEEN THERE, you would have seen nine of Jesus' disciples
acting somewhat restless and adrift in the absence of their Master. He had
gone with Peter, James, and John on a kind of mountain retreat. A father
arrives, bringing his afflicted boy. He's looking for Jesus. He wants the Master to drive out the evil spirit that troubles his son. From time to time the
boy goes into convulsions, falls, grinds his teeth, foams at the mouth. His
life has been endangered when he has fallen rigid into a fire or some body
of water. The father is desperate. Where is Jesus? he asks. Can he help my
boy? He's not here now, the father is told, but he has empowered us, his
followers, to heal and to cast out demons. Bring the boy to us.

You draw closer with the growing crowd to see what will happen. The
disciples are trying to cast out this evil spirit. They say the words of exor-
cism. They invoke divine authority. They do what they can, but nothing happens. They try again and again, each time with more vehemence,
but the boy remains unchanged.

Quite a discussion follows. Some visiting scribes are quick to point
out that Jesus' followers have no authority to attempt such signs. What
has their training been? Where are their credentials? Others see this failure as reflecting unfavorably on Jesus. He must not be all that people say
he is. See, his followers are helpless. The claims made about this Jesus
must be exaggerated.

Just then there's a commotion in the crowd. People are looking toward
the mountain. Some are running in that direction. Soon you see Jesus

and three of his disciples making their way towards them. Everyone is excited. The Master seems to be arriving at just the right time.

"What's the discussion about?" asks Jesus. The father speaks up in reply, telling about his son's difficulties and about the failure of the disciples to cast out the evil spirit. You sense the tension building as the story is told. What will Jesus' response be? What will he do?

His first reaction is a kind of lament. "O faithless generation," Jesus exclaims, "how long am I to be with you? How long am I to bear with you? Bring him to me." Isn't that striking? The first observation Jesus makes about this situation bears on faith. He sees it as tragically lacking in this generation. That troubles him greatly. How long, he wonders, will he go on living in this kind of environment? How long will he have to bear with the unbelief of his contemporaries?

To whose faithlessness was Jesus referring here? Some say it must have been that of the scribes who were criticizing his disciples. They were the faithless ones who clung to their tradition but refused to welcome a great new religious movement. Others say it must have been the crowds who were concluding from this failure of the disciples that Jesus himself was impotent. All of that may be true, but it doesn't say nearly enough.

The faithlessness with which Jesus is most familiar is that of his friends. It is their slowness to believe, their failure to learn and grow, their dullness of heart that pains his spirit. He is grieved because they have proved unable to help this suffering boy. The whole scene, full of pathos and disappointment, saddens Jesus and tests his endurance.

We can't help noticing how important faith is to Jesus. It's the one thing he especially praises when he sees it ("Great is your faith"), and misses when it's lacking ("O you of little faith, why did you doubt?"). We sense that he's always looking for faith in people. When he finds it, he speaks words of joy and promise. Where faith is absent, on the other hand, few of his mighty works become evident. He seems especially saddened when those who ought to know better still act in faithless ways, when even his disciples prove backward in believing.

I wonder if he calls our generation faithless, if he says now, how long can I put up with these people? I wonder if he's looking for something in us that he doesn't find and if our little faith grieves his Spirit.

Jesus asks that the boy be brought to him. At that moment the boy has a kind of seizure. He falls to the ground, rolls about, foaming at the mouth. It's unnerving to watch this and to see the father looking on in helpless anguish. "How long has he had this?" Jesus asked. "From childhood," the answer came. "It has often cast him into the fire and into the water, to destroy him; but if you can do anything, have pity on us and help us." The father is at the breaking point. He has almost abandoned hope. He seems now to be grasping at straws, "If you can do anything..." It's as though he said, this is terrible, Jesus, and I'm not sure you can make things different, but if there's anything at all that you can do to help my boy, please have a heart and do it.

Now all eyes are upon Jesus. Will he heal the boy now or will he agree that nothing can be done? Suddenly Jesus is doing the unexpected again. He's turning the man's words around. The man had said, "If you can do anything..." Jesus says, "if *you* can." (If you can believe.) In other words, Jesus' ability and adequacy are not in question. That will be demonstrated soon enough. The question is can the man making the appeal find the strength to believe. Is he up to this, or will his gloom and hopelessness stand in the way of a miracle? The man's faith is the only thing in doubt here.

Now you hear Jesus startling everyone. He makes a sweeping promise, a bold pronouncement. "All things are possible to him who believes." This is perhaps the highest tribute that Jesus ever gives to belief. According to him, it has a kind of delegated omnipotence. There are no achievements too great, no obstacles too forbidding for the person who believes. Believing, it seems, brings people into the stream of God's power and puts them in touch with his resources. There is nothing too hard for the Lord. If this father can only believe that, the future will be bright with hope.

That's the problem. Can we believe as we ought? How do we get the faith we need? Listen to the father's response. He cries out with a loud voice, "I believe." I trust in you, Jesus. I believe you can help. I really mean it. But then comes the plea, "help my unbelief." He confesses to doubts. He's been disappointed many times before. This problem has persisted for a long time. He's gotten his hopes up again and again, but no miracle has come. The long agony of concern for his son has gone on and on. Sometimes it's hard to believe, Jesus. I don't want to be weak and wavering. I don't want to be a doubter. I surely don't want my unbelief to stand in the way of my son's healing. So please, Jesus, help me in my struggle, free me from my fears, and give me what I need. "Help my unbelief."

Have you ever felt that way? You know that faith is important, that God wants you to believe, but sometimes it seems beyond you. You wish you could shake your doubts, but they keep cropping up. What can you do? You don't want to be skeptical or cynical, but you don't want to hide your head in the sand, either. You have moments in your life when it seems easy to believe, when you know that you really do trust the Lord. You know there's nothing he can't or won't do for you. But at other times he seems far away. You face situations that seem unchangeable and barriers in your way that laugh at your best hopes. You've known a lot of other religious people who tried to believe or said they believed, but nothing happened. You find yourself saying, too, I believe, Lord; help my unbelief.

Now as you stand watching, people come running from all directions. They sense that something marvelous is about to happen, and it does. Jesus rebukes the evil spirit. "You dumb and deaf spirit, I command you, come out of him, and never enter him again." Suddenly from the lips of this boy who has been deaf and mute comes a terrible cry. His body shakes with violent convulsions. The lad slumps to the ground and lies completely still. "He's dead! He's dead!" the people around you are saying. Can that be? Is the evil spirit too powerful for Jesus? Does Jesus' attempt to help the boy actually destroy him? Everyone is crowding around for a closer look.

Meanwhile, Jesus seems amazingly calm. He stoops over, takes the boy by the hand, and raises him to his feet. He is alive, and what's more, completely delivered. The crowd gasps, then cheers. You see tears of joy all around you. What an astonishing thing you have witnessed this day!

Now for a closing scene you probably would not have witnessed. The crowd has gradually dispersed. Jesus, with his reunited disciples, has gone into a house. They reflect together on the things that have just occurred.

The same question is on everybody's mind. Away from prying eyes and curious ears, the disciples wonder aloud, "Why could we not cast it out?" They're happy over what they have seen, of course. They are as awed as the rest at this sign of Jesus' authority, but they are puzzled too. What went wrong, Lord? Where did we fail? Why couldn't we help? Here was Jesus' response: "This kind cannot be driven out by anything but prayer."

There's no hint in this account that Jesus stopped to pray before casting out the oppressing spirit. What prayer is he talking about? Whose prayer? Jesus had just been on the Mount of Transfiguration. Luke tells us that he went up on that mountain with his inner circle of disciples to pray, and that while he was praying, his countenance was altered and the disciples beheld his glory. He had come from that place of prayer into this valley of the demon-possessed. Jesus, as we sometimes put it, was "prayed up." He was prepared by communion with his Father for this encounter. He went into the conflict filled with the Holy Spirit's power, sure in the strength of the Lord. And it was that prayer, Jesus said, that opened the way for the miracle.

Apparently the disciples had not prayed. At least, not in a way that prepared them. They were not spiritually ready for the moment of crisis. They were not in the kind of vital touch with God that would make their lives channels of redeeming power. They had learned from Jesus the central significance of prayer in the life of discipleship. They had become learners in his school of prayer. They had been practicing the high art.

And what about Jesus' earlier words when he had called them a faithless generation? Weren't they believers? Hadn't they confessed through their spokesman Peter that Jesus was indeed the Christ, the Son of the living God? Yes, they had, and they had meant it. They were men of faith, all of them, with the possible exception of Judas. Jesus sometimes chided them as men of little faith, but he never treated them as unbelievers. He knew they were true-hearted men who trusted and loved him.

We're a mixed bag, all of us. We can be believers and still sometimes act faithlessly. We can be praying people and still at times live without prayer. Sometimes we remember to pray and sometimes we blunder on as though God doesn't exist. Sometimes we rely on the Lord; sometimes we forget. We're like that brokenhearted father. "Lord, I believe; help my unbelief. Lord, I pray, help my lack of prayer."

And maybe that's just the attitude he wants to see in us. If we get complacent at the state of our faith or confident that we know all there is to know about prayer, then we're a people without power. But if we are always coming back to the Lord, affirming our faith and also our struggle, our willingness and also our weakness, if we're crying out to him to strengthen our faith and to teach us to pray, then we're on the right track. It may be also that when other people look to us for help in their moments of crisis we'll have something to give them.

Study Questions

1. What or whom do you think Jesus had in mind when he lamented the "faithless generation"?
2. Jesus said, "All things are possible to him who believes." What do you think he meant? Are there any limits to faith?
3. The father said, "I believe; help my unbelief!" How can people be believing and unbelieving at the same time?
4. What kind of praying was needed in this situation?

22

Encountering Jesus: A Rich Inquirer

◆

And as he was setting out on his journey, a man ran up and knelt before him, and asked him, "Good Teacher, what must I do to inherit eternal life?" And Jesus said to him, "Why do you call me good? No one is good but God alone. You know the commandments: 'Do not kill, Do not commit adultery, Do not steal, Do not bear false witness, Do not defraud, Honor your father and mother.'" And he said to him, "Teacher, all these I have observed from my youth." And Jesus looking upon him loved him, and said to him, "You lack one thing; go, sell what you have, and give to the poor, and you will have treasure in heaven; and come, follow me." At that saying his countenance fell, and he went away sorrowful; for he had great possessions.

[Mark 10:17–22]

WE OFTEN CALL HIM "the rich young ruler," but nowhere do we find in the Gospels that exact description. Only Matthew tells us he was young. Only Luke lets us know that he was a ruler. The point at which all agree is that he was rich. His encounter with Jesus was poignant and memorable.

There's much to admire in this young man. He comes running to Jesus, apparently eager to find him, happy to be in his presence. And when he comes, he kneels in the dust, expressing great respect, perhaps even reverence. He obviously has a high regard for the man from Nazareth. Further, he addresses him as "Good Teacher." To this man, Jesus was a rabbi with the wisdom to give instruction. He sees him also as a person of character, a teacher who lived what he taught, who embodied a good life.

His question tells us that he is concerned about important issues. He wants to know about eternal life and the future that God has in store for his people. He wants to be able to inherit God's kingdom, to become a child and heir of the most high God. That's a goal eminently worth seeking.

This young man has sought earnestly to keep God's commandments. When Jesus reminds him of what we call the second table of the law, God's order for how we are to treat other people, the man expresses his zeal, "Teacher, all these I have observed from my youth." For as long as he can remember, he has been aware of God's commandments and earnest about keeping them. Not everyone can say that about the turbulent years of childhood and adolescence. This man was like the apostle Paul in his early years, zealous beyond his peers in fulfilling the law. Apparently, it's no idle boast. Jesus doesn't contradict him. He seems to accept the truth of his claim but says that the young man still lacks one thing.

I see one more thing to admire. The ruler is honest. When the cost of discipleship is presented to him, he does not profess a commitment he isn't ready to make. He doesn't promise in a careless, superficial way to be a follower. No bravado with him: Lord, I'll follow you wherever you go. This man counts the cost and finds it too much to pay. He doesn't try to serve two masters. He is straightforward enough to know that he can't have it both ways.

What an outstanding young man! He is eager, reverent, and concerned about spiritual things. He tries to keep all of God's commandments and he won't compromise his integrity. What more could you want? Along with these impressive credentials, the man shows some areas of weakness. He seems supremely self-confident, at times unrealistically so. He wants to learn from Jesus how to inherit eternal life—a worthy quest—but he seems to believe that he can bring this off by something he does. What must I do for this to be mine? Then, when Jesus ticks off the commands, the man claims to have obeyed them all. There is no acknowledgment of wrong, no hint of shortcoming. He's done it all. What room is left for improvement? If it would be too severe to call him arrogant, we have to say at least that he is naïve.

What is more jarring about this young man is that when Jesus tells him one thing that he needs to do and invites him, "Come, follow me," the young man's face falls. Suddenly he's disappointed and turns away. How could that happen? How could anyone come to Jesus full of questions and good intentions, hear his word, and then turn away sad?

Mark tells us it was because the man had "great possessions." Jesus had said, "Sell what you have, and give to the poor." If this man had been destitute, that directive surely wouldn't have made him sad. With nothing to lose, he would have consented in a moment. But this young ruler had a lot to sell. This would have involved a major giveaway. Whether it was an estate received from his parents or the profits of a highly successful business, this fellow had a fortune, and the thought of giving it all away made him sick.

We could call him selfish or greedy, but are we sure we would have reacted differently had we been in his shoes? People of wealth tend to take very seriously what they have. It may have taken a lot of years and a lot of effort to accumulate. The thought of renouncing it all seems irresponsible to them, even intolerable. People just don't do things like that, at least not without a lot of careful consideration. Would you have been willing, right on the spot, to sign it all away? That's a pretty final thing to do—and scary.

Apparently, riches represented security for this man. The thought of losing it all was terrifying. He had always been secure in the fact that he would never have anything to worry about financially. He would always have the power to buy what he needed, to provide for his family, and to live well. Jesus' call sounded like radical insecurity.

According to Jesus, this transaction wouldn't be a total loss. The promise was "You will have treasure in heaven." Out ahead there would be a better kind of riches, something supremely valuable. The man couldn't imagine, however, that some future benefit would be valuable enough to warrant letting everything go now, so his heart sank. A great heaviness settled over his spirit. He turned to go away. The zest and eagerness he had shown in coming was gone. His head was down.

Notice a few things about the way Jesus dealt with this inquirer. He began by testing him. To the address, "Good Teacher," Jesus answered, "Why do you call me good? No one is good but God alone." Some have seen these words as a rebuke. Jesus regards the greeting as flattery and rejects it. Others think Jesus is denying that he's ultimately good or that he is one with the Father. Those explanations are unsatisfying to me. He did not take the man's greeting lightly, and he did not want to deny the deep mystery of who he was. He's inviting this inquirer to think carefully about what he's saying. Ultimately, the wisdom to teach and the power to be good come from God. Jesus wants the man to realize that the answer to his question and his search is in God alone.

Then notice how Jesus dealt unerringly with the sensitive area in this man's life. In listing the commandments, Jesus did not include, "Do not covet." He knew the heart of this man's problem. When the ruler replies that he has kept all these from his youth, Jesus begins to talk about selling what he has and giving to the poor. This was a personalized call, as the call of Jesus always is. Jesus knew that for this man the key issue was his possessions. Some have argued from this that Jesus wants everyone to sell his or her belongings and give the proceeds to the poor, but the Lord did not give this instruction to everyone who offered to follow him. Apparently some who were rich were not urged to take this drastic step.

Jesus said to him, "You lack one thing." Was this one thing poverty? In one sense, yes. In another, his possessions were only a pointer to "the one thing." The all-important thing for this man and for us is a single-hearted devotion to God—obedience to the first commandment. The fact that this man went away with a darkened countenance makes it clear that he had made riches a kind of idol from which he couldn't bring himself to part.

Jesus makes the call personal and specific for each of us. We are each tempted to serve a master. For each of us there is a darling idol that threatens to capture our hearts. The call of Jesus to you will zero in on that. It may be wealth or possessions. It could be popularity—having the good opinion of others may mean more to you than just about anything you can think of. You'd be willing to keep quiet about your convictions or even go against your conscience to be well thought of by certain important people. Jesus might say to you, sell that and follow me.

There may be a hobby or a pleasure that has so grown in importance for you that you shape everything else around it. Indulging yourself there takes priority over your vocation or your relationships with your loved ones. Jesus might say to you, sell that. Or you may have been trusting in your own performance to make you acceptable to God. Your confidence is in your record rather than in his grace. The Lord may be saying to you, sell all that and follow me.

With him the command is also a gift. When Jesus said, "Come, follow me," he was offering himself to the man. Jesus is the answer to this man's question and to ours. He is the way to eternal life. To inherit life, to take hold of it, is to receive the gift offered to us in the person of Jesus Christ and to welcome him as our Savior and our King.

Mark writes that as Jesus looked on the young man and gave him this charge, he loved him. He saw his weakness, knew the idol he was clutching, felt his spiritual peril, but he loved him and wanted him to have life. Jesus' love is the kind of love that would not force him but let him walk away sorrowfully. There was no pleading from Jesus, no compromising of the call, no adjusting of the terms. The man was free to walk away and live with his decision.

We don't know what happened after that, but I have a hunch the rich young ruler eventually became a follower of Jesus. The word of the Lord had really reached his heart. He was sad when he turned away. Perhaps his inner distress brought him back later to make a deep, real, and lasting commitment.

In the first church I served, I invited a man named Art to a pastor's class for church membership. At the end of those classes I would customarily ask the people involved if they were ready now to make a commitment to Christ and his church. I knew that Art had been listening intently, so I was surprised when he answered no, he wasn't ready. He didn't give me much light on why. Later on I learned. Art had been a man much given to profanity, especially at his work. He knew that would have to change if he were to live as a Christian. He wasn't sure that he wanted to be different or even could be.

One day several weeks after our conversation, someone on the job said, "What's the matter with you, Art? You don't talk like you used to." Somewhere along the line, the profanity had all dropped out of his speech and he hadn't even been aware of it. That settled it for Art. He came to me and said, "I'm ready now." And he was. When I visited that congregation recently, almost thirty years later, Art was a key officer in the church, still serving Jesus Christ. I hope it was that way for the rich young ruler.

Study Questions

1. Do you think this man was as upright as he claimed to be? Explain your answer.
2. What was the "one thing" he lacked?
3. How was his turning away a failure of faith?
4. Does Jesus mean for everyone to sell all they have and give to the poor? Explain.

23

Encountering Jesus: A Blind Beggar

◆

And they came to Jericho; and as he was leaving Jericho with his disciples and a great multitude, Bartimaeus, a blind beggar, the son of Timaeus, was sitting by the roadside. And when he heard that it was Jesus of Nazareth, he began to cry out and say, "Jesus, Son of David, have mercy on me!" And many rebuked him, telling him to be silent; but he cried out all the more, "Son of David, have mercy on me!" And Jesus stopped and said, "Call him." And they called the blind man, saying to him, "Take heart; rise, he is calling you." And throwing off his mantle he sprang up and came to Jesus. And Jesus said to him, "What do you want me to do for you?" And the blind man said to him, "Master, let me receive my sight." And Jesus said to him, "Go your way; your faith has made you well." And immediately he received his sight and followed him on the way.

[Mark 10:46–52]

MOST OF US ENJOY the priceless gift of vision. Have you ever pondered what it would be like to be blind? What life must be like for the friend or acquaintance who is sightless? Sometimes the effort to put ourselves in someone else's place can open up for us a new dimension in life.

I remember reading years ago a book titled *Black Like Me*. It told the story of a white man who had his skin so treated that he seemed, even to close observers, to be black. He wanted to find out how it would feel to be seen and treated as a member of a minority group and to learn first hand about racial prejudice. I've heard also of psychologists who, in an effort to appreciate a small child's view of the world, creep on the floor for long periods of time.

My closest touch with the experience of blindness came once in what is called a trust walk. I was securely blindfolded and then led about by a guide. My instructions were to relax and commit myself completely to his care. I remember how I began to notice acutely the messages coming through my other senses and also how dependent I felt on the person leading me. An experience like that can give just a hint of what it would be like to be blind. We discover that there are dangers of which the blind cannot be aware, beauties they cannot appreciate, and most of all, dearly loved faces they cannot recognize.

Blind Bartimaeus lived in the ancient city of Jericho. He was a beggar. In his day, there was nothing a blind man could do but beg. In our time, many blind people enjoy opportunities that Bartimaeus never knew. Especially since the days of Helen Keller, sightless people are often able to develop their skills and live richly productive lives.

At first Bartimaeus, sitting by a dusty thoroughfare outside the city of Jericho, seems like just another beggar, but after reading about his encounter with Jesus, he's somehow transformed. I see him now as a man in deep need who seized a great opportunity. His need was great, an aching, poignant human need, one which he felt deeply, which every blind person must feel deeply. I have read that once a mighty emperor, after having accidentally put out the eyes of one of his servants, offered to compensate him with royal gifts. The servant seemed unaffected. All he kept saying was, "I wish I had my eyes! I wish I had my eyes!"

This is the kind of need no friend, no doctor, no human agency can possibly meet. All of us have some needs like that. We may be physically whole but we may feel afflicted in our spirits. We may have missed the way in life and need to be forgiven. Or we may crave release from some bondage but have been seeking it in vain. Perhaps we need a sense of meaning, some purpose in life, which nothing around us seems to supply. There's something in our life and situation we long to change but we feel helpless to do it.

One day, to this man Bartimaeus, there came a once-in-a-lifetime opportunity. It was one of those rare occasions in an otherwise humdrum, routine existence when things can suddenly change dramatically, when life can be different, when something new can open up before us. Bartimaeus heard a commotion around him; he sensed excitement in the air and asked what it was all about. It's Jesus of Nazareth, said someone. He's going by now. The words went through Bartimaeus like an electric shock. He had heard strange tales of this man's deeds, how the crippled had thrown away their crutches, how the deaf heard, the blind saw, and how funerals had been canceled. He trembled with excitement. Here's my chance, he thought. Without a moment's hesitation, he began to cry out at the top of his voice. "Jesus, Son of David, have mercy on me!" When a group of bystanders tried to quiet him, he shouted all the more loudly.

This was a man who longed for help, cried out for it, and refused to be discouraged or intimidated. He believed that though others didn't care about him, perhaps this Jesus would. And so this obscure, afflicted man becomes a picture for us of what it is to seize life's greatest opportunity, what it is to act in faith.

Look for a moment at the crowd that tried to silence him. They were sure that nothing could be done for this man anyway. Perhaps some were hostile to Jesus and resented the title of honor that Bartimaeus gave him—Son of David. Shut up, blind man. You blasphemer! They may have railed.

Others may have thought he was only after money. Quit your begging, they jeered. They didn't understand his cry. They didn't know what he really wanted. How easy it is for us to assign the worst motives to people who cry out in their distress. Some interpret the appeals of welfare mothers, for example, only as pleas to be lazy and promiscuous. Some dismiss as troublemakers the prophets who call for social justice.

I suppose there were others who saw Bartimaeus simply as a nuisance. They were in the crowd to see the famous prophet, not to be disturbed by one more beggar. What did this man matter? What did his condition have to do with Jesus anyway? Perhaps even the disciples wondered about that. They were concerned for their master, eager to protect his privacy, to shield him from being bothered. They knew that tremendous things were on his mind. At times they even tried to keep children away from him.

In our day, some well-meaning people in our churches often act in a similar way. Please, let's not have anyone poorly dressed or noisy or disruptive here in church. They might be offensive to the Lord—as though God would welcome less heartily people who aren't middle class, conventional, and neatly dressed!

Note how Jesus reacted to the situation. The cross was only a few days away. His face had been set toward Jerusalem with a determination that struck his disciples with awe. Gethsemane and Golgotha loomed up before him, and so his mind and heart were occupied with enormous issues. If ever anyone could be excused for being preoccupied, caught up in his own thoughts, it would surely have been Jesus at a time like this. And yet he heard the blind man's cry. In spite of all the noise around him and his own thoughts, he heard the cry of one man. He listened with a love that singled out that one person. That seems strange to us. What is this incident by the road compared to the vast panorama about to unfold in Jerusalem? Nothing, it would seem. Yet it was something significant and crucial to Jesus. That's good to know, isn't it? It can almost make us believe that our own cries for help will be heard and answered.

Jesus didn't just hear Bartimaeus's cry, he actually stopped. Think of it—a blind beggar could stop Jesus on his way to Jerusalem to accomplish the salvation of the world! Others had tried to stop him—his enemies and his well-meaning friends—but no one could. Jesus stopped, and it was as though he were saying to the blind man, I'm turning all my attention on you. You are an important person to me.

How much all of us need to know that! We crave respect. We long to know that we're people of worth, that we matter to someone. And Jesus' stopping on the Jericho Road says that to all of us. Imagine it: the Lord can be interrupted. Apparently the great issues can wait. The Lord of heaven and earth has time for us. Jesus demonstrated here that every kind of human need is his urgent business.

Jesus said to his disciples, "Call him." He was testing the blind man's faith, his eagerness, and Bartimaeus was equal to the test. We see him throwing off his mantle, springing up, and coming to Jesus. What an act of faith that was—for a blind man to jump up and start running!

Jesus' first word to him was a question, "What do you want me to do for you?" That seems a strange thing to ask. The blind man's need must have been obvious. Bartimaeus could have been asking for money, of course, but Jesus' question probed to a deeper level. Did he really want to be healed? Was he ready to leave his begging and step out into a new world of responsibility? That wasn't a question to be shrugged off.

What about us? Do we want deeply to be healed, cleansed, set free? Sometimes we can hug those problems of ours to ourselves. We can become almost dependent on them. We can make them an excuse for copping out and hiding from the pressures of life. But Bartimaeus knew what he wanted. He asked for it. He received it. And then he gladly followed the one who had given him light.

Now it's true that this man lived long ago and far away, but there's something about his encounter with Jesus that is fresh and contemporary. People wonder today, and maybe you do too, what the church really is, what's it all about. What's the point of all these religious organizations, these evangelistic efforts, these gospel broadcasts? What do they have to say to people nearing the end of this century, this millennium?

The heart of our message is the same as what someone said to Bartimaeus that day, "Jesus of Nazareth is passing by." The one who died once for us is alive again and is here right now. Wherever Christians gather—in cathedrals, in chapels, in homes, in caves—wherever the Word is preached, wherever the Good News is offered, wherever God's people walk and witness, Jesus Christ is there, passing by. He is the living Lord, the present one, mighty to save.

The presence of the Lord is never obtrusive. Jesus doesn't force himself on you or on anyone else. He waits for you to call on him, just as Bartimaeus did, and, just as Jesus did for the blind beggar, he'll stop for you. People around you may try to discourage you, pressures may distract you, and voices may seem to say, This is not for you. You may hesitate because you feel unworthy or insignificant. Don't worry about that. Lift your prayer to him anyway. Jesus Christ will hear you. Why, he would suspend the stars in their courses to listen to one person like you!

Study Questions

1. What do you think are the most difficult aspects of blindness?
2. How do you see faith expressed in Bartimaeus?
3. How have others discouraged you from reaching out to Christ?
4. What is amazing about the fact that Jesus stopped for Bartimaeus? What encouragement does it give you?

24

Encountering Jesus: A Scribe

◆

And one of the scribes came up and heard them disputing with one another, and seeing that he answered them well, asked him, "Which commandment is the first of all?" Jesus answered, "The first is, 'Hear, O Israel: The Lord our God, the Lord is one; and you shall love the Lord your God with all your heart, and with all your soul, and with all your mind, and with all your strength.' The second is this, 'You shall love your neighbor as yourself.' There is no other commandment greater than these." And the scribe said to him, "You are right, Teacher; you have truly said that he is one, and there is no other but he; and to love him with all the heart, and with all the understanding, and with all the strength, and to love one's neighbor as oneself, is much more than all whole burnt offerings and sacrifices." And when Jesus saw that he answered wisely, he said to him, "You are not far from the kingdom of God."

[Mark 12:28–34]

IT MUST HAVE BEEN REFRESHING for Jesus to meet a questioner like this one. He had been dealing with people whose motives were suspect. They came to him with mock respect, asking their "loaded" questions. He knew they wanted to embarrass him, to catch him in his words, to gain some pretext for putting him out of the way. Should they give tribute to

Caesar or not, they asked. They hoped to turn his answer, whether yes or no, into some kind of charge against him. Or what about this woman who had married seven brothers in the same family? In the resurrection you talk about, Jesus, which one's wife will she be? These wiseacres planned in this way to make his teaching appear ridiculous.

Sometimes Jesus would confront such carping questioners with a rebuke. "You are very far from the truth." Sometimes he would leave them hanging with a cryptic remark or penetrate their defenses with a searching question of his own. But after this encounter with a man Mark describes as a scribe, Jesus spoke with warm approval: "You are not far from the kingdom of God."

What was there about this man that was so encouraging? What was different about him? Notably the difference was the attitude with which he approached Jesus. Whereas others had been seeking to embarrass or entrap him, this man came with evident respect and admiration. In answering the questions about paying taxes to Caesar or marriage ties in the resurrection, Jesus had responded with consummate wisdom. He had confounded his critics, thwarting their schemes to make him look bad. This scribe (that means an expert in the Jewish law, someone well versed in the Scriptures) had been listening with evident approval. He saw how well Jesus had answered. The word could be translated also: "how honorably" or even "how beautifully." The scribe was impressed.

With him there was not the slightest desire to put Jesus at a disadvantage. He saw where the truth lay in the discussions that had been going on. He recognized Jesus as a master teacher, and wanted to hear more. Let him continue expounding the ways of God with men, bringing the truth to light! That was the scribe's attitude.

If you've ever taught a class or led a discussion or been plied with questions, you know how varied in tone these inquiries can be. Some are trivial, hardly worth spending time on. Some are asked for purposes of self-display, by people confident they already have the answer. Some are trick questions designed to call forth a laugh at your expense. Some are downright hostile, suspicious, and sneering. But then there are some you delight to hear. Someone really believes that you have something to contribute, a worthwhile insight to share. They want to hear from you. Perhaps it's a friend who wants to give you a chance to say something he knows is important to you. Questions like that make you feel relaxed, relieved, and grateful.

This man asked Jesus about a vitally important matter. Of all the things that God requires of people, what stands at the top of the list? What does the Almighty look for most in us? How Jesus must have welcomed that kind of search! Here was a man not working an angle, not covering up a hidden agenda. He really wanted to know about something that mattered deeply. He wanted to hear how human beings can fulfill the purpose of their existence, how they can please God.

And since the question was frank and genuine, Jesus responded directly, giving the man just what he asked for. God's first requirement is that we know him, the one true living God, and that we love him with all our being. That's it. That command comes first. And the second, Jesus went on to say, from which the first can never be isolated, is that we are to love our neighbors as ourselves. Then Jesus added, "There is no other commandment greater than these," as though to say, this is what you've asked for. Nothing takes priority over this call from God to walk in love.

Now notice how the man responded: "You are right, Teacher; you have truly said that he is one, and there is no other but he," and so on. Here is a ringing affirmation of Jesus and his message. This scribe, whose profession was the study of God's law, who was looked on as an expert in what pleases God, said to Jesus, Well done! Honorably, splendidly answered! Among many who were murmuring, criticizing, searching for a basis to accuse, here was a distinguished scholar-teacher, trained in the schools of his day, who said in effect, Jesus, you could not have said it better.

Then he demonstrated that he had been listening carefully. He repeated what Jesus had said, recasting, paraphrasing, showing that he had clearly understood. His approval, in other words, was not thoughtless and superficial. He put Jesus' response in his own words and then proceeded to amplify and apply it. To do this, he went on, "is much more than all whole burnt offerings and sacrifices."

That's the kind of thing a teacher looks for in his or her students: understanding of what has been communicated, an ability to articulate it for themselves, and a keen grasp of its implications. Teachers want students who can grasp the truth, internalize it, and apply it to life. Jesus had spoken earlier about how obedience is better than sacrifice, how God wants mercy and kindness more than he wants animal offerings. How cheering it must have been for him to hear this now from the lips of the scribe!

The man must have known that he was taking a risk here. This open affirmation of Jesus could hardly have been popular among the Lord's critics and enemies. And there were doubtless some in the audience to whom the words about the burnt offerings and sacrifices would have been shocking. Why, the man seemed to be calling into question the value of the whole sacrificial system! Many in Israel believed that by offering the appropriate sacrifices in the worship conducted in the temple, they were fulfilling the major part of their duty to God. The scribe made a lot of people feel uncomfortable that day, but he didn't seem worried about that. He was ready to say amen to Jesus' words and to follow the truth wherever it would lead him. Some of the other scribes in the group must have wondered whose side their colleague was on.

Then came this word of Jesus, "You are not far from the kingdom of God." What was he saying to the scribe? His words seem very different from those spoken to Nicodemus, another inquirer he encountered. He too had been a respected leader of the Jews, learned in the things of God. But Jesus had brought Nicodemus up short when he told him that he could not enter the kingdom of God or even see it unless he were born again. Nicodemus would have to be totally transformed, made new, to get near God's kingdom. Now this scribe, Jesus says, was already close to it. How so?

According to Mark, Jesus saw that the man had answered wisely. Or as another translation puts it, "thoughtfully" or "with understanding." Jesus sensed in this man an openness, a receptivity, a welcoming of the light. That impression was deepened when he heard the scribe's response.

How was he "not far" from God's kingdom? It was evident that he responded positively to Jesus himself. He respected him and sought his counsel. That was important. Beyond that, he wrestled seriously with the command of God and its implications for life. Where people are open to Jesus, willing to be taught by him, and where they let themselves be engaged by his Word, and seek to apply it in their own situations, they're surely on the right track, moving in the right direction.

Jesus said on one occasion, "He who is not with me is against me." This man was in no sense against Jesus. He was rather a truth seeker. He was open to whatever Jesus had to teach and to give. He gave thoughtful attention to the word of Jesus and showed himself willing to affirm it openly, to become himself a witness to what Jesus had declared. But still, the man wasn't in, apparently. He wasn't far from the kingdom but there was still some distance remaining. He was not yet on the inside. What was still lacking?

I spent a sizable portion of my life in theological seminaries. I attended one for three years after graduation from college, spent another two or three years in a different one pursuing doctoral studies, taught full time in still another for ten years, and I've had various part-time involvements with seminaries since. One of the things I became aware of in that milieu is the difference between talking theology and living it, between discussion and discipleship. Sometimes we find it easy in a seminary setting to listen to lectures and sermons, to comment about them, to express our approval or disapproval, and to become capable articulators of the Christian message. None of that guarantees that we will live it out. It's possible for us to become hearers of the Word but not doers, experts in describing God's way who never get around to doing much about it.

That's not a peril confined to seminary classrooms. It can happen just as easily within the church. We may be very enthusiastic about the Word and affirm all that the Bible teaches yet never really function as salt in the earth and light in the world. Talking about the will of God is not the same thing as obeying it.

This man's openness to Jesus, though encouraging, was only a beginning. Would he go from respect for his teaching to a real personal commitment? Would he remain an admirer at a distance or would he become a disciple? Would he throw in his lot with Jesus? Would he put his whole trust in him?

These words, "You are not far from the kingdom," were meant to be affirming, yet also inviting. Jesus was saying to him, you're on the right track. You're moving in the right direction, but don't stop there. Keep following that line and see where it leads you. The words, "You are not far from the kingdom," expect a question. How do I get closer? How do I actually enter in?

Maybe the response of Jesus to this scribe was not so much different from the one he made to Nicodemus, after all. Something more was needed in both cases: a miracle of grace, the new birth, the new life. All who have repented and believe the gospel, submitting themselves to Jesus' lordship, are kingdom people. They are in.

Study Questions

1. How was the questioner different from many others?
2. What did Jesus seem to appreciate about his question?
3. What does the scribe's response to Jesus' answer show about him?
4. Where are you if you are "not far" from the kingdom?

25

Encountering Jesus:
A Devoted Woman

◆

And while he was at Bethany in the house of Simon the leper, as
he sat at table, a woman came with an alabaster flask of ointment
of pure nard, very costly, and she broke the flask and poured it over
his head. But there were some who said to themselves indignantly,
"Why was the ointment thus wasted? For this ointment might have
been sold for more than three hundred denarii, and given to the
poor." And they reproached her. But Jesus said, "Let her alone; why
do you trouble her? She has done a beautiful thing to me. For you
always have the poor with you, and whenever you will, you can do
good to them; but you will not always have me. She has done what
she could; she has anointed my body beforehand for burying. And
truly, I say to you, wherever the gospel is preached in the whole
world, what she has done will be told in memory of her."

[Mark 14:3–9]

THIS LITTLE ACCOUNT from the Gospels always moves me. It's about
extravagant devotion, about the criticism extravagant devotion sometimes arouses, and about the gracious Lord who appreciates what his
people do for him.

Mark doesn't tell us the woman's name. In John's Gospel, Mary, the sister of Lazarus, anoints Jesus' feet at Bethany. Luke tells us of a sinful woman who anointed Jesus in the home of Simon the Pharisee and washed his feet with her tears. Mark does not identify this woman or say anything about her character. For him, she's a person to whom many names might be given. She stands for all who are truly devoted to Jesus Christ. It would be a grand thing if any one of us ever found ourselves acting in this way.

Let's look first at just what it was that she did. The setting is Jerusalem, and it was two days before the Passover. The chief priests and scribes had already decided that things had gone too far. Jesus had to die. They were searching for a way to seize him quietly, away from public view. Crafty foes with murder in their hearts were closing in on Jesus. This woman's simple act of love shines all the more brilliantly against that somber background.

Jesus was dining at the home of Simon the leper in Bethany (Simon may have been healed by Jesus). While Jesus was reclining at table, the woman came up to him, carrying an alabaster jar of ointment. Mark tells us that it was pure nard, very costly. Its equivalent today would be the most exquisite perfume. It was probably a family heirloom passed down through the family from mother to daughter—surely the greatest treasure this woman possessed.

The guests noticed her standing behind Jesus. Did she plan to touch the ointment with her fingers and offer him its fragrance? Would she sprinkle it on him? To everyone's astonishment, she broke the jar and poured the entire contents on Jesus' head. The aroma instantly flooded the room. She had not announced in advance what she was about to do and no explanation followed. She let her act speak its own poignant, powerful message.

How can we call this anything but extravagance? A few drops would have been a lovely tribute, but the whole jar? Most of it could have been saved for other special occasions, but now the jar was broken. Nothing could be retrieved. It was all poured out, used up. It was like water slipping through your fingers into the thirsty earth. All at once it was gone.

Have you ever received a gift like that? When someone gives us something expensive, or a gift that required a great deal of time and labor, we are awed by it. We say, "You shouldn't have done it!" But every now and then someone may bestow on us a gift that is so priceless and involves such a sacrifice that we're simply speechless. We don't know how to respond.

Have you ever given something really extravagant to a loved one? You couldn't afford it. You went in debt to do it, but you knew it would make that special someone happy, so you threw caution to the winds and bought it anyway. Just to see his or her delight was more than worth the cost.

King David was once thirsty in the heat of a battle. He let his men know that. Some of them risked almost certain death to break through the enemy lines and bring their king a drink from a familiar well. David was so moved by that that he couldn't drink the water they had brought. He poured it out instead before the Lord, the only one worthy of such devotion.

We can only imagine what was behind this woman's gift of precious ointment. She must have known Jesus' pardoning mercy, his healing love. Somehow she had glimpsed who he really was. Overwhelmed with grateful love, she brought the best she had and poured it all out for him.

Not everyone was favorably impressed. Some were shocked. They thought it was a shame. "Why this waste of the ointment?" they complained. The magnitude of the tribute offended them—all that expense for one teacher at one meal! It made no sense to them. They had no capacity to understand or appreciate devotion like that. Next came the weighty charge: "This ointment might have been sold for more than three hundred denarii and given to the poor." Why was this woman so foolish and wasteful as to break the flask and pour all the ointment on Jesus' head? She showed no sensitivity to human need, they implied. If she didn't care to keep this expensive perfume, why didn't she use it for something worthwhile? Why didn't she sell it and give the money to those in desperate need?

That sounded pious and humane, didn't it? They were so concerned about good stewardship and so sensitive to the needs of the underclass! They would have made much better use of such a treasure. They would have sold it all and given it to charity. At least, that's what their objection implied.

This is a strange spectacle. Some of those sitting around the table in Simon's house reproach this dear woman. They heap on her scorn and blame. You can almost see her there wilting, withering under their disapproval. This storm of accusation reveals a good deal about those who object to the woman's sacrifice. It's interesting that they should use the term *waste*. Pouring ointment on Jesus in a kind of lavish, single-minded devotion was offensive to them. They didn't see him (and this is the real indictment against them) as especially worthy of this. They didn't see the teacher from Nazareth as this thankful worshiper saw him. They apparently saw nothing in him to call forth such an outpouring of grateful love.

We can wonder, too, about their talk of giving the proceeds of a sale to the poor—can we take that seriously from them? Is that what these critics were doing with whatever of value they had? Often the people most truly generous in giving to the poor are those who talk least about it. The tone of the accusation does not appear to be altruistic but heartless. They were quite ready to put down a person who had shown a truly generous heart and manifested a sacrificial spirit.

We may be like those grumbling guests, uncomfortable when someone is evidently, enthusiastically devoted to the Lord—much more than we are. Do we find ourselves ready to carp at a Christian commitment that seems to go beyond prudence, at a love for Christ that takes risks we would never consider? Do we sometimes look for ways to disparage those people who embarrass us by their flaming zeal for Christ, their witness for him? We can sometimes put ourselves in the position of judging people whose shoes we aren't worthy to untie. Or, with high-sounding words, we pretend to be a good deal better than we really are.

Jesus didn't leave the woman defenseless. "Let her alone," he said. "Why do you trouble her?" He told them to stop picking on her. Their blame was undeserved, to say the least. She had nothing to apologize for. Why should anyone trouble her over what she had done?

They had been speaking on behalf of the poor, and that, Jesus said, is always appropriate. You have the poor among you always and you can help them whenever you like, he said, pointing them to their own responsibility. They should do what they could with their resources for the poor, not just at that moment but all the time. This woman, on the other hand, had captured a special moment. The poor are always here but Jesus was with his followers for only a very short time. This woman had sensed that. Her critics had not.

She did something more, according to Jesus, than to express her devotion. She had anointed his body in anticipation of his burial. Perhaps the woman realized that Jesus was about to die, perhaps not. But knowing what awaited him in the next few days, Jesus received her gift as an anointing for the great work he was about to do in bearing our sins and dying that we might have life. Some thought this outpouring of love a waste. Jesus saw in it a high and holy purpose. Further, what they were quick to criticize, Jesus saw as worthy of praise and celebration. He tells them that. "Truly, I say to you, wherever the gospel is preached in the whole world, what she has done will be told in memory of her." When these critics have long been forgotten, this woman will be remembered. What they called a shameful waste will be lifted up for her honor.

Jesus, about to be condemned to death and crucified, knew that the good news of his saving love would be proclaimed in all the earth. He knew that his followers would do that. They would preach his message, and they would so understand the meaning of his death and resurrection that they would tell the story everywhere of this woman's loving preparation for it. There are thousands of languages into which this Gospel according to Mark has been translated. There are hundreds of millions of people in the world today who have read or heard of how this woman anointed Jesus. She is a model to all of them of what it means to be a devoted disciple. It has happened, just as Jesus said it would.

He summed up his reaction to the woman's gift in these words, "She has done a beautiful thing to me." This could also be translated a "fine" or an "honorable thing." What the other guests despised, Jesus esteemed highly. What they called wasteful, he called wonderful. Where they saw something blameworthy, he saw beauty. And his evaluation, needless to say, is what really matters.

What's the real difference between this woman and those chided her? It's in what she saw in Jesus. She saw him as someone supremely worthy. She looked on him as Master and King. She trusted him as God's anointed one and expressed that by what she did. And most deeply, she felt a sense of debt to him that the richest of gifts could not possibly discharge. All of that was lost on those who found fault with her.

It's still true today that genuine believers, those who realize who Jesus is and what he has done for them, are always those who feel a measureless indebtedness to Jesus, a grateful devotion to him that knows no bounds. They are ready to sing, "What language shall I borrow to thank Thee, dearest friend, for this thy dying sorrow, thy pity without end? O make me thine forever, and should I fainting be, Lord, let me never, never, outlive my love to Thee!"[†]

Study Questions

1. How would you explain the seeming rashness of the woman's act?
2. What's right and what's wrong with the objections of her critics?
3. What was the most humbling and overwhelming gift you were ever given. How did you feel about the giver?
4. How might people today extravagantly express their love for Christ?

[†] From "O Sacred Head, Now Wounded."

26

Encountering Jesus: Judas Iscariot

◆

And immediately, while he was still speaking, Judas came, one of
the twelve, and with him a crowd with swords and clubs, from the
chief priests and the scribes and the elders. Now the betrayer had
given them a sign, saying, "The one I shall kiss is the man; seize
him and lead him away under guard." And when he came, he went
up to him at once, and said, "Master!" And he kissed him.

[Mark 14:43–45]

MOST PEOPLE HAVE HEARD the story of Judas, the most notorious traitor who ever lived. King David had his Ahithophel, Caesar his Brutus,
Charles I his Cromwell, but no other name has ever etched itself in
infamy like the name of Judas. He, the one-time disciple of Jesus Christ,
has become for all the world the chief symbol of treachery.

Judas was the treasurer of the apostolic group and in that role he consistently stole from the common funds. Judas was one who protested
loudly when the grateful woman poured precious ointment over the head
of Jesus. He thought the ointment should have been sold and the money
given to the poor. That is, he feigned a concern for the impoverished
while seeking his own advantage. He listened to Jesus, his master and
teacher, speak of someone who would betray him, and then Judas went
out brazenly to do it himself. He conspired with Jesus' worst foes. For

thirty pieces of silver, he handed him over to die. And it was his idea to identify Jesus to those who would capture him by the sign of a kiss. In the darkness of Gethsemane, he went up to Jesus, saying "Hail, Rabbi," embracing him as though he were a faithful friend. Judas went along as the soldiers led Jesus away to mockery, torture, and death.

Is there any wonder that Judas is so universally despised, that Dante pictures him in the deepest recesses of hell? "What a monster he was!" we exclaim. "How could he do such a thing?"

Was he always so detestable? There must have been a time when Judas showed promise. From among many would-be followers, Jesus chose him—after much prayer—to be one of the twelve. He must have been trusted by the band of disciples, as they placed their resources in his hands. At the end, after he had betrayed the Lord, Judas was stricken with remorse. He felt so wretched about what he had done that he took his own life. Before that, he had gone to the authorities who hired him and tried to give back the money he had been paid. He confessed to them and to the whole world, "I have betrayed innocent blood," and so he bore his witness to the integrity of Jesus.

Judas was not a monster. He was a man, made in God's image, precious in God's sight. He was someone called by Jesus, trusted by Jesus, befriended and loved by the Lord. Jesus sought to the last to win Judas, stooping to wash his feet, warning him of his spiritual peril, yearning over him even as he went out into the darkness. What can help us penetrate the mystery surrounding this man? How can we understand, at least in a measure, what he did, why he became a traitor, and how he could resist such moving overtures of love?

Some suggest that Judas's problem was money. Perhaps so. "The love of money," the apostle Paul reminds us, "is a root of all kinds of evil" (1 Tim. 6:10). In pursuit of it, he goes on, "some have wandered from the faith and spiked themselves on many a painful thorn" (author's translation). Paul may have had Judas in mind when he wrote that. Judas, eager to possess, found himself possessed. The money he was called to manage became his master. For the sake of it, he cheated his brethren. He despised actions by others that were truly generous. For thirty silver coins, he sold the best friend he ever had. His career is a sobering witness to what covetousness can do to a human heart.

After Jesus had been arrested, however, Judas didn't want the blood money. He tried to give it back. When the authorities wouldn't take it, he threw it on the ground before them. Covetousness was a terrible snare for Judas, but I don't think it was the ultimate reason for his fall.

Far more sinister was the deceit that crept into his life. In order to steal from the common treasury, he had to start by lying about what was on hand. That must have happened again and again. Have you ever thought about how every kind of evil either begins with deceit or involves it somewhere along the line? We have no idea, any of us, what we open ourselves to when we knowingly tell an untruth, when we misrepresent the facts. Someone has said that "every lie, great or small, is the brink of a precipice, the depth of which nothing but omniscience can fathom." The Bible speaks of Satan, the enemy of God and man, as "the father of lies." Every time we compromise the truth, every time we knowingly deceive, we open ourselves to evil's frightening power. We invite the arch-deceiver to dwell with us.

It's true that one lie leads to another. We find ourselves needing to multiply falsehoods in order to shore up the first one we tell. This becomes more than a matter of tactics and embarrassment; it becomes an inner compulsion. The more we lie, the more we find ourselves driven to deceive. It becomes the pattern for relating to other people, and is desperately hard for us to break. It so affects us that we find it increasingly hard to distinguish any longer the false from the true.

If we had any idea of the dangers to which falsehood exposes us, we would tremble at the thought of starting out on its pathway. We would shrink from the least of lies. People learn to tell big lies by starting with little ones. The more we lie to people, the less we like them. We commonly end by despising those we have deceived, or even doing them ill. Did something like that happen with Judas? Was it that long-continued habit of lying, that pattern of deceit, that made him the man he became?

Sitting with the Twelve at the Last Supper, Judas listened to Jesus talk about the one who would betray him. Judas didn't blush. He gave no evidence of being the one. In feigned innocence, he asked like all the others, "Lord, is it I?"

He let Jesus wash his feet, while plotting all the time to destroy him. It was Judas's own suggestion that the sign by which Jesus would be identified to the soldiers was a kiss. There in Gethsemane, Judas could speak words of endearment and offer a token of friendship, even as he took part in a judicial murder.

Had Judas become totally false and deceitful? Perhaps. What happened after Jesus' arrest, however, shows us that Judas had not lost all capacity to discern the truth. He said truthfully that Jesus was innocent and he acknowledged having betrayed him.

What is most mysterious and most tragic about Judas is that though he encountered Jesus and was close to him, he never really knew him, never truly trusted him, never opened his heart to the Lord's great love. Judas lived in the company of the Twelve and in daily fellowship with Jesus. He was a man called, trusted, and loved, with whom Jesus shared his heart. He heard from Jesus' lips all that the rest of the disciples heard. He watched the same miracles. He saw sick people healed, blind ones given back their sight. He saw the paralyzed walk again and even the dead return to life. All of that never won his allegiance. That which eventually led the other disciples to become such heroic, faithful servants of God did not have the same effect on Judas. While they grew, he shriveled. While their hearts opened up increasingly, his became more and more closed. While they received new life from Christ, he died by his own hand.

What if Judas, after acknowledging his wrong and leaving the money on the temple floor, had gone looking for Jesus? What if he had come alongside him on the way to Golgotha, pouring out his heart, admitting his treachery, appealing to be forgiven? Who can doubt that the mercy of the Lord would have been extended toward him then? How the angels about the throne of God would have rejoiced if this sinful wanderer had come back from the far country of his covetousness, his deceitfulness, his hideous betrayal! There is more than enough grace in the heart of the Lord to welcome back a million Judases, if they will only come to their senses and turn their faces toward home.

Judas couldn't do that. Peter, after denying the Lord three times with oaths and curses, could go out and weep bitterly but still be there with the others at the cross, in the upper room, and when the Lord appeared on Easter night. He could say three times over out of brokenhearted trust and gratitude, "Lord, you know that I love you." Apparently Judas wanted nothing to do with his fellow disciples. He had nothing to say to Jesus. He died in the deepest loneliness that can be imagined.

There's a lot about this that no one understands. Surely I don't. I don't know how someone could live for three years in such close association with the Son of God and then deliver him over to die by betraying him with a kiss. I don't know how Judas could resist so many gifts of grace, so many tokens of God's faithful love. Thinking about him puzzles me, saddens me, frightens me. I can't dismiss him as an inhuman menace, an evil dragon. I know that he too is a man, a man like me. I'm vulnerable to the same craving to possess, the same temptation to deceive that proved so dreadfully compelling for Judas. It would be foolish as well as self-righteous for me to say that I could never fall like that, that I could never stoop to what he did.

Troubled as I am by Judas, I can't cut him out of the Bible story, can't pretend that he didn't exist or act as though his story couldn't somehow be repeated. Judas is a standing reminder to us that we can be very near to the kingdom of God but not enter it, that we can see marvelous things and hear great truths and not have our lives transformed. We can encounter Jesus, interact with him, even know that he's a good man and still die a hopeless death.

But as surely as I know that Judas's evils could be mine, far more surely do I know that they don't have to be. I can turn to the Lord whom I have failed, denied, or in some ways betrayed and, acknowledging my sins, can receive his gracious forgiveness and experience the renewing power of his Holy Spirit. And so can you.

Study Questions

1. How does the love of money become "a root of all kinds of evil"?

2. In what sense is deceitfulness involved in almost every kind of evil in our lives?
3. What for you is the most sobering lesson of Judas's career?
4. Even as we realize our own vulnerability, what is our great comfort?

27

Encountering Jesus: Simon Peter

◆

And as Peter was below in the courtyard, one of the maids of the high priest came; and seeing Peter warming himself, she looked at him, and said, "You also were with the Nazarene, Jesus." But he denied it, saying, "I neither know nor understand what you mean." And he went out into the gateway. And the maid saw him, and began again to say to the bystanders, "This man is one of them." But again he denied it. And after a little while again the bystanders said to Peter, "Certainly you are one of them; for you are a Galilean." But he began to invoke a curse on himself and to swear, "I do not know this man of whom you speak." And immediately the cock crowed a second time. And Peter remembered how Jesus had said to him, "Before the cock crows twice, you will deny me three times." And he broke down and wept.

[Mark 14:66–72]

WE'VE BEEN THINKING in these recent chapters about people who encountered Jesus of Nazareth and the effects that had on their lives. For the last of these in Mark's Gospel, it's fitting to think about Simon Peter, the great apostle, and what happened in his life because of his association with Jesus. We remember how he was called by the Lord from his fishing trade by the Sea of Galilee. We rejoice in his great confession of faith in Jesus, "You are the Christ, the Son of the living God." We think of how he was a leader in the apostolic group, usually the first among them to speak, prominent both in his devotion and at times in his dullness of mind and heart. But the true revelation of his character and the transforming influence of Jesus on his life is best seen in the closing chapters of the gospel, in connection with the Lord's passion and resurrection. Peter denies knowing Jesus and this represents the low point of Peter's entire life.

Peter's denial of Jesus in the Gospel according to Mark reads like a drama in three acts. In the first, Jesus predicts what is going to happen. After the Last Supper, when Jesus and his followers have gone out to the Mount of Olives, he says to them, "You will all fall away; for it is written, 'I will strike the shepherd, and the sheep will be scattered.' But after I am raised up, I will go before you to Galilee" (Mark 14:27–28). The Lord is speaking here about the sufferings that lie just ahead for him: his arrest, his shamefully unjust trial, the beatings at the hands of the soldiers, and the agony of crucifixion. He as the shepherd will be smitten and his flock will be scattered.

As Jesus speaks about that, he doesn't single out any one disciple for special responsibility and blame. He says, "You shall all become deserters." When their Lord and Master is taken, they will all scatter as frightened, unattended sheep, but he will not reject them as a result of that. He will still go before them to Galilee and lead them as their faithful shepherd. That will happen after he has been raised from the dead. In the time when they are apart from him, without his leadership, they will only flounder and fail.

Peter objects to this prophecy of Jesus. He doesn't insist that the others will not deny the Lord. In fact, he concedes that they may well do so. But not he. "Even though all become deserters," he insists, "I will not." We can't escape the impression that Peter sees himself as more courageous and more loyal than the rest. In the matter of staying with Jesus, come what may, he stands head and shoulders above his brothers. Or so he thinks.

After Jesus repeats the prophecy, Peter maintains that even if he should have to suffer death with Christ, this is certain: He will not deny the Lord. And, following Peter's lead, all the rest make the same affirmation.

Here the stage is set for the action to follow. Jesus has prophesied Peter's denial; Peter insists it will never happen. The Lord knows what is ahead; Peter thinks he knows better. Once again, this fisherman disciple is contradicting his master. No, Lord, he says (a peculiar combination of words!), it will not be as you have said. Peter has set himself up for a fall.

In the next act, described in Mark 14:32–42, Peter, James, and John are invited to be with Jesus when he withdraws from the others in Gethsemane. As the Lord goes apart to pray, he asks the three to stay near by and watch with him. The Lord needs their support and wants them to fulfill the ministry of caring friends. But while Jesus is praying in great agony, his sweat falling to the ground as great drops of blood, Peter and the others fall asleep. Jesus, returning, asks him about this, "Simon, are you asleep? Could you not watch one hour?"

Then comes a charge, "Watch and pray that you may not enter into temptation; the spirit indeed is willing, but the flesh is weak." This is our great defense against temptation, what keeps us from coming under its power: We keep on watching. We keep on praying. We stay vigilant and we stay dependent. Our problem is that though we are willing to stand up for Jesus, as Peter surely was, though we want to, intend to, and are sure we will, we are still woefully weak.

Peter doesn't heed the call and doesn't stay awake. He doesn't pray and thus guard against temptation. He goes back to sleep. For Jesus the intensity is building. He asks for Peter's support and doesn't get it, so he gives him a loving warning, which Peter doesn't heed. The Lord is saddened and alone. For his part, Peter seems to have no awareness of his spiritual peril and vulnerability. Anxious, confused, depressed perhaps, he seeks refuge in sleep. The Master's need and the Master's word are forgotten.

Now for act three. It's in the passage with which we began. When the servant girl says, "You also were with Jesus," Peter gives ground for the first time. He tells the first lie. He says he wasn't with Jesus, that he had nothing to do with him. Perhaps we could say at this point that Peter felt he was simply being prudent, avoiding a public commotion, keeping his options open. Who could quarrel with that?

We seldom can stop with one untruth. Pressure inevitably comes again at the same point. The servant girl began to talk to some others. A wider circle of people became involved and curious. Now the possible difficulties loom larger to Peter. He has to say again, more loudly and vehemently this time, that he hasn't been with Jesus.

Next, a group of bystanders takes up the inquiry. You are one of them, they say. Here's the evidence: You're from Galilee, right? Under this stepped-up attack, Peter is pushed to make even more vehement denials. He begins to swear. He even invokes curses on himself if what he says is not true. And then he lies again. He not only wasn't with Jesus, he says; he doesn't even know him. This Jesus, Peter is saying in effect, is nothing to me. The denial and the renunciation seem complete.

Just then the cock crows again. The sound must have gone like an arrow to Peter's heart. He remembers the words of his Master, the prophecy he had so stubbornly resisted, and he feels overwhelmed with shame. The big fisherman breaks down and weeps bitter tears. End of act three.

Happily, that's not the end of the drama. Peter's name appears once more in this gospel. It's after that terrible day on Golgotha when he watched his Master die. It's after the time of desolation that followed. It's after Easter morning and the thrilling news of resurrection. This is the word of the angel to the women who came to the tomb at dawn that day:

> "Do not be amazed," he said, "you seek Jesus of Nazareth, who was crucified. He has risen. He is not here, see the place where they laid him. But go, tell his disciples and Peter that he is going before you to Galilee; there you will see him, as he told you."
>
> [Mark 16:6–7]

Did you hear that? "Go, tell his disciples and Peter." The Lord apparently wasn't through with his fallen follower. In spite of all the falsehood, all the presumption and arrogance, all the insensitivity and even disobedience, Jesus still numbered Peter among his followers, still had a work for him to do. That was the thrilling message of Easter for the man who had denied his Lord, and for all of us. Later, as we learn from the Book of Acts and other parts of the New Testament, Peter became a bold preacher of the gospel and a faithful servant of Jesus, and he eventually sealed his testimony with his life blood. That was the final, wonderful fruit of Simon Peter's encounter with Jesus Christ.

What gives special power and poignancy to this account is the fact that it is recorded in Peter's own memoirs. Biblical scholars uniformly believe that Mark's Gospel rests on Peter's reminiscences. Imagine it! Simon Peter greatly influenced the writing of this Gospel, and it tells the whole story of his shameful failure! Peter's telling his story is a beautiful expression of repentance. What a difference it made when he encountered Jesus of Nazareth! At first it led to commitment and then to a great confession of faith. In the long run it led further, to depths of self-discovery, to a shattering of pride and to new discoveries of the Lord's marvelous grace.

And so here in Mark's Gospel, Peter tells his story so that no one who has failed the Lord terribly need feel there's no hope for him or for her. Peter wanted everyone to know that the mercy of the Lord is very great and that he is able to transform the most dull, backward, stubborn and vain disciples and make them faithful witnesses to his saving power. Isn't that a marvelous thing?

You may hear Christians telling of the wonderful changes Christ brings about in their lives and in the lives of his people. They are speaking the truth. He really does that. Don't get the impression that he brings about this transformation all at once. He imparts new life, yes—that happens in a moment, instantaneously—but the new birth isn't the end of the story. As with every new birth, it's followed by a long and sometimes perplexing and painful process of growth.

Peter was a true believer from the very start, but the Lord, even after three years, still had a lot of work to do on the life of this rugged follower. We all need further remodeling. The Lord's patience and mercy are wonderfully great. Trust him. Don't feel because you've stumbled and fallen that you're out of the running. Don't feel because you've shamefully

failed the Lord that he has counted you out. The risen Christ offers forgiveness and a new start. He still has a work for you to do.

Study Questions

1. What character traits emerge in Peter's refusal to accept the word
   that he will deny Jesus?
2. What did Peter learn, by sad neglect, about "preventive prayer"?
3. What does it mean that we usually get involved in compromise
   and denial of Christ by degrees?
4. How is the heart of the gospel expressed in the words of the risen
   Lord, "tell Peter"?

28

Listening to Jesus When He Preached

◆

Now after John was arrested, Jesus came into Galilee, preaching the gospel of God, and saying, "The time is fulfilled, and the kingdom of God is at hand; repent, and believe in the gospel."

[Mark 1:14–15]

SUPPOSE YOU COULD BE TRANSPORTED back in time to hear some great performance or speech just as it was given. What event would you choose? Would it be the singing of the great Caruso or President Lincoln actually giving his Gettysburg Address? What about the first rendition of Handel's *Messiah* or the opening night of Shakespeare's *Hamlet*? To hear any of those would be a fantastic treat for me, but if I had to choose one event at which to eavesdrop, I would go further back in history. I would stand among the people of Galilee almost twenty centuries ago and listen to the very first message proclaimed by Jesus of Nazareth.

That's not possible, of course. We have no time machine to take us back through the centuries and no devices, at least currently, to pick up voices from the distant past. What we do have, however, in the pages of the New Testament, is a brief summary of our Lord's first public address.

Jesus had just passed through an exalted, unforgettable experience. After his baptism in the river Jordan, heaven had seemed open before him. He had heard a voice from heaven saying to him, "You are my beloved Son; in you I am well pleased." That was the sure sign to him that his mission had begun. Then had followed his forty days in the desert where he was weak with hunger and assailed by strong temptation. He had resisted all the attacks of the evil one, and now, strong in the Spirit of God, he was returning to the world of men to begin his ministry. When the crowds gathered to hear him, this was his inaugural theme, his keynote address: "The time is fulfilled, and the kingdom of God is at hand; repent, and believe in the gospel."

We don't know all that he said on that day. We can't see the light in his eyes or sense the power in his voice. But how thrilling it is that we can know the essence, the burden, of his message! If we can understand these few brief words, we will have grasped the core of the New Testament gospel. And far better, if we respond to them in faith, we will have found the way of life.

The preaching begins with a twofold announcement: "The time is fulfilled, and the kingdom of God is at hand." Jesus is saying here that something momentous, something climactic, has occurred. The long-awaited time has come! We're accustomed to using that word *time* in more than one way. Perhaps most often we think of it in a linear sense, as chronological time. Here is a particular event. Something happened before it; something happened after it. All are points on a line of time. By that use of the word, we express order and duration.

But there's another usage with a different flavor and emphasis. I'm thinking now of what we call the appropriate time, the right time, the moment of opportunity, the moment of truth. That's what Jesus has in mind here. Sometimes what happens in a five-minute period may be more weighted with meaning for life than the preceding five years. When Jesus proclaims that the time has been fulfilled, he is telling his hearers that they have come to a crisis in human history. This is the hour for which everything else has been preparatory. This is the fulfillment of all that had up to now been only hinted at and held out as promise. This moment in God's purpose is what all the world has been waiting for.

And just what is that? someone asks. What is the meaning of man's history, if it has any meaning? Is there a special time that helps us to understand all the rest? Can any one event or series of events give us a clue to the whole mystery? According to Jesus Christ, the answer is yes. The days of his ministry were the special ones and the decisive event above all others was this: The kingdom of God has drawn near.

What is this "kingdom" of which Jesus speaks? We usually think of a kingdom as involving several elements. There is, of course, a king or queen who is sovereign over a kingdom, which is made up of the subjects and the domain, over which he or she rules. The phrase "the kingdom of God" involves much more. Here we are referring not only to the Lord and to the extent of his dominion but also to his active, reigning power. This is something present, alive, dynamic. God's kingdom means the mighty expression of his lordship in the midst of human history. That's why the word of Jesus takes the form of a dramatic announcement. Hear ye! Hear ye! The time is fulfilled, and God has come in person to rule!

But what's new about all that? Hasn't God always been the king? Certainly he has, in the sense that he's the creator and owner of this world—and of all worlds. But according to the Bible, the rebellion of his human creatures has produced a new situation. We who rightfully belong to him have come under the dominion of sin, under the sway of evil powers. By misusing our freedom and choosing to go our own way, we have become hopelessly enslaved.

The Old Testament foreshadows and prepares for what God is going to do about this situation. We can sense on many of its pages the yearning expectation that God will come to set things right. Psalm 96:11–13 is an example of this.

> Let the heavens be glad, and let the earth rejoice;
>> let the sea roar, and all that fills it;
>> let the field exult, and everything in it!
> Then shall all the trees of the wood sing for joy
>> before the LORD, for he comes,
>> for he comes to judge the earth.
> He will judge the world with righteousness,
>> and the peoples with his truth.

Or again, here are the longings for an ideal king in Psalm 72:2, 7–8:

> May he judge thy people with righteousness,
>   and thy poor with justice!
> In his days may righteousness flourish,
>   and peace abound,
>   till the moon be no more!
> May he have dominion from sea to sea.

In the Old Testament that hope is only a vision and a prayer. The message is: Take heart! God is going to do something wonderful for his fallen world.

The New Testament, on the other hand, announces that he has come in person to do it. That is the throb and thrill of this tremendous claim: The kingdom of God has drawn near! Here is a world groaning under alien rule. We are gripped by a tyranny we chose and now cannot escape. In the fullness of the time, God comes to free us. He comes, astoundingly, in a genuinely human life—in the person of Jesus of Nazareth. The Lord of Glory, the King of all Kings, comes as a humble obscure man straight into enemy-occupied territory. He throws down his challenge to the entrenched powers of evil, all the malignant forces that hold mankind in bondage. These are the rival kings he comes to dethrone. Jesus has met the prince of darkness in his wilderness temptations. In a kind of hand-to-hand combat, he threw back every assault. Now begins the strange and awesome divine offensive. Jesus rebukes the demons and they are driven out. He commands the diseases and they disappear. He speaks to raging seas and they quiet down like docile puppies. He even meets King Death in funeral processions and sets its captives free.

As he moves along, the opposition against him mounts. Wily men taunt him. Enemies plot against him. The powers of hell finally engineer his murder. This is their hour and power of darkness. They seem to win. They have him where they want him—rejected, betrayed, mocked, whipped, spat on, and strung up to die before a howling crowd. He claimed to be the king! What kind of king is that, dying in ignominy outside the city walls?

There God's reign comes breaking in. By his cross Jesus smashed hell's power. Rising, he broke the back of death. About to ascend to his throne, he could say, "All authority in heaven and on earth has been given to me." Victor over all his foes, he is now the exalted one—King of Kings and Lord of Lords.

Now think of it, that whole drama of divine action is wrapped up in the phrase, "the kingdom of God has drawn near." And still today, it's the central theme of all who proclaim the gospel. We Christian preachers are announcers of the reign of God, heralds of the lordship of Jesus, witnesses to the Holy Spirit's transforming presence in this world. The kingdom of God has come near. Sin is conquered! Death is doomed! Hell is overthrown! What great good news we have to tell!

That isn't all. Jesus brought more than a grand announcement. In the light of that announcement, he called his hearers to repent and believe. He summoned them to renounce all false lords and welcome their rightful king. They were to turn from darkness to light, from death to life, from the power of Satan to God.

The call to repentance has two sides. One is a warning of our great peril. We human beings are in danger vulnerable, immersed in a sea of troubles. We live in a bondage that now robs our lives of meaning and will finally destroy our hopes of happiness. Worse still, we are estranged from our one source of life and help, barricaded in against the only one who can rescue us. Any message, therefore, that lulls us into false security is criminal and traitorous. To whisper to people, all is well, when they are enemies to their own peace is the height of cruelty.

Jesus warns us of judgments in this life. The everlasting peril breaks into our world in wars, slums, racial strife, broken homes, political corruption, and decaying cultures. In our personal lives, it comes as anxiety, bitterness, emptiness, and despair. Jesus warned that bondage, estrangement, and danger extend beyond this life. There comes a colossal judgment of which all earthly dooms give only a glimpse. Do we recognize that? Whoever we are—unschooled or sophisticated, prudent or profligate, moral or reckless—we're all pursued by danger. We all plunge on toward tragedy if we refuse the seeking God.

Yes, the seeking God. That's the other side of Jesus' call to repentance. Sure judgment is ahead, but a yearning God pursues from behind, calling us to stop and turn. Return, rebel children! The Father waits with outstretched arms. The Savior with wounds in his hands is searching for you!

So with the urgent warning comes the invitation to believe. As Jesus summons us to turn, he holds out to us the royal gifts of the gospel. God's new reign means for us adoption as children by the Father, cleansing from all guilt, liberation from the prison of our self-concern. To serve him brings us a share in a new loving fellowship, a sense of purpose, hope, and joy abounding in our pains, a fresh capacity to love, and a more abundant life.

Christ calls us to receive and rest on his promise of salvation. To believe in him is to accept the love he offers and enjoy the mercies he gives. The great word of the prophet Isaiah is, "Ho, every one who thirsts, come to the waters" (Isa. 55:1); and of Jesus, "Come to me, all who labor and are heavy laden" (Matt. 11:28); and of the apostle, "Believe in the Lord Jesus, and you will be saved" (Acts 16:31). He is the King who died to redeem you. Commit yourself now to his lordship, to follow him all the days of your life.

No, we don't have a time machine and no one of us was privileged to hear Jesus speak in the days of his flesh but by his Spirit, through his Word, he is still speaking to us. The grand announcement of the gospel is coming to your heart today.

Study Questions

1. In what sense was the "time fulfilled," as Jesus put it?
2. What is the meaning of the phrase "the kingdom of God"?
3. How does this relate to the powers of evil on this earth?
4. What are repentance and faith? How do they work themselves out in your life?

29

Listening to Jesus
When He Called His Followers

◆

And passing along by the Sea of Galilee, he saw Simon and Andrew
the brother of Simon casting a net in the sea; for they were fishermen. And Jesus said to them, "Follow me and I will make you
become fishers of men." And immediately they left their nets and
followed him.

[Mark 1:16–18]

WHAT DID JESUS SAY when he called people to be his disciples? How
did he go about getting them to throw in their lot with him? It was quite
a commitment he was expecting of them. How did he make his appeal?
We don't know about that in the case of some of the disciples. We are
simply told that Jesus appointed them. He said to them, "Follow me," or
"Come and see." But in the case of a little group of fishermen, Simon
and Andrew, the sons of Jonas, and James and John, the sons of Zebedee,
we are told exactly what Jesus' call was. "Follow me and I will make you
become fishers of men"—come along with me and I'll have you fishing
for people.

There are four things about that simple call that impress me deeply.
The first is that the call is always at Jesus' initiative. It always starts with

him. This is how Mark introduces the account: "And passing along by the Sea of Galilee, he saw Simon and Andrew the brother of Simon casting a net in the sea; for they were fishermen. And Jesus said to them . . ."

What Mark is recording here was preached and taught many times before it was ever written down. This account of the calling of the disciples was probably proclaimed hundreds, maybe thousands of times, before the Gospels were put in written form. That's how the message of Christ spread at first. It was by oral tradition. It was the Word preached and taught, and when significant events are told in this way, over and over again, all the trivial data come to be trimmed away. Everything left is rich with significance.

With that in mind, look at the account again. Everything starts with Jesus. The fishermen are in the midst of their daily labors. They don't go to Jesus. He comes to them. Before they are aware of him, he sees them. Before they speak, he addresses them. The Lord is always ahead of his people.

To Jeremiah God said "Before I formed you in the womb I knew you, and before you were born I consecrated you; I appointed you a prophet to the nations" (Jer. 1:5). Jesus' call to his disciples is similar: "And he went up on the mountain, and called to him those whom he desired; and they came to him. And he appointed twelve" (Mark 3:13–14). We hear the same note in the first Scripture verse I ever memorized, given to me on a little card by the person who introduced me to Christ: "You did not choose me, but I chose you and appointed you that you should go and bear fruit and that your fruit should abide" (John 15:16).

In other words, none of the disciples were volunteers. They were all draftees. In each case, their service was God's idea. It began with his call.

It still happens that way today. Jesus, the risen, living Lord, is here among us powerfully at work by his Spirit, taking the initiative with us. Just a few weeks ago, I heard a young woman in my home congregation confessing her faith in Christ. She told of how she had had no interest in the church. She had only attended a worship service because her fiancé had invited her. As soon as she came into the congregation, however, she had a sense of God's presence. Before the service was over, she knew that she wanted to follow Jesus. This is how she described it, "When I wasn't even looking for the Lord, he found me."

Jesus still comes to us in the midst of our everyday life as he did to those fishermen by the lake. He has his eye on us and through his Word and by his Spirit he invites us personally to belong to him.

Here's the second thing that comes to me from this passage: Whenever Jesus calls us, he always directs us to other people. Peter, Andrew, James, and John had been trying to catch fish. Now they were going to be reaching out for people. Maybe if they had been shepherds, the Lord would have said, You've been taking care of your sheep; now I want you to look after my flock. Or, Matthew, you're interested in investments; what about investing your life in other human beings? Or, you there, you're a builder; come along with me and build a church of redeemed lives. God's priority is always people.

I am an astronomy buff. My technical skills in that field are almost nonexistent, but I have an amateur's keen interest. I love to read books about the starry heavens and let my mind be stretched and numbed by the vastness out there. I like to remember that our galaxy, the Milky Way, has in it some hundred billion stars, many of them much larger than our sun, all of them light years away from each other. That, the experts tell us, is just one galaxy out of billions, each containing billions of individual stars, and they're all traveling away from each other at colossal speeds.

When we begin to ponder facts like those, we can feel insignificant. What is this little chip that we call Earth in the midst of all this immensity? Can our brief lives here possibly matter very much? But then I remember this: As far as we know, God never sent his Son to straighten out the orbit of the Milky Way or to bank the fires of a great star like Betelgeuse. But he did send him down here to our planet to share our humanity and bear our sins.

That's amazing, and what it assures me of is this: A million of those blazing stars out there are not as important to God as one of my grandchildren, or the oldest person in your family, or the poorest person you pass on the street. Human beings are supremely precious to God.

When Jesus calls us then, it's not only for our blessing and benefit, but he wants to make us channels of his grace to other people. Why didn't he take you straight to heaven the moment you first believed, since from that moment you were totally acceptable through Christ? He left you here because he has a work for you to do, a work that involves other people. He calls you to love them, to serve them, to reach out to them, and in the magnetism of his love and joy, to bring them home to him. That's what we're here for: caring about and catching people for Christ.

Now for the third great theme in this call of Jesus. When he calls you, there's only one thing that you need to do in response. Jesus said it simply: "Follow me." He doesn't call you to a multitude of new responsibilities but he calls you to a relationship with him.

To follow a leader could mean many things in the ancient world. Sometimes students would follow a rabbi until they had heard all he had to teach and then they would go out on their own. Sometimes to follow meant complete imitation, even mimicking a leader's eccentricities. Jesus wasn't looking for that in his disciples.

In the Old Testament, to follow sometimes meant a supreme religious commitment. Elijah on Mount Carmel thunders at a people prone to idolatry: "How long will you go limping with two different opinions? If the Lord is God, follow him; but if Baal, then follow him" (1 Kings 18:21). In other words, make your choice. Choose your ultimate allegiance.

That's close to the heart of Jesus' call. Jesus called his disciples to a lifelong companionship. They were to walk along with him, listening to his words, watching what he did, and sharing in his ministry. They were to get to know him better and better and to love him more and more. More than anything else, they were to be his own ones, his devoted companions, his loyal friends.

Today, when people follow Jesus, that's what they want—a relationship with him. That's what's behind a regular reading of his Word, letting him speak to us afresh by his Spirit. That's what's behind daily times of prayer in which we get to know him better and invite him into every part of our lives. That's the greatest thing about the fellowship of the saints. Together we draw nearer to the Lord and learn better how to live as his grateful people.

In Galilee that day the fishermen didn't know all that Jesus would do for them—how he would love them to the end, suffer for their sins, die in their place, and rise again to give them forgiveness and a new life. We know that from his Word, so we have many more reasons to cleave to him than they did.

There's one more element in Jesus' call of tremendous importance. It's the remarkable promise that the Lord makes. "Follow me," he says, "and I will make you fishers of men." That word *make* is the same word that in the original language means "create." Follow me, Jesus says, and I'll recreate you. Follow me and I'll fashion your life and ministry into something it could never be otherwise.

That's what Jesus does for his people. When we come to him, he forgives and cleanses us. Wonderful! But he doesn't simply leave us the way we are. He imparts to us new life. By his Word and Spirit he works in us amid the circumstances of our lives. He gradually transforms us into the people we are meant to be. He takes our lives and makes them over, and especially, he creates our ministry.

When there were five thousand hungry people needing to be fed and only a few loaves and a couple of fish available, the disciples didn't know what to do. Jesus said, "Bring it to me." They did. He took the bread and the fish, lifted his eyes toward heaven, blessed and broke the food, and gave it back to the disciples. When they had passed it out, they found there was enough for everyone—with basketfuls left over. Jesus was saying to them, bring what you have to me, however inadequate it seems, and watch what I can do with it!

You don't have to be a superstar before God can do a wonderful thing in your life. In fact, if you're all taken up with what a star you are, he may not be able to use you. You don't have to have a certain kind of personality or a great deal of education or remarkable gifts. You simply need to bring what you have to him.

I think of a lady who felt that her only gift was that of baking pies, a humble, simple ability. She devoted that to the Lord. She took her pies to people all over her community who were having a celebration or going through a sorrow or had just moved in. She was instrumental in bringing several of those families into our church. A number of those people came to Christ through her gift.

I know a man who trusted Christ late in life. He called himself an eleventh-hour laborer. Wanting to make the remaining years of his life count for the Lord, he went to seminary. He served three churches and had a beautiful, fruitful ministry before God called him home. These people simply placed their lives and all they had in the Lord's hands, and he made them into fishers of men. He'll do that for each of us. He'll create in us something truly wonderful. He will make our lives really count.

Study Questions

1. How has it been evident in your life that Jesus is ahead of you, leading the way?
2. How does your calling as a Christian involve ministry to others?
3. As you understand it, what is the central meaning of "following" Jesus? What does that involve?
4. In what sense does the Lord create our ministry?

30

Listening to Jesus: His Mission

◆

And in the morning, a great while before day, he rose and went out to a lonely place, and there he prayed. And Simon and those who were with him pursued him, and they found him and said to him, "Every one is searching for you." And he said to them, "Let us go on to the next towns, that I may preach there also; for that is why I came out."

[Mark 1:35–38]

And when Jesus heard it, he said to them, "Those who are well have no need of a physician, but those who are sick; I came not to call the righteous, but sinners."

[Mark 2:17]

JESUS SAID A NUMBER OF THINGS about his mission, about the mandate he had received from his Father, and about what he was in the world to do. I want to focus on two of them. Jesus had a strong consciousness of his personal destiny. This overpowering awareness lay behind everything Jesus said and did. He had been sent by God on a mission. He was not in the world by chance, nor was he moved, as many are, by merely personal ambitions. He had a race to run, a work to do, a calling to fulfill.

Did you notice how he said in each of the passages above that such and such was why he came? Jesus was born of a human mother. He entered the world as we do, along a birth canal. But the language he almost always used to describe his life here was that of a *coming*. Think of what that means. When a person says, "I came," the clear implication is, I was somewhere else before. I was there and now I'm here, and to get from there to here, I came.

Jesus was the only human being who ever lived before he was born. He is the everlasting Son of the Father. He is the eternal Word of God. He was in the beginning with God. All things were made through him. Then at a certain moment in our history, he entered into time and space. He ventured down, we might say, to share our humanity and live among us. From the glory of the Father's presence, from the throne room of the universe, he came to planet Earth.

This awareness of being sent into the world appears also in the way that Jesus prayed. He prepared for the choosing of his disciples by spending a whole night in prayer. At the threshold of every new experience and after each season of ministry, he went apart to commune with his Father. In the Bible text for this chapter we see Jesus rising up a great while before day, going out to a solitary place, and there praying. It was the Father who had sent him and Jesus was determined to live his whole life in fellowship with the Father, seeking his direction and invoking his aid. For him God's work was to be done in God's way, by God's power, and for God's glory. So everything was begun, continued, and ended in prayer.

Let's review what led up to this early morning prayer vigil. Jesus had been in the house of Simon and Andrew. On the day before, he had healed Simon's mother-in-law, who had been sick with a fever. Then at sundown, people had come from everywhere bringing their diseased, afflicted, and demon-possessed loved ones. A great crowd had gathered around the house and Jesus had healed many people. He had delivered many from demonic power. He must have been exhausted from the labors of that day, but long before daybreak the next morning, he rose from sleep and went out to pray.

When Simon Peter and the others woke up, they saw that he was gone and went looking for him. When they finally found him, they said, "Everyone is looking for you." In other words, there are many who still need your healing and help, Jesus. Crowds of people want to see these wonderful works that you do. They seem to be asking, what are you doing out here? There may be even a hint of chiding, as though to say, the recognition you deserve, Master, is already coming your way. Everyone is talking about you. Everyone wants to see you. This is your big moment, Jesus. Why do you leave? Why do you pull away at a time like this?

They must have been stunned at the Lord's reply. "Let's go on to the neighboring towns," he said, "so that I may proclaim the message there also. For that is what I came out to do." For some, miracles were the centerpiece of Jesus' ministry. That's what really got the world's attention. People were amazed and overjoyed at the marvelous things Jesus did. They praised God. They said, "We have seen wonderful things today." The disciples wanted Jesus to keep at this ministry until the whole world marveled.

But that, apparently, was not the Lord's way. The miracles, the healings, the deliverances were never ends in themselves. They testified to his divine power and were expressions of his compassionate heart, but most of all, they were signs of God's coming kingdom. They were confirmations of Jesus' message.

It's good to remind ourselves of that. Sometimes we get the idea that people can be dazzled into repentance, amazed into faith. Jesus, however, had little confidence in signs and wonders as a way of converting people. It's sobering to recall that many who saw his mighty works never trusted in him. Some of them even arranged for him to be crucified. Creating a sensation among the masses is not the same thing as turning peoples' hearts to the living God. So why did he come? Why had the Father sent him into the world? Jesus affirms in these passages that it was to preach. For Jesus, the message was always primary. The wonders, the mighty works, were confirmations of the Word he brought. If the people didn't hear God speaking, if they didn't welcome the Good News of the Kingdom of God, the miracles would have little lasting meaning for them.

"Let's go on to the neighboring towns," he said. Jesus had the burden of a missionary and the heart of an evangelist. He wanted more and more people to hear the gospel of God's love, to know what he was doing for them and for their salvation. He wasn't content to settle down in one place permanently. He wanted to press on, sowing the seed and spreading the message as far as possible. Only as people heard God's word of judgment and grace, of warning and invitation, could genuine faith be awakened in their hearts. For this the Father had sent Jesus into the world—that he should proclaim the message of the Kingdom.

In the synagogue at Nazareth one day he spoke the word in which he related his own ministry to Isaiah's prophecy.

> The Spirit of the Lord is upon me,
>   because he has anointed me to preach good news to the poor.
> He has sent me to proclaim release to the captives
>   and recovering of sight to the blind,
>   to set at liberty those who are oppressed,
>   to proclaim the acceptable year of the Lord.
>
>   [Luke 4:18–19]

Notice what he says: "to preach good news" and "to proclaim." That was the heart of his mission. Out of that proclamation, every other gift and grace would flow. The creative word would save and transform, calling God's people to himself.

The preaching and teaching of the gospel must never be minimized. Special programs and innovative church services cannot take the place of preaching and teaching the gospel. Demonstrations and even signs and wonders should never take precedence. Jesus was on a mission to preach. He didn't let anything distract him from that. He has commanded his followers to see that everyone on earth gets to hear his message. Let's not let any competing cause, however worthwhile, distract us from obeying his command.

Jesus has another word about why he came, this one having to do with the people he sought to reach. There came a day when Jesus went to the home of a despised tax collector for dinner. He had actually chosen this man Levi to be one of the inner circle of his followers. Imagine it! The man threw a party to celebrate. He invited many tax collectors, along with others of doubtful reputation. It was a gathering of outcasts, rejects, and moral lepers. And there Jesus was, laughing, talking, and eating with these people.

The religious leaders of Jesus' day were scandalized. They asked his disciples indignantly, "Why does your teacher eat with tax collectors and sinners?" Why does he seek out the company of these abandoned people? When Jesus heard of their objection, he said, "Those who are well have no need of a physician, but those who are sick; I came not to call the righteous, but sinners." Jesus came to preach—we've already seen that—and especially, he says here, he came to preach to sinners. He came to call them to repentance and restore them to fellowship with God.

Jesus reasons with his objectors. He lets them see their arguments in a different light. With some homely analogy from life, he often beams the light of truth on the cavils they raise. He tells them to think about the work of a doctor. The doctor's mission is to heal people. With what group, then, would you expect him to spend most of his time—with those in sound health or with those suffering from some malady? The answer, of course, is too plain even to be spoken. How ridiculous it would be for anyone to criticize a doctor because he was spending most of his time in hospitals and sick rooms!

Jesus presents himself here as a kind of doctor and his ministry as a work of healing. He comes to bring God's forgiveness, to cleanse the impure, to lift the fallen, and to restore lives that have been broken and marred by sin. To what element in society, then, should he direct his ministry? Should he go to the righteous and the law-abiding, those who are sound in faith and love, or should he rather seek out the lost ones, the transgressors, the estranged people, the ones without hope? With that Jesus rests his case. "I came not to call the righteous, but sinners."

Some suggest that there is an irony in Jesus' use of the word *righteous* here. He is said to be chiding the Pharisees and others like them who only imagine themselves to be righteous and pride themselves on their own performance. That element may well be present. Jesus may be saying to them that if they're willing to recognize their sin, then they too can know the joy of his calling.

Jesus' main concern is to emphasize the positive. Since he's a Savior for sinners, no one should be surprised or shocked when he seeks them out. The Pharisees may have thought that Jesus went among such people because he enjoyed their company or endorsed their lifestyle. They didn't understand that Jesus went among tax collectors and sinners as the Messiah. The basis of his table fellowship with them was the Messianic forgiveness he came to bring. The meal was an anticipation of God's great feast in the life to come. Here was Jesus, the Messiah, the Savior, breaking bread with the outcasts and bringing to them genuine fellowship with God on the basis of forgiveness.

That's why Jesus came. He came to preach to sinners, to the guilty, the defiled, the bound, and the driven. He came to call them out of judgment and bondage, out of misery and into the joy of eternal life and restored fellowship with God.

The most heralded theologian of this century is Karl Barth. Christians disagree widely about his theological work. Many do not realize, however, one of the most significant things about this church leader. Barth was a preacher to prisoners. He went again and again into jails and prisons, bringing the good news of Jesus Christ to people behind bars. Some may question his orthodoxy on other points, but here the learned doctor surely had the mind of Christ, for Christ came to call sinners to repentance.

Study Questions

1. Why did Jesus speak of his birth and ministry as a "coming."
2. What is the relationship between Jesus' message and his miracles?
3. Why was Jesus happy to socialize with sinners?

31

Listening to Jesus: The Sabbath

◆

And he said to them, "The sabbath was made for man, not man for the sabbath; so the Son of man is lord even of the sabbath."

[Mark 2:27]

THE SABBATH WAS A SPECIAL DAY for rest and worship. To the people who heard him, Jesus' words must have sounded astonishing and revolutionary. What did Jesus mean when he said this about the most hallowed institution in the life of his people—the sabbath day?

In seeking to understand what Jesus said, we need to remember first of all that Jesus observed the sabbath day. An incidental reference in the Gospel according to Luke brings this out. It's from chapter 4, verse 16: "And he came to Nazareth, where he had been brought up; and he went to the synagogue, as his custom was, on the sabbath day." Jesus went to the synagogue for public worship on the sabbath day. It was his custom to do that, a regular consistent part of his life. He joined himself to the people of God. He shared in the worship of God. He listened to, and at times proclaimed, the Word of God—all on the sabbath day.

And that's what we would have expected. "Remember the sabbath day, to keep it holy," was one of the commands in the decalogue, the Ten Commandments. Since it was Jesus' lifelong purpose to do the will of

God, he always endeavored to honor the sabbath. "Six days you shall labor, and do all your work," was the command; "but the seventh day is a sabbath to the LORD your God; in it you shall not do any work . . . for in six days the LORD made heaven and earth, the sea, and all that is in them, and rested the seventh day; therefore the LORD blessed the sabbath day and hallowed it" (Exod. 20:9–11). It was a day to celebrate God's mighty works, a day to remember the redemption of his people from bondage, and a day to be refreshed and begin life anew.

It was never Jesus' intention to disobey or abrogate any of God's laws. He announced that he had not come to destroy the law but to fulfill it. He taught that no part of the law would ever fall to the ground, that all would be accomplished. Whoever kept and taught God's commandments, he promised, would be great in the kingdom of heaven.

At the same time, Jesus was against certain interpretations and applications of this fourth commandment. He did not agree with many of his contemporaries about how the sabbath commandment should be kept. He resisted especially human attempts to control the behavior of others on the sabbath day.

For example, when Jesus healed the man with the withered hand in the Capernaum synagogue on the sabbath, some people were furious and they began immediately to conspire together as to how they could destroy Jesus. What upset them was that he had done this thing on the sabbath day. In their judgment, this healing was a form of work and therefore ought never to be done on the sabbath.

These are two strikingly different ways of keeping the sabbath! Jesus was loving; they were hating. He was longing to heal, and they were eager to harm and kill. Jesus asked them a question about this contrast: "Is it lawful on the sabbath to do good or to do harm, to save life or to kill?" The suspicious onlookers were silent. What could they say?

On another occasion Jesus met a man who had been blind from his birth. He stopped and reflected aloud about the situation. Jesus presented himself as the light of the world, and then he spat on the ground, made mud, spread it on the man's eyes and said, "Go, wash in the pool of Siloam!" The man went, washed, and came back, marvelously able to see. Again, the religious authorities were indignant. Why? Because this had happened on the sabbath day. Their reaction was, "This man [Jesus] is not from God, for he does not keep the sabbath" (John 9:16). He didn't keep it their way. Jesus' manner of keeping the sabbath was very different from theirs.

Here's a third incident. Jesus and his disciples were going through the grain fields one sabbath day, and as they made their way, his disciples began to pluck heads of grain, rubbing them in their hands and eating them. It was a perfectly lawful activity for people walking through the fields. The Pharisees, however, raised a question about it to Jesus: "Look, why are they doing what is not lawful on the sabbath?" (Mark 2:24). It wasn't wrong to pluck the grain and eat it, but in their eyes this was work. They saw it as a form of reaping and of preparing food; and any kind of work was forbidden on the sabbath. They made their objection to Jesus, considering him responsible for the behavior of his disciples.

Here was the Lord's response:

> Have you never read what David did, when he was in need and was hungry, he and those who were with him: how he entered the house of God, when Abiathar was high priest, and ate the bread of the Presence, which is not lawful for any but the priests to eat, and also gave it to those who were with him?
>
> [Mark 2:25–26]

David, of course, was Israel's greatest king. Flawed and failing at times, he was still a man after God's own heart. There came a time, Jesus reminds his critics, when David did what was forbidden by the law. He ate the bread of the presence from God's sanctuary, the food that only those of the priestly tribe could eat. And he gave some of it to his companions also. Note the parallels here: David and his companions, Jesus and his disciples. In each case, something was done that seemed to be a legal violation. And, in both situations, the people involved were hungry. In Jesus' eyes, what the ceremonial requirement of the law seemed to forbid, the urgency of human need made lawful. What was technically illegal was essentially and morally right.

Now the Lord gives expression to the principle involved: "The sabbath was made for man, not man for the sabbath." Let's look at the negative side of that first. Man, or humankind, says Jesus, was not made for the sabbath. The sabbath is not God. Man was not created in order to keep the sabbath. People were created for God, to live in communion with him, to know him, love him, honor him, and serve his purpose in the world. To say that the sabbath has ultimate significance, that man was made for it, would be to put the day itself in the place of the Lord, would make a certain way of sabbath observance our supreme duty, our chief good, but sabbath observance is not the ultimate meaning of our lives. The sabbath imposes no absolute claim on us. It has been instituted by God for his purposes, and only he can legislate how it is to be observed.

Jesus was a sabbath keeper because he loved the God who had ordained the sabbath. He delighted to do his will, to seek his face, and to give him praise. If we want a model for keeping the sabbath day holy, we have an unfailing one in Jesus of Nazareth.

In a church I once served, a lady told me excitedly about a recent experience she had had. She said she had witnessed to her neighbor. Since I tried to encourage the people in my congregation to share the good news with others, I was happy to hear that and asked the lady to tell me about it. "Well," she said, "my next-door neighbor was washing his car, and I told him he ought not to do that on Sunday." I waited, but that was the end of the story. That was all she had said. For her, witnessing meant just that, telling someone what not to do on Sunday. Presumably, if he had heeded her words, his life would have been complete! That's like saying that people are made for the sabbath.

Jesus turns this around. The sabbath was made for man, for humankind. It was instituted for our good, for our benefit, for our refreshment. Keeping the sabbath was never intended to be an end in itself. It was meant to minister to the wholeness, rest, and renewal of human lives in communion with God.

The sabbath command involves restriction and limitation, of course. People are not to work or have family members, servants, or employees work, not because God has some arbitrary whim against people working seven consecutive days and not because he simply wants to test and see if we will do it or not. It is wholly for our benefit. The sabbath, says Jesus, was made for us, that we wouldn't be so caught up in the world of work as to forget the real meaning of our lives, so that we wouldn't idolize our work or be enslaved by it. What a boon the sabbath is to all who labor! What a tragedy when its place is lost, its importance forgotten!

There are penalties for breaking this command. We can see them all around us. Those who work all the time, never stopping at an oasis of refreshment, wear themselves out and fall by the way. Societies that have no time for worship become increasingly shallow and superficial as the ties that bind people together tend to weaken. Further, those who will not submit to God's gracious ordering of human life often find themselves the victims of human tyranny. We bring these evils on ourselves when we reject God's good way or when we neglect to our great loss the kind provision he has made for us. The sabbath was made for us. God, who created us and understands us altogether, knows that we work best when one day out of seven is set apart for rest and worship. This commandment, like all the rest, is always for our good.

Then comes the Lord's closing word: "So the Son of man is lord even of the sabbath." Since the sabbath is made for humankind, then the Son of man, God's idea of a human being, the representative person, reigns over the sabbath. He is high above it. It is subject to his lordship and under his authority. He holds the final say as to its observance.

This phrase "the Son of man" is Jesus' favorite name for himself. It speaks, of course, of his humanity and his representative role. But it has far more meaning than that. The Son of man in the Old Testament Book of Daniel is a heavenly figure:

I saw one like a human being coming with the clouds of heaven.
And he came to the Ancient One and was presented before him.
To him was given dominion and glory and kingship,
that all peoples, nations, and languages should serve him.
His dominion is an everlasting dominion that shall not pass away,
and his kingship is one that shall never be destroyed.

[Dan. 7:13–14 NRSV]

Jesus now presents himself as this one coming with the clouds of heaven, to whom all sovereignty belongs, and yet he shares our humanity. He is one of us. As this heavenly Son of man, Jesus has authority even over the most cherished and sacred institution in the life of his people, the sabbath. To many of his Jewish hearers, this may have been the most astounding and offensive claim that Jesus ever made.

Have you noticed how everything Jesus taught points us finally to who he is? His words lead us to worship, his doctrine to devotion. We only appropriate the heart of what Jesus teaches when we submit ourselves to his reign. Jesus is the Lord, the Lord of everything. He's the one who has shared our humanity and borne our sins while dying in our place. He has conquered death for us and lives today to offer us forgiveness and new life.

Study Questions

1. How was Jesus a sabbath-keeper?
2. How did his approach to keeping the sabbath differ from that of his enemies in the synagogue?
3. In what sense is the sabbath created for us?
4. What does it mean that the Son of man is Lord of the sabbath?

32

Listening to Jesus: His Relatives

◆

And his mother and his brothers came; and standing outside they sent to him and called him. And a crowd was sitting about him; and they said to him, "Your mother and your brothers are outside, asking for you." And he replied, "Who are my mother and my brothers?" And looking around on those who sat about him, he said, "Here are my mother and my brothers! Whoever does the will of God is my brother, and sister, and mother."

[Mark 3:31–35]

SOME OF THE THINGS Jesus said about his relatives and the significance of family ties were quite surprising. In this passage Jesus is apparently teaching his followers in a house crowded with people. They're gathered around him so tightly that no one else can possibly squeeze into the building. Quite unexpectedly, Mary, the mother of Jesus, and his brothers arrive and want to see him. When their efforts to reach him prove hopeless, they send a message through someone near the door. The word gets passed along until finally someone in the inner circle around the Lord says, "Your mother and your brothers are outside, asking for you."

What will Jesus do? Will he rise immediately, excuse himself and go out to meet them? Probably some in the crowd expected that. They thought he would interrupt his teaching, leave the circle of his follow-

ers and hasten to his family members. If that's what they were antici-
pating, they must have been shocked at his reaction. He responded with
a question to those around him, "Who are my mother and my brothers?"
What do you mean, Jesus? You know who they are. Your mother is Mary,
your brothers James, Joseph, Simon, and Judas. They're your family and
they're right outside. Why are you asking us who they are? Those must
have been some of the thoughts of people around him.

Jesus didn't wait long for a reply. After he had given them a moment
to think about it, he answered his own question. "Whoever does the will
of God is my brother, and sister, and mother."

We know that people are not automatically close to their family members. Sometimes that happens and sometimes it doesn't. Sometimes those
who grow up in the same home, as members of the same family, remain
for a lifetime distant from each other. There may be fierce enmity, long-
standing distrust, or simply a staying out of each other's way and a living apart.

Children can't be compelled to love their parents and delight in their
company. Parents can demand obedience, conformity, and expressions
of respect, but close ties of affection are another thing. Parents cannot
enforce shared values, genuine friendship, or joy in being together. The
warm and friendly response of our family members to us is a gift of grace,
not subject to our coercion or manipulation. It's a blessing that cannot
be bought.

The gospel records make it clear that Jesus' family members didn't
always understand him. Early in this third chapter of Mark, we're told
that they feared at times that he was out of his mind. His brothers sometimes suspected the motives behind his ministry. They thought he wanted
to make a name for himself, to become famous. At that point, they didn't
believe in him. Perhaps they shared the skepticism of others in Nazareth
who couldn't imagine where he got his teachings or how he did these
remarkable things. Apparently his brothers were not especially eager to
listen to his words. Though they were his siblings, reared in the same
home, their relationship to Jesus was not always close.

What makes people close if being born into the same family and living in the same house doesn't automatically make them close? In C. S.

Lewis's book *The Four Loves*, the author speaks of how deep friendships are formed. He notes that people who are always trying to find a friend often fail in the search.

Ties of friendship are formed, according to Lewis, in a more indirect way. We discover one day, for example, that we share a common interest with someone. We enjoy the same activities. At an even deeper level, we find that our basic values are in harmony. We care about the same concerns; our hearts beat for the same cause. And as we stand shoulder to shoulder, working for the same goal, we discover that a wonderful thing has happened. We are friends.

This may happen between siblings, and often does. It may become a reality between parents and children. Blessed are those families where that occurs! But it doesn't necessarily happen—we're not necessarily friends—because we're in the same family or live in the same neighborhood or are citizens of the same country.

In 1978 I had an experience in the Soviet Union that I'll never forget. My wife, Helen, and I, with our friends the Sergeys, were in Moscow on the Fourth of July. That year it fell on a Sunday. In the morning I was privileged to preach in a Moscow church with John Sergey, our Russian language broadcaster, as my interpreter. That afternoon we had a communion service in the same congregation. I was asked to pray, holding the cup of blessing aloft. We partook together, all those Russians, a handful of Americans, and perhaps a few from other nations as well. It was a moving experience. At the close of the service, many of the Russian believers gathered around us, full of smiles, weeping tears of joy. Several burly men threw their arms around me and kissed me. Now this was a time when relations between the U.S. and Russia were severely strained. I hadn't known what to expect when I arrived there, and the welcome and warm affection of these Russian Christians was almost overwhelming to me.

Later that same day, because it was the Fourth of July, there was to be a kind of celebration at the U.S. embassy in Moscow. Americans who happened to be in the city were invited to attend, so we went along. It was a grand occasion. The embassy personnel were all there, some of them splendidly uniformed. There was an abundance of good food, tastefully prepared. Guests strolled around comfortably. The conversation was polite and pleasant.

As I stood in that circle of people, this thought came powerfully to my mind: I had felt closer to those Russian believers in that communion service than I felt to these Americans in the U.S. embassy. The tie was not national, not racial, not cultural or political, but spiritual. The basis of fellowship and friendship around the table of the Lord was Christ and his love.

What makes for closeness to Jesus Christ? What in our lives promotes genuine kinship with him and brings us near to his heart? Jesus spells it out clearly, "Whoever does the will of God is my brother, and sister, and mother." As he says this, he looks around at the circle of his followers. These are his family members.

As the beloved Son, Jesus' sole ambition was to do the Father's bidding, to accomplish the Father's work and so to honor his name. "My food is to do the will of him who sent me, and to accomplish his work." "I have come down from heaven, not to do my own will, but the will of him who sent me." Even in Gethsemane, facing the agony of being forsaken, he prays, "Nevertheless, not my will, but thine, be done." Jesus recognized as kinfolk those who felt the same way, who had the same life objective.

It wasn't that his disciples were totally obedient to God all the time. Most of them were struggling and had a long way to go, but their basic heart attitude was right. They had responded to his call and submitted themselves to his lordship. They were learning his ways and listening to his word. They were open to God and his rule. As Jesus saw it, they were sharing his vision and burden. They were doing the will of God.

So take heart, friend, even though you feel you're fumbling and failing and are a long way from a totally obedient life. If you are sitting at the feet of Jesus to hear his word, then you are close to his heart. To him, you're a family member.

Maybe you don't have a family now in the biological sense. Your parents are gone. You have no brothers or sisters. You're a single parent or you're just single. What family you have may be badly fractured. Sometimes you feel that because you're not a part of a nuclear family, that there can be no close ties for you. Even in the church of Jesus Christ you may feel left out because it seems so family-oriented. However it seems, that's not the way it is. You are just as much a part of God's family as anyone. If you are listening to the Lord's Word and following him, you belong in the most profound sense. You are a beloved child of your heavenly Father. You're a member in Christ of God's family.

I've noticed this about friendships: My best friends are those who not only love me but also love my cause. They care about my well being and want to see the work of my life prosper. The attachment is based, then, not only on agreeable personal traits but on a living sympathy of purpose. A relationship can go just so far when it isn't grounded in a shared commitment, so if your aim in life is different from that of Jesus, it simply isn't possible to be close to him.

If the kingdom of God is what you prize most highly, if doing God's will is what's most important in the world to you, and what you pray about most fervently, then you're truly close to Christ, and your very best friends are those who join with you in giving themselves to see God's will realized.

As I've reflected on the passage in Mark, I've wondered why Jesus said what he did. It was surely not to put down his family members or to disparage the importance of family ties. But on the positive side, it was to lift up the blessedness of discipleship and the closeness that his devoted followers might have to him. The gospel, the good news, in this text is that anyone can be near to the Lord's heart, closely related to him. Jesus is no respecter of persons. You don't have to belong to the right family or come from the right part of town or be a certain color or speak a particular language. Jesus welcomes as a brother or sister anyone who has a heart to do the will of God.

Jesus was not speaking against love and loyalty toward family members, but he wanted us to see that an ultimate loyalty to one's biological family may prove to be exclusive of other people, even idolatrous if carried to an extreme. An ultimate loyalty to Christ, on the other hand, brings us near to him and into closeness with his people.

The love of God perfects every other love. We truly love our family members best when we love them in him. When Jesus' mother and brothers responded to Jesus' word and trusted in him as the crucified and risen Savior and Lord they were far closer to him than they were at this time. They were one with him in a new way.

Study Questions

1. What can parents compel from their children, and what must be freely given?
2. In your relationships, what seems to contribute to closeness?
3. Jesus called his disciples his family because they were "doing the will of God." We know they were not always perfect, so in what sense was this true?
4. Was Jesus' comment a reflection on his bioligical family members? Explain.

33

Listening to Jesus: How People Hear

—————————— ◆ ——————————

A sower went out to sow. And as he sowed, some seed fell along the path, and the birds came and devoured it. Other seed fell on rocky ground, where it had not much soil, and immediately it sprang up, since it had no depth of soil; and when the sun rose it was scorched, and since it had no root it withered away. Other seed fell among thorns and the thorns grew up and choked it, and it yielded no grain. And other seeds fell into good soil and brought forth grain, growing up and increasing and yielding thirtyfold and sixtyfold and a hundredfold. And he said, "He who has ears to hear, let him hear."

[Mark 4:3–9]

The sower sows the word. And these are the ones along the path, where the word is sown; when they hear, Satan immediately comes and takes away the word which is sown in them. And these in like manner are the ones sown upon rocky ground, who, when they hear the word, immediately receive it with joy; and they have not root in themselves, but endure for a while; then, when tribulation or persecution arises on account of the word, immediately they fall away. And others are the ones sown among thorns; they are those who hear the word, but the cares of the world, and the delight in riches, and the desire for other things, enter in and choke the word, and it proves unfruitful. But those that were sown upon the good soil are the ones who hear the word and accept and bear fruit, thirty-fold and sixtyfold and a hundredfold.

[Mark 4:14–20]

THIS IS A STORY from the farm that has become familiar the world over. Some call it the Parable of the Sower and the Seed. Others say it's a story about different kinds of soil. All agree that to Jesus and his apostles it was an extremely important message.

More verses in the Gospels according to Matthew, Mark, and Luke are devoted to this parable than to any other parable. Jesus gives a detailed interpretation of the parable, and he does this only one other time. Further, he seems to say that this one parable is a key to the understanding of all the others. He asks his followers in Mark 4:13, "Do you not understand this parable? How then will you understand all the parables?"

This story is loaded with significant clues concerning God's purposes in the world and the life and ministry of his church and of individuals like you and me. This parable is vital because it deals with the proclamation of God's Word, an activity that Jesus always saw as central to his own ministry and that of his disciples. The seed, he says, is the Word of God. The sowers are God's messengers who proclaim it. This is how the secret of the kingdom is made known and how the mystery of God's purpose is unveiled. God speaks. He breaks the silence and draws back the veil. He makes himself known. In the proclamation of Jesus and his witnesses, a miracle of revelation is happening. The preaching of the Word is central to God's purpose and his saving work. Hearing the Word is the most important thing that ever happens in the lives of human beings.

In telling us about the different kinds of soil into which the seed falls, Jesus is helping us to understand what goes on when the word is proclaimed—why responses to it are so varied. More than that, he wants us to ask ourselves what kind of soil am I? and how do I receive the seed of God's Word?

By the wayside, along the beaten path, the ground is hard packed. The seed finds no entrance. It's like trying to grow something on concrete. The seed just lies there on the surface, exposed and vulnerable. Soon the birds come and make off with it. Nothing happens. There is no growth and no crop.

There are people like that, Jesus says. They never let the Word of God get into their minds and hearts. They remain closed to it. Before long the evil one has removed every trace of the Word, and they scarcely give it a thought.

Do you know people like that? You can't get them to go to church or listen to the Word preached. They refuse to open a Bible and read it for themselves. And if, while tuning the television or radio dial, they should come upon someone heralding the Word of God, they quickly switch channels or stations. They seem determined not to let the Word of God get to them.

Some seed, Jesus continues, falls on the rocky ground. There's a thin layer of soil on the top, then a massive ledge of rock. The seed drops on the ground and almost immediately, it seems, we see some green growth. But it doesn't last. As soon as the sun is high, the little seedling withers. Its problem: no depth of earth and therefore no root system.

Jesus says these are the people who are enthusiastic when they hear the Word. They come to church. They celebrate their new faith. A few weeks later, however, they're nowhere to be found. They've fallen away completely and are living just as they lived before. The response and growth were only on the surface. Nothing ever went deep and when it became difficult to be a Christian, when some cost was involved in discipleship or when someone spoke against them because of their faith, they had had enough. Their discipleship was shallow and brief.

Do you know anyone like that? I'm afraid I do. I can think of people I've known who seemed to me at one time to be genuinely converted. They said they believed. They were happy in their newfound faith but very soon they seemed to lose interest. They had no heart at all for the disciplines of the Christian life and so as soon as the going got rough along the Christian way, they dropped out.

Then there was that seed that fell among the thorns. That seemed promising, too. But the soil already harbored other seeds and they began to sprout and grow along with the good seed of the Word. They grew up with it, cut off its air and light, and choked it out so that it never matured enough to bear any fruit.

Jesus doesn't leave us in doubt about what these thorns are, at least some of them: the cares of the world, the deceit of riches, the desire for other things. Some people get sidetracked in the Christian race because they're consumed with worries. Will I be able to keep my job? What about my health? How are we going to make ends meet? They're so pre-occupied with anxiety about what's going to happen to them that everything else in their lives suffers. Their Christian growth is stunted.

For others the distraction is the deceit of riches. People pursue the will-of-the-wisp of wealth. They believe it's the secret of happiness, and so to make more money, to strike it rich, they compromise conscience. They may walk over others. They forget the Lord.

The desire for other things can also hinder the Christian walk. We get caught up in the rat race of consumerism. We have to have what everyone else has—the latest thing we see advertised. We're so busy acquiring possessions and taking care of them, so bent on the next acquisition, that our spiritual lives never get a chance to grow.

At times all of us have given in to these pressures. Who can say that he's free from anxiety, that she never worries about the future? Who of us hasn't been fooled at times, as King Midas was, with the false promises of wealth? And most of all, who hasn't allowed the desire for other things to crowd out an appetite for the things of Christ? That happens to all of us in some ways, but for some, it goes on unchecked until it seems that every vestige of faith and obedience has been squeezed out.

Then there's the good soil, the fertile soil, the welcoming earth. As soon as the seed drops there, growth starts. Soon there's grain above ground. It grows, flourishes, and multiplies, yielding thirty times more than anyone would expect, even sixty, even a hundredfold. Who are these people? Jesus says they are the ones who hear the Word and accept it. They take it into their hearts. They let it go deep. They won't tolerate anything that chokes it out.

Do you know some Christians like that? Maybe you are one yourself. They're not perfect people. They're flawed and fumbling like all the rest of us, but they are good listeners to the Word of the Lord. They take seriously what he has said. They dwell on it and try to translate it into life. As you watch them, you can tell the difference, for they are growing in the likeness of Christ and are becoming fountains of good works. They are helpful servants who have a way of attracting other people to the Lord.

Remember now what Jesus said when the parable was ended: "He who has ears to hear, let him hear." And again, "Take heed how you hear." It's as though he's saying, you have a capacity to take in the Word of God. Now use that capacity. And again, you're responsible for what you do with the Word, so handle it with care.

Do you know what that says to me? It suggests that whatever kind of soil we may be in at the present moment, we're not locked into that. Things can change. With real repentance we can plow up that hard-packed ground. We can dislodge those rocks and even root out the thorns. The Lord can make the most unpromising terrain into good earth, a garden for the Lord. So be careful how you listen when the Word comes to you and pray as it does, "God, help me to prepare the ground. Lord, change my heart and make it receptive to your Word."

But this is not only a parable for those who hear the Word, not only a call to take heed how we hear. It's also a message for proclaimers. It's a word for those followers of the Lord who try to sow the seed, to preach, teach, and witness. It's a word meant for our encouragement.

All of us who seek to share the gospel with others meet with disappointments at times. Some people turn us off right at the start. Maybe they laugh and mock like some of the Athenians did when Paul preached on Mars Hill. Sometimes people seem to give us a hearing, nod pleasantly, and act as though they're responsive, but nothing ever comes of it. They tell the pastor they're coming to church next Sunday, but something always interferes and they never quite get there.

Or maybe they do come to church. Maybe they're members, even officers in our congregations. They sit under our ministry week after week and we keep bringing the Lord's Word to them, but we sense more and more that we're working against some kind of opposition. There seem to be powerful forces in the lives of these people that negate the effects of the Word: their worries perhaps, their pursuit of wealth, their thousand and one distracting interests. We go through the agony of watching these things strangle out God's Word in their lives. It can be disheartening to preach the Word and see that many of our hearers are so little changed for the better.

But, thank God, that's never the whole story. One of the great themes of this parable is that whenever the sower goes out to sow there's always some seed that falls on good ground. Some of it produces a bountiful harvest and some an exceptional crop. Some respond in a way that's almost beyond belief, that brings tears of joy to our eyes. That's the good news for those of us who preach: God's Word never comes back empty. It always brings forth fruit. When we proclaim the gospel, there may be people who shrug it off, who deal with it shallowly, who take it in only to snuff it out. There may be those people, but there will be some who hear the Word and accept it, who hide it in their hearts and bear fruit. There will be some hearts changed, some lives dedicated, and some people blossoming as God's beautiful children. So we don't lose heart. We keep on preaching, keep on asking the Holy Spirit to bless the Word. We know that whatever else comes from that ministry, some of that seed will always fall on good ground. Take heart, Christian. No sharing of the Word, no witness to Jesus Christ and the gospel will ever be in vain.

Study Questions

1. What are the evidences that this parable had central significance for Jesus and his followers?
2. Try to evaluate your own life as to "soil quality" for the Word.
3. What can we do if we have been unproductive soil thus far?
4. What great encouragement is here for all who preach and teach the gospel?

34

Listening to Jesus: The Human Heart

◆

And he said to them, "Then are you also without understanding? Do
you not see that whatever goes into a man from outside cannot defile
him, since it enters, not his heart but his stomach, and so passes on?"
(Thus he declared all foods clean.) And he said, "What comes out of
a man is what defiles a man. For from within, out of the heart of man,
come evil thoughts, fornication, theft, murder, adultery, coveting,
wickedness, deceit, licentiousness, envy, slander, pride, foolishness.
All these evil things come from within, and they defile a man."

[Mark 7:18–23]

DO YOU KNOW WHAT the Bible is referring to when it speaks of the
heart? It's not the same as the definition found in a medical book. *Heart*
in the Scriptures does not mean merely the physical organ that pumps
blood. *Heart* means the inmost center of our lives, the essential person
that we are. God says to his people, "If with all your heart you truly seek
me, you will ever surely find me" (see Jer. 29:13). We're to love the Lord
our God, we're told, "with all your heart." We believe in him in our
hearts. Those who are single in heart, Jesus says, shall "see God." Those

who can dwell in his presence are those who have "clean hands and a pure heart."

The heart is that central place in all of us to which God looks and where all our experience of him is rooted. It's the inner fountain from which all the streams of our life flow forth. It's the inner center in us beneath all pretense and deception: the real you and the real me. What we are in our hearts is what we really are in the sight of God.

That's what makes it so shocking when Jesus says this about the heart. "From within, out of the heart of man, come evil thoughts, fornication, theft, murder, adultery, coveting, wickedness, deceit, licentiousness, envy, slander, pride, foolishness. All these evil things come from within, and they defile a man." Think of that. All that evil comes from within human hearts, hearts like yours and mine. How then can a heart be cleansed? How is it ever possible to have a pure heart?

That's the kind of question Jesus is dealing with in his controversy with the scribes and Pharisees in this passage in Mark. What is it to be defiled and unclean, and what can we do about it?

The religious authorities found fault with Jesus' disciples because they sometimes ate without first carefully washing their hands. For the Pharisees, one of the leading marks of true piety was ceremonial washing. For the strictest Pharisees, purifying themselves meant washing not only their hands but also their various utensils: cups, pots, and vessels of bronze. This was not merely a matter of sanitation; it involved character and commitment. If you didn't go through with the prescribed washings before a meal, you were viewed as a bad person, lacking in righteousness, and disloyal to God's covenant. The Pharisees asked indignantly, "Why do your disciples not live according to the tradition of the elders, but eat with hands defiled?" (Mark 7:5).

Jesus rejects their view. "Hear me," he says, "all of you, and understand: there is nothing outside a man which by going into him can defile him" (v. 15). In other words, nothing we eat can possibly make our hearts unclean, defile our lives or render us unacceptable to God. For Jesus, purity of heart has nothing whatever to do with the kinds of foods we eat, nothing whatever to do with elaborate external washings. The reason is that food and drink, though vital to sustain our bodies, do not affect the inmost springs of our lives.

When his disciples asked him about this later, he developed the thought more fully. "Are you also without understanding?" he asked. "Do you not see that whatever goes into a man from outside cannot defile him, since it enters, not his heart but his stomach, and so passes on?" (vv. 18–19). When food goes through the digestive system, nourishing elements are assimilated by the body and the rest is eliminated as waste. All of this is merely physiological. It has nothing to do with the condition of a person's inner life. It has nothing to do with the state of his or her heart. In fact, as Jesus could tell the very people who were so scrupulous about these washings, though they honored God with their lips, their hearts were far from him.

The Lord does not mean to say by this that cleanliness is unimportant or that we shouldn't be concerned about good nutrition. Obviously, contaminated foods can cause disease and the wrong kind of diet can undermine health. The point Jesus makes, however, is that our relationship to God is not determined by how we eat or what we eat or even the quantities we consume. Nothing I take into my body can make me more or less acceptable to God, because nothing I eat or drink can change my basic personhood. It cannot touch my heart.

There is so much said and written today about good nutrition, about cholesterol and food additives, that eating and drinking can become a moral issue for people. Many in our society feel uncomfortable about being overweight. Often others also make them feel guilty, as though the slender and the trim were the more godly and obesity were a cardinal sin. How many of the eating disorders that young adults suffer with are related to this tendency to assign moral judgments to matters of diet? Don't believe that, urges Jesus. No food you eat, however prepared, can make you better or worse in God's sight. Meat and drink cannot change the inner springs of anyone's personality. You cannot be defiled by what you eat.

According to Jesus, real defilement comes about in quite a different way. There's nothing outside a man that by going into him can defile him, but the things that come out of a man are what defile him. He goes on to develop that thought: "For from within, out of the heart of man, come evil thoughts, fornication, theft, murder, adultery. . . ." Defilement, Jesus insists, is from the inside out. It's what comes forth from within us that makes us unclean, because that proceeds, he says, from the heart.

Evil thoughts, for example, defile us. They originate within our minds and are harbored there. Acts of fornication, theft, murder, and adultery begin as passions in the heart, which then are acted out in life. Coveting, deceit, envy, and pride are attitudes of the heart. Even the foolishness, the slander, and the lies that we speak represent the outflow of our inner life. The heart, you see, has to do with character—a person's inmost thoughts, motives, and attitudes toward others and toward God. Outward acts bring to light these inward dispositions.

Jesus is saying to his critics, don't worry about these external details. Don't be so concerned about ritual cleanliness. What really matters is what we most deeply believe within us, the major motivations that shape our lives and the patterns of conduct that flow from them. These are the things that make us unclean, that cause guilt, that alienate us from God and from each other. It's that inward defilement that you and I ought to be most concerned about.

It's important to realize that Jesus was not challenging the written Word of God but the oral traditions, which had been superimposed upon it. The Pharisees asked, "Why do your disciples not live according to the tradition of the elders?" In response, Jesus charges them with leaving the commandment of God and holding fast the traditions of men.

Why, we wonder, were these elaborate traditions added to the written Word? The attempt at first may have been praiseworthy, to clarify the law's demands, to make practical applications of it for everyday life. The effect, however, was often quite different. Men often used the oral law to gain control of and manipulate the law of God. That law, when we take it seriously and let our consciences feel its inner demand, is a devastating thing because it shows us how far we've fallen short, how much in us rebels against God's standard. So our tendency always is to blunt its effects. Instead of allowing the law to show us that we are sinners who can only live with God on the basis of his forgiveness, we try to make the law establish our own righteousness and show us to be always in the right.

We try to make the law into something we can live with on some other terms than the forgiveness of sins, something that fits in with our self-righteousness and complacency. We substitute for God's law a kind of human legalism. We spell out details of proper observance. We set up our own codes. Then, having complied with them, we manage to blur the fact that we have ignored the main thrust of God's law. What a trap!

All of us who try to make the law prove us right seem to end by modifying or perverting it. It's our thinly veiled attempt to escape from the law, to void its authority. We learn to obey it technically even while we disregard it essentially. Now we see how people can be superficially religious and yet be far from God, how they can be careful about details of behavior and still live wickedly. External rituals cannot change the heart.

The heart is like the root and trunk of a tree. The branches that the tree puts forth, the leaves, the blossoms, the fruit, all of that is a direct result of the kind of tree it is. Again, the heart is like a spring. All the water that flows forth from that fount, however far it may go, is like the source from which it comes. If the spring is impure, everything that comes from it will carry the same impurity. In a similar way, all the thoughts, motives, attitudes, and actions of our lives arise from and are tinctured by the state of our inner lives, by what we are in our hearts.

That brings us to the all-important question: What can be done about a defiled heart? If our inmost being is impure, if the central source of our behavior is wrong, and if the outward fruit of our lives is constantly separating us from God, what can we do? We feel ready to cry out as the apostle Paul did once, "Wretched man that I am! Who will deliver me from this body of death?" The traditions of the elders about foods and washings didn't touch the problem of inner uncleanness. They only masked it. The way to deal with a defiled heart is not to pretend there's nothing wrong with it. If an apple is rotten at the core, you can't make it a better apple by painting it red, can you? If human life is flawed at the center, you can't improve it by polishing the surface. The only way is the way of confession, of brokenheartedness over our sins and turning away from them to God. That becomes possible because the kingdom of God has drawn near to us, because the Lord has come in Jesus his Son to save us from our sins. Jesus bears the load of our guilt. He takes on himself the stroke of our condemnation. He dies in our place so that we can be forgiven. Through trusting in him and his perfect work for us, we are forgiven, we are justified, we are accepted completely before God. And grander still, we are given the gift of his Holy Spirit to make us new on the inside, to cleanse our hearts.

That's the gospel. We don't need to pretend we're something we're not. We don't need to develop elaborate kinds of ritual to prove that we're all right. In Jesus Christ, God accepts us just as we are and then undertakes to make us new from the inside out. In Christ, we're becoming a new creation.

Study Questions

1. How would you sum up the biblical meaning of *heart*?
2. Why, according to Jesus, can eating with unwashed hands not defile us?
3. As the Lord teaches, where does real defilement come from?
4. Is there anything that can be done for a defiled heart? Explain.

35

Listening to Jesus: Discipleship

◆

And he began to teach them that the Son of man must suffer many things, and be rejected by the elders and the chief priests and the scribes, and be killed, and after three days rise again. And he said this plainly. And Peter took him, and began to rebuke him. But turning and seeing his disciples, he rebuked Peter, and said, "Get behind me, Satan! For you are not on the side of God, but of men."

And he called to him the multitude with his disciples, and said to them, "If any man would come after me, let him deny himself and take up his cross and follow me. For whoever would save his life will lose it; and whoever loses his life for my sake and the gospel's will save it."

[Mark 8:31–35]

BILL BRADLEY used to be a famous basketball player, first with Princeton University and later with the New York Knicks. Now he is a distinguished U.S. senator. When he was moving from one career to the other, he wrote a book about the first: *Life on the Run*. Bradley tells how professional athletes who have reached the summit of achievement and fame in their early years must live out the rest of their days in a kind of prolonged anticlimax. They can never hope to feel again the exhilaration of their youthful stardom. The great performer who retires at age thirty-five asks himself, where do I go from here? What can I possibly do next? Perhaps all of us are in some way to blame for this dilemma. We've made too much of our athletes. We've had young men thinking that they were people of stature just because they were physically tall or that they were especially important because they had been gifted with superb hand-eye coordination.

Are there parallels to this in religious life? Indeed there are, especially if the beginning of that life was sudden, dramatic, and deeply moving. How can anything that follows possibly equal the thrill of that newfound faith? I've known young people, for example, who became enthusiastic Christians back in the late 60s and early 70s. They were all aglow with a wonderful new radiance. They spoke of their faith, they sang about it, they were eager to attract others. Their gifts and their joy brought them into the public eye. People flocked to listen to their music; hundreds of teenagers hung with rapt attention on their words. What a tremendously exciting thing it was then for them to believe! And, as with our athletes, we sometimes put new believers on a pedestal. We listen to them as though they are oracles. We praise them at the start of the race as though they had already crossed the finish line. We haven't taught them about, or equipped them for, the long haul. Then, when the party's over, the sparkle has faded, and the crowds are gone, the hard realities of making a living, working at a marriage, and struggling through difficult days take the place of those enchanted beginnings.

Jesus was careful not to put people on a pedestal. Remember when Simon Peter made his great affirmation of faith? Jesus had asked his followers what the people were saying about him and who they believed that he was. They had answered, "Some say John the Baptist, others say Elijah, and others Jeremiah or one of the prophets." Then, when he addressed the question to the disciples themselves, "Who do you say that I am?" Peter answered for all the rest, "You are the Christ." In other words, you are the long-awaited Messiah. You are God's appointed King and Savior. You are the Lord.

What a marvelous moment that was! Here was Simon Peter voicing a revolutionary conviction. He was saying, Jesus, you are more than a prophet, more than a religious leader. You are the Son of the living God.

This faith, Jesus responded, was a divine gift, a heaven-born confession. We admire this rugged fisherman Peter for making it. He dared to believe. You would think that Jesus would have been immensely gratified by that. Here was someone who believed in him, who saw who he really was and was willing to declare it. This surely was a time to celebrate. You would think that Jesus would commend Peter and that all his fellow disciples would congratulate him for the stand he had taken.

But none of that happened. As soon as he heard what Peter said, Jesus cautioned all the disciples to tell no one about it. That was surprising in itself. But they were even less prepared for what followed.

> He began to teach them that the Son of man must suffer many things, and be rejected by the elders and the chief priests and the scribes, and be killed, and after three days rise again. And he said this plainly. And Peter took him, and began to rebuke him. But turning and seeing his disciples, he rebuked Peter, and said, "Get behind me, Satan! For you are not on the side of God, but of men." And he called to him the multitude with his disciples, and said to them, "If any man would come after me, let him deny himself and take up his cross and follow me. For whoever would save his life will lose it; and whoever loses his life for my sake and the gospel's will save it."
>
> [Mark 8:31–35]

Jesus rejoiced at the witness of his followers, but he wanted them to understand clearly what it meant for him and for them. After we believe and declare that Jesus is the Christ, the Savior, the Lord, what then? Jesus teaches first that we need to know the kind of Christ he is. Sometimes we can say the right words sincerely but have little awareness of what they involve. Jesus announced that he was one destined to suffer, to be rejected and killed. But Peter, the man who had made the great confession, was scandalized at that. He thought there must be some mistake. Didn't you hear what I said, Jesus? You're the one we've been waiting for. How can you talk about such a gloomy future? That's never going to happen to you. And Peter began to rebuke the one whom he had professed to trust.

It's difficult for any of us to hear about a suffering, rejected Christ. We would much rather fashion in our minds some heroic, conquering one who was hailed by the crowds. Didn't he come to rescue us, to meet our needs, to make our world what it ought to be? Yes, but for Jesus that meant agony and hatred, a crown of thorns and a cross of shame. That was his destiny—God's path for him. It was the only way in which he could be our Savior. Sometimes in the first glow of faith we miss the depth and force of that. We don't realize that our rebellion was such that it rejected and crucified the Lord who came to us. We don't see that our need is so acute and our peril so grave that only a suffering, dying Lord can possibly redeem us. We stumble, all of us at times, at the offense of the cross.

We're ready to stand with Peter, ready to correct the Lord. Surely there's some other way, we protest. Then his words to Peter pierce us too. "Get behind me, Satan! For you do not mind the things of God but those of men" (author's translation). What about you? Has the truth of Jesus' mission come home with power to your heart? Even his matchless example and beautiful teaching can never save you. He must bear your judgment and die your death if you are to have hope. The only Christ there is to believe in is God's Christ, the real one, who came to suffer and die.

After you believe in the crucified Christ, what will it mean for your life? What does Jesus say about discipleship? He wanted everyone to know just what they were getting into if they decided to follow him. And so after this exchange with his disciples, he called the crowds together and then said to all of them, "If any man would come after me, let him deny himself and take up his cross and follow me" (Mark 8:34). He's saying, in effect, that if we want to follow him, we need to walk the same road. That shouldn't take us by surprise. He often said something like that. The disciple is not above his master, neither is the servant above his lord. It is enough for the disciple that he be as his master (see Matt. 10:24).

But this is precisely what many have missed in their early Christian experience. No one told them about the way of discipleship, or if someone did, they have somehow blocked out the stern reality of it. That may be why they've been surprised, discouraged, or disappointed at times.

Jesus says to follow Christ means to deny ourselves. For Jesus, the way of the cross meant saying no to his own plans, wishes, and hopes. It means the same for us. Just as it meant resisting the temptation to play it safe and look out for himself, so it must be for us. Following Christ means a radical change in the way we approach everything. It involves shifting the center of gravity from concern for ourselves to a single-hearted pursuit of God's will. It means renouncing and disowning the sovereign claims of king self and relinquishing all right to run our lives as we please. According to Jesus, we cannot say a realistic yes to God's way without saying a repeated no to our own.

If that seems strong, even ominous, what comes next is far more so. "Let him . . . take up his cross." That phrase could have meant only one thing to Jesus' contemporaries. In first century Palestine, if you saw a man with a cross on his back, you knew he was headed for execution. He had just shouldered the stake on which he was soon to be nailed. Jesus' obedience to the Father was to carry him all the way to crucifixion. Those who were serious about following him might well meet the same fate. They were to deny themselves and come after him even if it meant facing death.

Usually, people aren't told that when they become Christians. When I first believed in Jesus, I learned that he had died for my sins and that I could be forgiven through trusting in him, but no one told me that following him meant renouncing all rights to myself and obeying him even at the risk of my life. Had I known that at the start, would I have been as responsive as I was? I'm not sure about that. But if I had known it, I would have seen the Christian life much more realistically and would have been able to make a far more responsible decision.

Jesus wanted people to follow him, of course, but he loved them too much to hide the cost and struggle of it. When we tell others today that their faith in Christ will lead them to success, prosperity, and fame, we distort his plain teaching. We seem at times to say, if you follow Christ, you can indulge yourself and be secure from all inconvenience. No wonder people are dismayed and indignant when the going gets rough!

Why would anyone want to follow Christ if the road may be hard and painful? That's a good question. That's the issue we need to wrestle with.

Jesus offered precious little in the way of earthly inducements. There was nothing in his message that even remotely resembled a sales pitch. The only conceivable reason for those disciples to continue to follow him was their personal attachment to Jesus. Why would they follow him, deny themselves, and risk everything? Jesus said, "For my sake and the gospel's." In other words, do it for me. Do it because you trust me and my love for you. Do it so that the whole world can know me and my saving love. Now if you decide to come after him for those reasons, nothing will ever disappoint you. The Christian life won't be one big bang followed by a long fizzle. Rather it will be a growing, deepening, transforming adventure because you live it in fellowship with Christ himself and you live it for him.

What about the end of the road? What about the final choices we make? Jesus wants us to be clear about those: "Whoever would save his life will lose it; and whoever loses his life for my sake and the gospel's will save it" (Mark 8:35). Suppose you decide this path of discipleship is too hard, too unnatural? You don't want to deny yourself. You don't want to give up all your rights to someone else. You're not going to risk yourself for anyone. You'll pamper that life of yours and keep it for your very own. Jesus says no. Not that way. You'll end up losing your true life. The more tightly you grasp it—like drops of water or grains of sand—the more surely it will slip through your fingers.

Suppose you decide to follow Christ, to follow him because he's Lord and because he died for you? Suppose you're daily making the choice to say no to yourself and yes to him? You may experience ridicule, even rejection. Obeying him will cost you something and probably bring you reproach. You may seem at times as a disciple to be losing everything. But Jesus says that the self you give away will become for the first time truly yours. And out of what looks like death, you'll discover what it really is to live. That's what the Lord has in mind for his disciples.

Study Questions

1. Why was Peter resistant to Jesus' words about suffering?

2. How do you understand Jesus' call to follow? What practical steps are necessary?

3. Jesus said if we are to follow him, we must deny ourselves. What did he mean?

4. Compare Jesus' way of calling for commitment with the invitations of contemporary preachers you may have heard.

36

Listening to Jesus: The Scriptures

◆

And as they were coming down the mountain, he charged them to
tell no one what they had seen, until the Son of man should have
risen from the dead. So they kept the matter to themselves, questioning what the rising from the dead meant. And they asked him,
"Why do the scribes say that first Elijah must come?" And he said
to them, "Elijah does come first to restore all things; and how is it
written of the Son of man, that he should suffer many things and
be treated with contempt? But I tell you that Elijah has come, and
they did to him whatever they pleased, as it is written of him."

[Mark 9:9–13]

JESUS HAD A LOT TO SAY about Old Testament Scriptures. In the
accounts in the Gospels, Jesus quotes the Old Testament frequently, recognizes the ancient Scriptures as the Word of God, and accepts their
authority. Especially, he sees himself, his ministry, and his saving work
as the fulfillment of the Old Testament.

A few passages give us the flavor of this. The first is a kind of aside
recorded in John's Gospel. Jesus had been talking about his unique relationship to the Father. Some of his critics accused him of blasphemy
because, they said, he, being a man, made himself God. Here was the
Lord's answer:

Jesus answered them, "Is it not written in your law, 'I said, you are gods'? If he called them gods to whom the word of God came (and scripture cannot be broken), do you say of him whom the Father consecrated and sent into the world, 'You are blaspheming,' because I said 'I am the Son of God'?"

[John 10:34–36]

Note those words, "and scripture cannot be broken." To Jesus, the Old Testament revelation stands firm. He says: "one jot or one tittle shall in no wise pass from the law, till all be fulfilled" (Matt. 5:18 KJV).

For Jesus, this word from God had final authority. It settled every issue. Again and again he resisted the tempter in the wilderness by appealing to passages from the Old Testament. "It is written . . . It is written . . . It is written . . ." And right at the heart of what he said on that occasion were these words: "Man shall not live by bread alone, but by every word that proceeds from the mouth of God" (Matt. 4:4).

His major emphasis was on his own life and ministry as the fulfillment of the Old Testament Scriptures. He said to his challengers on one occasion: "You search the scriptures, because you think that in them you have eternal life; and it is they that bear witness to me" (John 5:39). Again, "If you believed Moses, you would believe me, for he wrote of me" (John 5:46). And after the resurrection, "beginning with Moses and all the prophets, he [Jesus] interpreted to them in all the scriptures the things concerning himself" (Luke 24:27).

The text for this chapter deals with a promise made in the prophetic writings. Let's see how Jesus dealt with it. The incident that is recorded occurred right after the experience we call the transfiguration. Having just seen Elijah conversing with Jesus on the mountaintop, the disciples asked, "Why do the scribes say that first Elijah must come?" It was apparently a popular belief among the religious leaders of Israel that the Messiah would not come until Elijah had first reappeared. They based this belief on the last verses in the Old Testament, these words from Malachi, chapter 4, verses 4–6:

Remember the law of my servant Moses, the statues and ordinances that I commanded him at Horeb for all Israel. Behold, I will send you Elijah the prophet before the great and terrible day of the LORD comes. And he will turn the hearts of fathers to their children and the hearts of children to their fathers, lest I come and smite the land with a curse.

In the religion of God's people, Elijah was an enormously important figure. As the champion of the holy Lord against the entrenched forces of Baal, Elijah became a great hero in the eyes of later ages in Israel. He represented all that was highest and best in the prophetic tradition. He was miraculously taken up to heaven, and the prophet Malachi assured the faithful that this man of God, Elijah, would return to earth before the awesome day of the Lord.

The disciples wonder what Jesus thinks about this promise. What does he say about the expectation of the religious leaders? Jesus agrees with them. Elijah will indeed come, Jesus says, to restore all things. This Old Testament prophecy, this promise from the God of Abraham, Isaac, and Jacob, will surely be fulfilled. But he doesn't stop there. He goes on to make a startling announcement, "I tell you that Elijah has come." Questions must have sprung up everywhere: When? Where? How has Elijah come? His answer was: in the life and ministry of John the Baptist.

In the Gospel according to Luke, we read these words, which an angel conveyed to Zechariah, John's father:

> You will have joy and gladness,
> and many will rejoice at his birth;
> for he will be great before the Lord,
> and he shall drink no wine nor strong drink,
> and he will be filled with the Holy Spirit,
> even from his mother's womb.
> And he will turn many of the sons of Israel to the Lord their God,
> and he will go before him in the spirit and power of Elijah,
> to turn the hearts of the fathers to the children,
> and the disobedient to the wisdom of the just,
> to make ready for the Lord a people prepared.
>
> [Luke 1:14–17]

That was the first inkling that the career of John the Baptist would be like that of Elijah.

John, like the great prophet, was a man of the wilderness, a child of the open spaces. His clothing bore a striking resemblance to that of the fiery prophet. Here is the Old Testament description of Elijah: "He wore a garment of haircloth, with a girdle of leather about his loins" (2 Kings 1:8). And here is the gospel writer's sketch of John: "John was clothed with camel's hair, and had a leather girdle around his waist" (Mark 1:6). Both men called the Israelites to repent and turn to the Lord. Both contended against kings with the word of God on their lips. Both were hated and opposed by powerful, malicious queens. And just as Elijah had ushered in a new day for Israel with his fiery, prophetic ministry, so John the Baptist came to announce that the time was fulfilled and the kingdom of God had drawn near. Jesus, noting these things, and knowing John well, had this to say about him one day: "All the prophets and the law prophesied until John; and if you are willing to accept it, he is Elijah who is to come. He who has ears to hear, let him hear" (Matt 11:13–15).

Note that. John is Elijah in the eyes of Jesus. The promise of God is not only certain to be accomplished, according to Jesus, but the fulfillment of it is now, for this generation, before their very eyes.

But Jesus' idea of this fulfillment was manifestly different from that of his contemporaries. They expected Elijah to come and identify himself openly. Everyone would know who he was. He would appear to set everything right, to turn the hearts of the fathers to the children, and the hearts of the children to the fathers. Under his ministry would come the restoration of all things. All Israel would surely rejoice when Elijah came at last.

John, on the other hand, was a controversial figure. He angered some of the best people in Israel with his urgent call to repentance, not seeming to recognize their piety and position. Further, when some of the Pharisees had expressly asked him if he were Elijah, he had denied it. All he said about himself was that he was a voice crying in the wilderness. He was preparing the way of one so great that he, John, was not worthy to stoop down and untie his sandals. He did no mighty works of healing and performed no wonders. Consistently he directed attention away from himself. If he were Elijah, they reasoned, he would surely have said so and acted accordingly.

To Jesus, then, the true fulfillment of the ancient Scriptures was sometimes surrounded by mystery, accomplished in quiet. That was true of his own ministry. Though he knew himself to be the Messiah, the son of God, he never seemed to advertise that. When people saw his mighty works and were overwhelmed with amazement, he charged them again and again not to make him known, not to tell anyone about what he had done.

Perhaps this reticence was due to popular expectations about the Messiah. The masses had their idea about what the Messiah would be like and how he would act. Jesus' conception of his role and work was quite different. He didn't want to encourage mistaken impressions. He didn't want people to hail him as the Christ until they understood what he had come to do. And so he gave occasional hints and glimpses of his glory but showed deliberate reserve in making himself known to the multitudes. For him the promised reign of God was visiting the earth not in pomp and display but in strange restraint, through the ministry of one who was meek and lowly in heart.

Thus Jesus agreed with the Pharisees and with the rest of Israel that the Scriptures would be fulfilled, but the manner of their fulfillment as he saw it would surprise many. The fulfillment would be recognized only by those who had inner ears to hear and inner eyes to see, only by those who could read the signs of the times, those who welcomed him in faith.

One theme in Jesus' view of fulfillment seemed to surprise everyone. It was the note of suffering and rejection. The common belief was that Elijah's coming would be attended by triumph and glorious manifestations of God's power. By contrast, see what happened to John the Baptist. After brief days of fame, when his preaching in the wilderness had caused a stir, he had gotten into trouble with King Herod by telling the monarch that he shouldn't have married his brother's wife. John was thrown into prison for this boldness. It wasn't long before the vengeful wife Herodias had conspired to have him murdered.

All of this was anything but Elijah-like. John seemed a pathetic figure, languishing in a prison and finally losing his head. Could this be

Elijah—the John who seemed to fail in his mission, who came to such a tragic end?

And what about Jesus himself? Remember what he said first in answer to that question about Elijah? "Elijah does come first to restore all things; and how is it written of the Son of man, that he should suffer many things and be treated with contempt?"

This seemed even more mysterious. Jesus was speaking of the Son of man, that heavenly figure described in Daniel 7, to whom everlasting dominion would be given. According to Jesus, this Son of man, trailing clouds of glory, was yet to suffer terribly and be treated with contempt.

This for Jesus' contemporaries must have been genuinely shocking. They looked for a triumphant Messiah. They expected one who, as the promised king in David's line, would deliver them from the Roman yoke and restore the glory days. Jesus appeared as a quite different kind of king, without wealth or magnificence, without fighting men or royal retinue. He rode into Jerusalem on a donkey. Though he was a king in David's line, he presented himself most of all as a suffering servant. He was to be wounded for our transgressions, bruised for our iniquities. The chastisement of our peace would be upon him, and with his stripes we would be healed. The Lord would lay on him the iniquity of us all. The servant of the Lord would endure rejection. He would suffer death (see Isa. 53:5–6).

So for John, the hoped-for Elijah, and for Jesus, the promised Messiah, glory would come only through humiliation and fulfillment through suffering. Our Lord saw this as one great lesson to be learned from the Old Testament Scriptures. Suffering is the appointed lot of God's faithful ones. First the groaning, then the glory; the cross before the crown.

Perhaps this surprises us, too. We had always thought that success, prosperity, and esteem would come to God's chosen ones—and surely it will be so in the end—but Jesus warns that in this world his followers will have tribulation. We are disciples of the crucified one, and ours is the fellowship of his sufferings. According to Jesus, this is the message of the Scriptures. This is the Word of the Lord.

Study Questions

1. What did Jesus say about the witness of the Old Testament to him and his ministry?
2. Why were the Israelites expecting Elijah to come?
3. In what sense, according to Jesus, had Elijah already come?
4. What pervading message of the Old Testament did Jesus' contemporaries seem to overlook?

37

Listening to Jesus: Marriage and Divorce

◆

And Pharisees came up and in order to test him asked, "Is it lawful for a man to divorce his wife?" He answered them, "What did Moses command you?" They said, "Moses allowed a man to write a certificate of divorce, and to put her away." But Jesus said to them, "For your hardness of heart he wrote you this commandment. But from the beginning of creation, 'God made them male and female.' 'For this reason a man shall leave his father and mother and be joined to his wife, and the two shall become one flesh.' So they are no longer two but one flesh. What therefore God has joined together, let not man put asunder."

And in the house the disciples asked him again about this matter. And he said to them, "Whoever divorces his wife and marries another, commits adultery against her; and if she divorces her husband and marries another, she commits adultery."

[Mark 10:2–12]

I COULD ENTITLE THIS CHAPTER, "A Christian View of Divorce and Remarriage." Note: not *the* Christian view. That would be presumptuous and dishonest. Presumptuous because I obviously don't have the last word and dishonest because in fact there are sincere differences of opinion on these issues among equally committed Christian people.

But I do call it a Christian view because I'm trying to make it just that, an outlook based on the way in which Jesus spoke about these issues and the way in which he treated the people who were involved in them. I'm trying to reflect the mind of Christ as clearly and fully as we may know his mind from the Scriptures.

One thing I have become convinced of is that a Christian view of this subject challenges other widely held views. When I look at the question, for example, what is Christ's attitude toward divorce? I find that the answer differs radically from the attitude of secular culture, here in America and in many other countries as well. When I ask further, what is Christ's attitude toward people who have been involved in divorce? I find his attitude very much at odds with the religious culture of today and with strongly held ideas in a community like mine. And when I ask, what is Christ's attitude toward remarriage? I encounter a challenge that cuts both ways and comes home powerfully to all of us.

Let's look with Christ at these three questions. First, what is the Lord's attitude toward divorce?

In two of the key passages in the Gospel where Jesus speaks about divorce, the occasion is an encounter with the Pharisees. They ask him if it is lawful for a man to divorce his wife—for just any cause. They make reference to a passage in Deuteronomy from the Old Testament on which they want Jesus to comment. The passage from Deuteronomy 24 is:

> When a man takes a wife and marries her, if then she finds no favor in his eyes because he has found some indecency in her, and he writes her a bill of divorce and puts it in her hand and sends her out of his house, and she departs out of his house, and if she goes and becomes another man's wife, and the latter husband dislikes her and writes her a bill of divorce and puts it in her hand and sends her out of his house, or if the latter husband dies, who took her to be his wife, then her former husband, who sent her away, may not take her again to be his wife, after she has been defiled.
> [Deut. 24:1–4]

There were two schools of thought among the rabbis as to how this passage should be interpreted. One felt that it opened the door for a man to divorce his wife on any grounds at all; the other felt that the only permissible ground should be adultery. What did Jesus think? They were out to test him on this.

Jesus' answer took them by surprise. He refused to buy into either of those interpretations. Neither one, he said, was really in line with God's original purpose. Moses' command had been given, Jesus says, because of "your hardness of heart," that is, to deal with the realities of life in a sinful world. God's original purpose, however, did not envision divorce at all. Jesus quotes Genesis, "From the beginning of creation, God made them male and female. For this reason a man shall leave his father and mother and be joined to his wife, and the two shall become one flesh."

In other words, Jesus takes the highest possible view of marriage. He sees it as ordained by God from the beginning, out of loving concern for human beings. "It is not good that the man should be alone." Marriage involves a public, legal event in which all of society has a definite interest. It also involves a commitment of love, affection, and fidelity. It means a total union of two people, creating a new reality. Marriage is a God-established bond, according to Jesus, which is meant to last for life. It is sacred and enduring. Divorce, from this standpoint, is a tragic deviation from God's original good design.

What a contrast to the view held commonly today! There are those who contend now for trial marriages. Give it a try for a couple of years with the option to renew at the end of that period! I read some time ago of a student from a college in Kentucky who won a scholarship but then decided to get married. If her marriage didn't work out, she asked the college authorities, could she still come back to school and retain the scholarship? A survey in England asked more than 2,000 married people if they had considered the possibility before marriage that they could always get a divorce if things didn't work out. For those willing to admit the thought, the people who had married in the late 1950s were more than twice as likely to say they had considered it as those married in the 1920s.

Countless books explore the various reasons for this, but the fact is: Multitudes in our time see marriage as a temporary, open-ended expedient without abiding significance. Divorce to them is simply a practical, legal exit from a situation that two people no longer find satisfying.

Jesus Christ is set against divorce, precisely because he is for us. The Creator who fashioned us knows us better than we know ourselves. He wills always what is for our good. He intended marriage for our happiness, knowing that normally the highest human joy and fulfillment is to be found in that relationship. It's his purpose that people know the grand human dignity of a lasting commitment to each other. And he makes that commitment the clearest human expression of an even deeper bond: the tie between Christ and his people, between the Lord and his church.

He knows too what a devastating trauma it is for people to pass through divorce. What a blow to their self-esteem! What a crushing sense of defeat, what loneliness, what inner anguish divorce can bring! The Lord knows what cruelty it can inflict, how it can tear apart the hearts of children who struggle helplessly to hold mom and dad together. From Jesus' viewpoint, knowing what marriage is meant to be and can be, divorce must always be an utterly heartbreaking thing.

It seems to me that a Christian seeking the mind of the Lord must always view divorce as the impossible possibility, the last resort. Those who work with married couples ought to be as eager to preserve marriages as a medical doctor is to preserve human lives, and even when they seem to be dead, they ought to call on the God of resurrection to revive them.

Now for the second question. What is Christ's attitude toward people who have been involved in divorce? We don't have a great deal of direct evidence in the Gospels for this answer, but what we do have is tremendously instructive. For example, Jesus converses with the woman by the well in Samaria. She has had five husbands and the man with whom she is now living is not her husband at all. How does Jesus deal with her? He initiates a conversation with her, asks her a favor, offers her living water, and reveals himself to her as Messiah. We note that he isn't ashamed in the slightest to be seen conversing with her.

Then there's the woman who comes into the home of the Pharisee Simon while Jesus is there to dine. Her marital status is highly questionable. She stands behind Jesus at his feet, weeping. She wets his feet with her tears and wipes them with the hair of her head. She kisses his feet and anoints them with ointment. Jesus accepts her offering. In fact, he says, "I tell you, her sins, which are many, are forgiven, for she loved much."

Here's one more scene. A woman has been caught in the act of adultery. The authorities tell Jesus about this. They point out that the Mosaic law commands that such offenders be stoned. What does Jesus say about this? First he bends down and writes with his finger on the ground, then stands up and says, "Let him who is without sin among you be the first to throw a stone at her." Soon all her accusers have slipped away. Only the woman is left standing before him. He looks up and says to her, "Woman, where are they? Has no one condemned you?" She says, "No one, Lord." Jesus says, "Neither do I condemn you; go, and do not sin again."

Now here are three instances where people have been through divorce or have committed offenses considered to warrant divorce. In each, Jesus is aware of what has happened. In each, he is socially accepting. In each, he seems totally noncondemning.

What a contrast here to a smug, judgmental religious culture! To most of Jesus' contemporaries in Israel, divorced people were to be avoided like lepers and held in contempt as evil doers. Here is Christ with a higher standard for marriage and divorce than Moses and the prophets, yet when it comes to people caught in the act of adultery, Moses says, "Let them be stoned," while Jesus says, "Neither do I condemn you; go and sin no more."

Haven't we seen something of the same contrast? There may be people in your community struggling with all the pain and grief of divorce, whom church people have made doubly miserable. They've made these sufferers feel like social pariahs, and they look down on them as contemptible.

Isn't it strange that where Christ is ready to forgive we are all too often ready to throw stones? We demonstrate the mind of Christ only when people whose marriages have been broken can feel as welcome among us as they did when they came to him.

Well, what about our last question. What is Christ's attitude toward remarriage? Here's where his words seem especially hard to understand: "Whoever divorces his wife and marries another commits adultery against her, and if she divorces her husband and marries another, she commits adultery."

Here the Lord seems to put all remarriage under an ugly shadow, but we need to remember, I believe, the setting in which these words were spoken. Pharisees are testing Jesus. People are looking for an easy way out of the marriage covenant. The Lord is dealing here with what is in a person's heart as he or she contemplates divorce. If the aim is to get out of one marriage in order to get into another, to drop one partner in favor of another, then the word *adultery*, without a doubt, best describes it.

For many, many people, I'm persuaded, the circumstances are much different. There has been a real struggle to make the marriage work. There have been years of pain and frustrated efforts with hopes strangled again and again. Sometimes divorce is seen as the only way out of a relationship that has become destructive for all the people concerned. Here, I think, is a very different situation.

Perhaps some of you have read the little book by Walter Trobisch entitled, *I Married You*. It tells of a Christian marriage counselor who spent four days in an African city helping people with their views of sex and marriage. At one point someone asked him, "Would you remarry divorcées without hesitation?" His answer was, "Not without hesitation, with much hesitation, but in some circumstances I would."

That's a significant question. "Would you remarry?" The answer of our secular cultures would often be yes, of course. The answer of our religious culture might be no, not unless it was the innocent party in the divorce proceedings. But Trobisch's answer was quite different. "In any case," he said, "I would remarry only the guilty parties."

What can that mean? It means this: If anyone claims he is entirely innocent, the fault totally his partner's, then it's certain that any subsequent marriage of his is doomed to failure too. This is true in any squabble between people. When people recognize their own failure and their need for forgiveness, and when they turn to Christ for grace and strength, there is forgiveness. There is a new beginning, and the future is open and bright with hope.

What's the mind of Christ about marriage, divorce, and remarriage? Let me put it this way: Honor marriage and do all you can to hallow and preserve it. Take to your hearts with genuine love and acceptance those who have met with pain and brokenness, and believe that in Jesus Christ all things can be made new.

Study Questions

1. How is the view of Jesus in these matters different from common ones in contemporary culture?
2. Why is Jesus against divorce?
3. How did Jesus customarily treat divorced people?
4. In what circumstances would you say that remarriage is appropriate for divorced people? Explain.

38

Listening to Jesus: Greatness

◆

But it shall not be so among you; but whoever would be great among you must be your servant, and whoever would be first among you must be slave of all. For the Son of man also came not to be served but to serve, and to give his life as a ransom for many.

[Mark 10:43–45]

I SUPPOSE THERE IS NO AMBITION among us more common or more compelling than the desire to be great. Who are the great people of our time? Are they the political figures whose names are often in the headlines—the Bushes, Yeltsins, and Husseins? Or are they perhaps the super athletes, the Joe Montanas, the Michael Jordans, the José Cansecos? Or could they be the men who appeared on the cover of a news magazine some time ago, all of whom had made a million dollars before age forty. Are they the great ones?

To bring it closer to home, who are the great people in your community, in your neighborhood? Are they those who own the most property, those who are highly influential, or those who are extraordinarily gifted? Are they the shakers and movers—those who have really made it in this world? In other words, is greatness just another name for what we call success?

All of us have an interest in that question because we've all felt something of the longing to be special, the ambition to be great. Every athlete or competitor, I suppose, at every level aspires to be number one. Every craftsman, teacher, and professional would like to be the best in his or her specialty. We long to be distinguished and stand out from the crowd.

Some are strongly aggressive in going after these things. Their ambitions are right out in the open. Take James and John, the disciples of Jesus, for example. These two men weren't called the Sons of Thunder for nothing. They had set their sights on the places of honor in the kingdom that Jesus was about to establish. First they prevailed on their mother to intercede for them with Jesus and were standing right beside her when the request was made. When Jesus came to his throne, they wanted to be his chief deputies—one at his right hand and one at his left.

You know people like that, don't you? They push for prominence. They know what they want and they are not in the least reticent about seeking it. They are aiming for the top and they don't care who knows about it. Not everyone is that forward, though. Many of us operate with a different style.

As far as we know, the other ten disciples hadn't asked for these favored positions in the coming kingdom. In fact, when they heard what James and John were up to, they were incensed. What's going on here? we can imagine them saying. Who do these men think they are anyway? Why should they get special treatment? What's behind all that indignation? Why the resentment? Think about the feelings we sometimes have. Why are we so annoyed when we sense conceit and self-advertisement in someone else? Is it partly because of our longings, our frustrated aspirations? Why do we resent the boy, the girl, the man, or woman who is always the "life of the party"? Maybe it's because down deep we would like to be like them but we don't know how or hesitate to try. Some of you may remember John Montefusco who used to pitch for the San Francisco Giants. They called him the "Count." He was a colorful ball player who, somewhat in the fashion of Mohammed Ali, used to talk about his exploits in advance. He would predict upcoming victories. He would announce on occasion that he would pitch a shutout and whom he would strike out and in what inning. For some years he was an effective pitcher, and sometimes his prophecies came true.

When asked by a sports writer about his seeming arrogance, he replied that every pitcher thinks those things, indulges those fantasies. The difference was that he, the Count, came right out and talked about them. Maybe that's the difference between, say, James and John and the rest of the disciples. We all have different styles, but belligerently or bashfully, openly or secretly, we all cherish our dreams of greatness.

I'm impressed at the way Jesus dealt with these men. He responded first, "You don't know what you are asking. Are you able to drink the cup that I drink, or to be baptized with the baptism with which I am baptized?" Their answer came back forthrightly, "Yes," as though to say, we can handle that. Jesus acknowledged that they were right but told them that what they were asking was not his to give. All of that was in the Father's hands. But it's noteworthy to me that Jesus didn't chide them for asking. He didn't say sternly, There's no room for such ambition and vainglory among my followers. He didn't put them down or treat them with the slightest note of scorn. He saw something worthwhile in their request. There was faith there—they believed he would have a kingdom—and there was a kind of love—they wanted to be as near to him as they possibly could. So he let them know that the path to greatness might take them through sorrow, rejection, and suffering, but he didn't blame them for wanting to walk that way.

Jesus would never discourage your ambition to be great, either. The desire in you to be a unique person, to make a significant mark in life, to be all you can be, there's something right, even good about that. There's nothing godly about passionless contentment with the mediocre. As the song from the musical "South Pacific" puts it: "You gotta have a dream. If you don't have a dream, how you gonna have your dream come true?" The God who puts eternity in our hearts and kindles those dreams in us never ridicules aspirations for greatness. Remember that. You don't need to be ashamed of those fires of ambition that burn deep within you.

What the Lord does here for his disciples and for the rest of us is straighten out our thinking about what it means to be great. There's a common way of looking at this that misses the mark entirely. Here it is. Jesus says, "You know that those who are supposed to rule over the Gentiles lord it over them, and their great men exercise authority over them."

According to this view, the great are those who throw their weight around and get others to jump when they snap their fingers. They are the people who seem to have the world on a string and everyone else at their service. They're the ones who are waited on, catered to, and fawned over. They seem to say by manner and bearing, if not in so many words, I've made it. Now let everyone else make room for me.

But Jesus said, "It shall not be so among you." In other words, that may be man's version of greatness but it is certainly not God's. It may be the world's pattern of things, but heaven has a different one. Then he says something so different and surprising that it's almost revolutionary. "Whoever would be great among you must be your servant, and whoever would be first among you must be slave of all."

You want to be great? Jesus asks. Then concentrate on doing for other people. The word means, literally, to be a waiter at their table. Attend to them. Fulfill their wishes. Meet their needs. Put yourself at their disposal. That's a strange kind of greatness, isn't it? Who do you know that's ambitious for that? Again, the Lord asks, do you want to be first, foremost, number one? Who doesn't? Then he urges, prepare to give yourself as a slave—one who is no longer his own. The earth's truest royalty wears the garb of a bondservant, a slave who lays aside his own rights to belong to someone else. What kind of distinction, what kind of prominence is that?

In the light of Jesus' words, look again at the question, "Who is truly great?" I think of a man in our congregation who, with his wife, was always arranging to visit some mission field—just to help in practical, commonplace ways. For thirty years or more he worked with young boys, teaching them how to play baseball. I think he was one of the great. I think of the mother I met some time ago who during the course of her life has had twenty-some foster children living in her home and has given to each a treasure of love and affirmation. I think of a doctor in our community who used to devote all kinds of time giving free medical care to migrant workers. You've probably never heard of those people, but they're on my list of the great ones. Maybe the great are people like that in your town, in your neighborhood, among your friends, people whom no one notices much, but who have learned in all kinds of hidden ways what it is to serve.

Wouldn't it be something if in this world the whole picture were somehow switched around? What if the great man on campus turned out to be not one of the star athletes but rather the assistant manager of the team who passed out towels and picked up orange peels? What if the greatest of women was seen to be not a headline winner but a quiet young lady in a hospital who smiles at patients and empties bed pans? Wouldn't that be something?

Yeah, that all sounds nice, says someone cynically, but what evidence do we have that that way would be better? When you come right down to it, no one operates like that. Everyone I know is scrambling for that other kind of greatness. What proof is there that this service business is a better way? Just this: Jesus said even the Son of man "came not to be served but to serve, and to give his life as a ransom for many." That's the key. Someone lived among us once who called himself the Son of man. He never seemed, as we say, to throw his weight around. He was meek and lowly in heart. He sided with the poor, the disadvantaged, even the outcast. He spent himself in loving ministry to the sick, the lonely, and the broken. When people wanted to make him a king, he withdrew from them. When his own friends became thoughtless and petty, he got up from a table one night and went around washing their feet. And when nothing else would help, he willingly gave himself up to die so that the broken people he loved could have true life.

Now he is alive again. The grave couldn't hold him. He rose from the dead by the power of God. They call him now King of Kings and Lord of Lords. They say that all authority in heaven and on earth belongs to him. His name is Wonderful, Counselor, Mighty God, Everlasting Father, Prince of Peace. They say that every knee will bow before him at the last day and every tongue confess that he is Lord.

When he lived, died, and rose again the world's idea of greatness was exposed as false. We still fall for it at times, still get fooled, but in our better moments we know that it's a lie. It's not what you get but what you give. It's not how you succeed but how you serve. It's not a crowned head that makes you great but a caring heart. The way to that for each one of us is in the footsteps and in the fellowship of Jesus Christ.

Study Questions

1. How would you evaluate the request of James and John? What was good about it? What not so good?
2. What does Jesus' response say to you? How did he treat these two?
3. What does Jesus say greatness involves?
4. How does he model it supremely?

39

Listening to Jesus: Forgiving Others

━━━━━━━━━━━━━━━━━━━━━ ◆ ━━━━━━━━━━━━━━━━━━━━━

Therefore I tell you, whatever you ask in prayer, believe that you have received it, and it will be yours. And whenever you stand praying, forgive, if you have anything against any one; so that your Father also who is in heaven may forgive you your trespasses.

[Mark 11:24–25]

SOMETIMES THE PROMISES JESUS MAKES about prayer seem sweeping and unconditional. "Ask, and it will be given you; seek, and you will find; knock, and it will be opened to you" (Luke 11:9). Then, lest anyone should miss the force of that, Jesus goes over the same ground once more: "For every one who asks receives, and he who seeks finds, and to him who knocks it will be opened" (v. 10).

Again, just before his death Jesus left this pledge with his disciples, "Truly, truly, I say to you, if you ask anything of the Father, he will give it to you in my name. Hitherto you have asked nothing in my name; ask, and you will receive, that your joy may be full" (John 16:23–24). It was one of Jesus' great assurances to his followers that their Father in heaven would unfailingly give good things to those who ask him.

The Lord's apostles pick up that theme and even expand on it. The apostle Paul, writing to the Ephesians, describes God as "able to do far more abundantly than all that we ask or think." James chimes in that the prayer of a righteous man has great power in its effects, and that the reason we do not enjoy the blessings of God more abundantly in our lives is simply that we do not ask. As we consider these words, they seem to assure us of limitless power in prayer. They seem to echo again and again, ask whatever you desire, and your request will be granted.

Another cluster of biblical passages, however, seems to teach otherwise. These propose certain conditions for effective prayer. The apostle John writes, for example: "This is the confidence which we have in him, that if we ask anything according to his will he hears us" (1 John 5:14). There the field is narrowed down; not just anything we ask, but anything that is according to God's will.

Sometimes the sins of God's people can negate the effect of their prayers. God speaks through the prophet Isaiah, "Behold, the LORD's hand is not shortened, that it cannot save, or his ear dull, that it cannot hear; but your iniquities have made a separation between you and your God, and your sins have hid his face from you so that he does not hear" (Isa. 59:1–2). The psalmist is alert to that same possibility. He says, "If I had cherished iniquity in my heart, the Lord would not have listened" (Ps. 66:18). And the apostle Peter reminds husbands and wives that if they do not live considerately with one another their prayers will be hindered (1 Peter 3:7).

Sometimes unworthy motives in prayer may be the problem. James writes, "You ask and do not receive, because you ask wrongly, to spend it on your passions" (James 4:3). Jesus seems to gather up all the conditions for answered prayer into one when he says this to his disciples, "If you abide in me, and my words abide in you, ask whatever you will, and it shall be done for you" (John 15:7).

In the text for this chapter, Mark 11:24–25, Jesus singles out two factors that are essential elements of genuine, effectual prayer: faith and a forgiving spirit toward others. Let's look first at the faith part. Jesus says, "Therefore I tell you, whatever you ask in prayer, believe that you have received it, and it will be yours."

Peter had been amazed at what happened to a fig tree. When Jesus saw that it bore no fruit, he had said of it the day before, "May no one ever eat fruit from you again." It seemed to be an action parable. The fig tree symbolized a people whom God had planted, watered, nurtured, and pruned but who, after all of that, had borne no fruit. When Peter saw that the tree had actually withered, he was awestruck. Jesus didn't use the opportunity to talk about responsibility and judgment but about faith. If Peter was astonished at what became of the fig tree, he would yet see things far more remarkable. Jesus said, "Have faith in God. Truly, I say to you, whoever says to this mountain, 'Be taken up and cast into the sea,' and does not doubt in his heart, but believes that what he says will come to pass, it will be done for him" (Mark 11:22–23).

Mountains seem to us about as secure and immovable as anything we know about, but Jesus says that the word of faith can move them. However massive and insurmountable the obstacles before us seem to be, we can say to them, be taken up. Be removed and cast into the sea. And we won't simply be speaking into the air. Jesus says that those mountains will depart. The obstacles will move.

Faith, however, seems to be the crucial factor. When we command the mountains to be cast into the sea, we are not to doubt in our hearts but rather to believe that what we say will come to pass. And then, Jesus says, it will be done for us. In a similar way, whenever we ask God for something in prayer, we are to believe that we have received it and then, Jesus says, it will be ours.

The heart of what Jesus is teaching here is summed up in the words "Have faith in God," or literally, "Hold on to the faithfulness of God." In other words, always keep as your primary conviction, your constant awareness that God is and that he is a faithful God. Prayer, therefore, is never to be looked on as magic, apart from the working of the sovereign, faithful God. Nor is it to be something we engage in mindlessly. Basic is the confidence that I never call upon God in vain, that his love is real and his faithfulness sure and that he will always respond to our asking in his own time and way.

If we pray without that basic confidence, James reminds us, we are double-minded people, unstable in all our ways. We will not receive anything from the Lord. It grieves God when we appeal to him in prayer without the slightest assurance that he will hear and answer. Our words may sound believing then, but our hearts give the lie to them. Let's call on him with the full confidence that we are loved, we are heard, and we are answered. We pray to the God who gives to everyone generously and without reproach.

The second element in Jesus' description of effective prayer is our readiness to forgive others. "And whenever you stand praying, forgive, if you have anything against any one; so that your Father also who is in heaven may forgive you your trespasses."

Jesus told an unforgettable story about this.

> Therefore the kingdom of heaven may be compared to a king who wished to settle accounts with his servants. When he began the reckoning, one was brought to him who owed him ten thousand talents [that's a fortune]; and as he could not pay, his lord ordered him to be sold, with his wife and children and all that he had, and payment to be made. So the servant fell on his knees, imploring him, "Lord, have patience with me, and I will pay you everything." And out of pity for him the lord of that servant released him and forgave him the debt. But that same servant, as he went out, came upon one of his fellow servants who owed him a hundred denarii [that's a trifling sum]; and seizing him by the throat he said, "Pay what you owe." So his fellow servant fell down and besought him [same words], "Have patience with me, and I will pay you." He refused and went and put him in prison till he should pay the debt. When his fellow servants saw what had taken place, they were greatly distressed, and they went and reported to their lord all that had taken place. Then his lord summoned him and said to him, "You wicked servant! I forgave you all that debt because you besought me; and should not you have had mercy on your fellow servant, as I had mercy on you?" And in anger his lord delivered him to the jailers, till he should pay all his debt. So also [Jesus concludes] my heavenly Father will do to every one of you, if you do not forgive your brother from your heart.
>
> [Matt. 18:23–35]

Apparently, there's a very close relationship between our receiving forgiveness from God and our extending it to others. Jesus taught us about that in the Lord's Prayer. We're invited to pray, "Forgive us our debts, as we also have forgiven our debtors."

What do we make of this? Is our forgiving others a kind of good work, a meritorious action, which deserves and gains for us God's forgiveness? That cannot be the case. Throughout the Bible, forgiveness is associated with God's great mercy. He provides it for us freely through the sacrifice of his Son. "Jesus paid it all," we sing. "All to him we owe."

At the same time, our readiness to forgive others seems to be the sign that we have truly known the forgiveness of God. The wicked servant seemed to have no awareness of how great a debt he had been forgiven or of what great kindness he had received, because in a similar situation he showed no inclination to extend mercy to his fellow servant.

We can see then that forgiving others is closely related to faith. Remember that other occasion when Jesus was teaching his followers about forgiveness? He said, "Take heed to yourselves; if your brother sins, rebuke him, and if he repents, forgive him; and if he sins against you seven times in the day, and turns to you seven times, and says, 'I repent,' you must forgive him" (Luke 17:3–4). The apostles responded to that hard word about forgiving others with this prayer: "Increase our faith!" Faith, apparently, is what frees us to forgive. Holding on to God's faithfulness means letting go of resentments. Knowing I am pardoned through God's great mercy releases me to pardon others.

Our forgiving others doesn't earn our acceptance, our forgiveness from God, but it opens the way for our receiving and enjoying his forgiveness. Think of how it is with confessing our sins. Confession is the sign that I'm aware of having sinned against God, and I tell him that. It's also the sign that I'm aware of his pardoning grace in Christ, and I trust him for that. Forgiving others involves the same double awareness: I too have sins that need forgiving and God has graciously forgiven me in Jesus Christ.

Vital aspects, then, of that genuine relationship with God from which prayer proceeds are our trust in God's faithfulness and our gracious openness to others. Prayer, faith, confession, forgiveness, all grow out of the gospel received into our hearts and the new relationship with God that follows. If we do not pray, we must have no sense of that incomparably wonderful relationship into which we've been brought. If we pray without faith, we must have no sense of the character of the one who stands behind the promises, the faithful one who always keeps his word. If there's no confession in our lives, then there must be no awareness of guilt, no turning of heart toward the Lord for grace and reconciliation. If there's no willingness on our part to forgive, then there must be no realization of how immense is our debt and how great his pardoning grace toward us. We haven't yet felt the soul's despair or its breathless gratitude.

It's striking how important to God it is that we should be willing to forgive. The same loving heart that longs to forgive us, longs also to see us learning his gracious ways in relating to others. Apparently one of the surest signs that we have internalized the gospel of God's grace is that we treat other people graciously. So hold on to the reality of God's faithful love in Christ and let go of every grudge and resentment. That's the way, Jesus says, to pray. That's the way to live. That's one of the secrets of genuine joy.

Study Questions

1. Which of Jesus' promises about prayer seem to you "unconditional"?
2. What teachings about prayer seem, on the other hand, to involve conditions?
3. How are faith in God and faith in prayer significantly different?
4. Why is forgiving others so vital for effective prayer?

40

Listening to Jesus: Life after Death

◆

And Sadducees came to him, who say that there is no resurrection; and they asked him a question, saying, "Teacher, Moses wrote for us that if a man's brother dies and leaves a wife, but leaves no child, the man must take the wife, and raise up children for his brother. There were seven brothers; the first took a wife, and when he died left no children; and the second took her, and died, leaving no children; and the third likewise; and the seven left no children. Last of all the woman also died. In the resurrection whose wife will she be? For the seven had her as wife."

Jesus said to them, "Is not this why you are wrong, that you know neither the scriptures nor the power of God? For when they rise from the dead, they neither marry nor are given in marriage, but are like angels in heaven. And as for the dead being raised, have you not read in the book of Moses, in the passage about the bush, how God said to him, 'I am the God of Abraham, and the God of Isaac, and the God of Jacob'? He is not God of the dead, but of the living; you are quite wrong."

[Mark 12:18–27]

CHRISTIANS BELIEVE that in Jesus God has made himself fully and finally known. That's what he said. "He who has seen me has seen the Father"

(John 14:9). Jesus is God come to dwell among us, sharing our humanity, living our life, and speaking our language. He is the Word of the Eternal made flesh.

We would expect then that when Jesus dwelt among us, he would have told us things about God and his purpose that we could not otherwise know and that he would have provided answers for our deepest questions. He who came from glory understands the ways of God with us. He knows about our origins, about the meaning of our life, and about our ultimate destiny.

One of the subjects that Jesus taught on is of great interest to everyone: life after death.

Note first how Jesus assured people that there is a life to come. There is life beyond death. The religious group in Israel known as the Sadducees apparently did not believe this. They held that when the body dies, the soul dies. Everything dies.

Curiously, they supported their view by appealing to the Old Testament Scriptures. The Sadducees, however, accepted as authoritative only the five books of Moses—what we call the Pentateuch: Genesis, Exodus, Leviticus, Numbers, and Deuteronomy. For them, these books alone had special, unique authority. The Sadducees would not accept any teaching that was not clearly set forth in these books. Since they contained, it was believed, no clear reference to life after death, the Sadducees were skeptical about any such doctrine.

The question they asked Jesus was clearly designed to poke fun at the teaching of a future life, to make a resurrection hope appear ridiculous. They pointed out that in the law of Moses the brother of a man who had died leaving his wife childless was to marry the widow and raise up children who would be the legal progeny of his brother. The Sadducees proposed a hypothetical case in which this kept on happening in a family of seven brothers. They all married the same woman and each successively died before she did. Now, in the resurrection, the Sadducees asked, with a scorn they made little attempt to disguise, "Whose wife will this woman be?"

The Sadducees have their modern counterparts. All of us know people who believe that death is a purely physical process and ends everything. When breathing ceases, when your heart stops, when the brain ceases functioning, you're dead and that's the end of you. Children may die of disease or starvation in their early years. Others may be cut down in midcourse. Some may survive to a ripe old age. But at the moment of death, the same nonexistence awaits them all. That's the doctrine. For people who see things this way, the sequel to all life in this world is oblivion. People may live on for a generation or so in the memory of their loved ones. The names of the exceptionally famous may be recorded in the history books or become household words. In each case, however, the essential person has forever ceased to be.

Bertrand Russell provides an eloquent expression of this view.

> That Man is the product of causes which had no pre-vision of the end they were achieving, that his origin, his growth, his hopes and fears, his loves and his beliefs are but the outcome of accidental collocations of atoms; that no fire, no heroism, no intensity of thought and feeling can preserve an individual life beyond the grave . . . all these things, if not quite beyond dispute, are yet so nearly certain that no philosophy which rejects them can hope to stand. Only within the scaffolding of these truths, only on the firm foundation of unyielding despair, can the soul's habitation henceforth be safely built.[†]

There you have it, unyielding despair, because, in his view, there is no possibility of a life beyond death, and that view does produce despair. There's no doubt about that. If all our individual selves at the moment of death come to nothingness, what difference does it make finally how we have lived, what causes we've supported, what values we've embraced? Ultimately, what significance do those relationships have that have warmed and nurtured us all our days? They are nothing now, according to this view, null and void. Do you see why people who believe things like that lose hope? Or even more ominously, why they sometimes lose all concern for others?

Archaeologists investigating some of the ancient Roman cemeteries have come across a common inscription on pagan tombs, consisting of

[†] Bertrand Russell. *Mysticism and Logic.* Longman, Green and Co., 1921, pp. 47–48.

the seven letters: NFF NS NC. They stand for a Latin saying, which can be translated like this: I was not. I was. I am not. I do not care.

Jesus says that people who hold that view are wrong—terribly, tragically wrong. They are wrong, he says, because they "know neither the scriptures nor the power of God." According to Jesus, the Scriptures clearly teach that God's people, even after they die, continue to live. We'll see in a moment the passage that he especially appeals to. He talks also about the power of God. That, for Jesus, is the basis of hope. We do not survive death because we are naturally immortal or because we can sustain our own lives or because we deserve to live eternally. We survive death because the God who made us is able, when everything about us has died, to recreate us and raise us from death to endless life.

What kind of life will that be? On that subject we are given few details in Scripture. One thing we know from this passage is that in the life to come there will be no marrying or giving in marriage. In other words the Sadducees' question was simply irrelevant. The woman will not be any man's wife in heaven. It's not that relationships between people will cease to exist or that love will have been done away. Real love is one of the things that abides forever. We'll be closer to our loved ones than we've ever been, but it will be different. It will transcend anything we now know within the ties of family.

We shall be, Jesus says, like the angels of God. We aren't told how. We don't know what the life of the angels is like. Certainly it is not more limited than ours. Angels are not necessarily sexless, loveless, or joyless. Jesus surely meant that being like the angels of God had to do with being in God's presence, sharing in his worship, celebrating his love, and doing his will. Human life in the coming age is not to be diminished but enlarged, not impoverished but enriched. The things that God has prepared for those who love him are unimaginably wonderful. The highest joys of this present life are but a hint and foretaste of what is to come.

What we know with assurance is that the life to come will be a life of resurrection. Notice how Jesus said to his questioners, "when they rise from the dead," not if, but when. There is no doubt in the mind of the Lord that the resurrection is a real, coming event. Further, Jesus argues that the Scriptures make this plain. He appeals to a passage in the Pentateuch, the very portion of Scripture that the Sadducees claimed to accept. In Exodus 3:6 God is speaking to Moses at the burning bush: "I am the God of your father, the God of Abraham, the God of Isaac, and the God of Jacob." Jesus points out that God speaks of his people as living, though they have died. Apparently, they are alive in his mind, heart, and purpose, alive to God. For God to call himself the God of Abraham, Isaac, and Jacob is clear evidence to Jesus that these Old Testament saints have a continuing existence because God is the God of the living. He is not the God of nonexistent people, mere names from the past.

When God calls himself "the God" of such and such a person, he means that he is the helper, the savior, and the hope of that person. He keeps his people and provides redemption for them. How could God, who has life in himself, who is supremely the living one, be the God of extinct phantoms? If he can protect his people, as he does, throughout all the perils of life but loses them to the last great enemy, death, where is his power? Where is his keeping? Where is his faithfulness? Why would he grant them partial tokens of deliverance only to give them over finally to oblivion?

If the death of the patriarchs were the last word in their history, this would be a breach of God's covenant, a denial of his revealed name as the living one. The salvation promised to the patriarchs and their descendants in the covenant contains at heart this assurance of resurrection. The Sadducees failed to grasp that God's faithfulness and resurrection are linked together, and this was at the root of their error. They forgot that God is the God of the living, that he keeps his promises to his people, that not even death can separate them from his great love.

What Jesus said on this subject was underlined in the most powerful way imaginable by what he did. Look at his teaching now in the light of his subsequent death and resurrection. Through Jesus' victory over death the hope of resurrection has become immeasurably more sure. Now it's not only a promise of something out ahead but a present reality in his person. Christ himself risen from the dead is the firstfruits of the resurrection life. We can look at him and see the reality of it.

If we thought it marvelous in the resurrection to be like the angels of God, here is something far more thrilling: We are to be like Christ. We are to be conformed to the image of God's Son. As he lives, we shall live also. We shall be like him, John writes, for we shall see him as he is. Of all the aspects of the Christian hope, this seems to me the most meaningful and precious. The heart of our salvation, the luminous center of our hope, is that we shall be with Christ at last and be like him forever.

Study Questions

1. How is human life affected by the view that death ends everything?
2. What do we know from Scripture about the nature of the life to come?
3. How does the passage from Exodus demonstrate that Abraham, Isaac, and Jacob are now alive?
4. What for you is the most comforting aspect of the Christian hope of life after death? Explain.

41

Listening to Jesus: God's Commandments

◆

And one of the scribes came up and heard them disputing with one another, and seeing that he answered them well, asked him, "Which commandment is the first of all?" Jesus answered, "The first is, 'Hear, O Israel: The Lord our God, the Lord is one; and you shall love the Lord your God with all your heart, and with all your soul, and with all your mind, and with all your strength.' The second is this, 'You shall love your neighbor as yourself.' There is no other commandment greater than these."

[Mark 12:28–31]

DURING JESUS' MINISTRY a number of people wondered what Jesus would teach as life's highest priority. They wondered what Jesus would say is the greatest of the commandments. On at least two occasions he was asked that question directly: "Which commandment, Jesus, is the first of all?"

It may be that they expected a surprising answer. Jesus had been known to say things like this: "You have heard that it was said to the men of old . . . (thus and so), but I say to you . . ." Would Jesus have a new and startling view about God's will? Would he set himself up in opposition to the thinking of his contemporaries?

It's interesting how Jesus responded to this question. First, he quoted directly from the Old Testament Scriptures. He reminded his hearers again that he had not come to destroy the law and the prophets but to fulfill them, that he viewed the Old Testament revelation with the highest esteem and acknowledged its divine authority. Jesus sometimes corrected mistaken interpretations of the law and the prophets, but he always honored their essential message.

Also, he combined the commands to love God and neighbor in a way that other Jewish teachers had already done. He was not the first to affirm the connection between these, but rather he underlined it in his own teaching. In other words, he never espoused the new just for novelty's sake. Wherever there was truth in the outlook of his contemporaries, he never hesitated to acknowledge it.

Isn't it striking that when asked to identify the first and greatest of the commands, Jesus answered by listing two? There was a clear priority in his mind—one was first, the other was second—but Jesus found it impossible to separate them.

Remember Leigh Hunt's poem "Abou Ben Adhem"? The hero wakes in the night to see an angel writing in a book of gold. Abou asks what is being written. The angel replies, "the names of those who love the Lord." "And is mine one?" he asks. "Nay, not so," replied the angel. "I pray thee then," says Abou Ben Adhem, "write me as one who loves his fellow men." When finally the book of gold is opened, the poet tells us, "Lo! Ben Adhem's name led all the rest."

Hunt is trying to say, of course, that love for our fellow men is the truest kind of love for God, that the two are inseparable. But the implication of the poem seems also to be that loving our fellow human beings is the only thing that really matters. Jesus, on the other hand, saw the two commands as closely related but gave primacy and emphasis to the first.

Let's look now at what Jesus called the first and great command. He begins his response to the questioner by quoting from Deuteronomy 6:4, a portion of Scripture called the Shema: "Hear, O Israel: The Lord our God is one Lord." The Lord is the one true and living God. The psalmist sings, "All the gods of the peoples are idols; but the LORD made the heavens" (Ps. 96:5). He is the almighty creator, the self-revealing one, in contrast to all the gods of merely human making.

Further he is described here as "our God" and as "your God." This is the language of covenant. Right at the heart of Israel's faith was the conviction that God had chosen them to be his special people and had drawn them into a covenant relationship with himself. He had acted first on their behalf, loving them, calling them, making himself known to them, and delivering them from bondage and misery.

In other words, the love for God commanded here is a response to the prior, steadfast love of God. God prefaces all his commands to his people by saying, "I am the LORD your God, who brought you out of the land of Egypt, out of the house of bondage" (Exod. 20:2). They are to obey him out of loyal gratitude. They are to love him because he first loved them.

Can you see what a difference this makes? There's a sense in which love cannot be commanded. No one can be compelled to love another person. Conformity can be legislated and enforced, perhaps, but love never. Think of a child growing up in a home where he or she is not loved. The parents may insist that this child show them love. They may require expressions of affection and may punish all disobedience, but the child who has not known love will scarcely be able to give it. Children learn what love is by feeling its warmth and power in the family circle, seeing it expressed, and hearing it spoken. Then from the heart they are free to give an answering love.

A god who did not love us first would not be the God of Abraham, Isaac, and Jacob, not the God and Father of our Lord Jesus Christ. A god who demanded love without giving it would be only a tyrant insisting on the impossible. The true God, the living God, who bids us love him, has first demonstrated to his human children what love really is.

Notice the kind of love he asks for: "with all your heart, and with all your soul, and with all your mind, and with all your strength." The love we're called to give is wholehearted (that is, undivided), and it's with all the soul (full of enthusiasm and zest). It's love with a desire to know God better and better and to be in closer fellowship. It's a love that compels us to pour all our efforts and all our energies in seeking after him. This, apparently, is the only fitting response to the total, intense love with which God has first loved us.

It's a love that excludes any rival, that holds back nothing, that keeps on growing and deepening all the time. Someone has said that by love we mean at least these attitudes and actions: rejoicing in the presence of the beloved with gratitude, reverence, and loyalty. God seeks from his beloved children all of that to the limit of their capacity and to the end of their lives.

The second command is also a call to love—to love our neighbors. The neighbor in Israel was usually considered to be a kinsman, one of the twelve tribes. For some, that was further extended to include proselytes. These were Gentiles who had thrown in their lot with Israel. When Jesus taught about neighbor love he made the hero of his story a despised Samaritan who showed compassion for an Israelite. To Jesus, then, the neighbor we are called to love is anyone in need.

We are to love that neighbor, he says, as ourselves. What does that mean? I've sometimes heard it said that this is an indirect command of God to love ourselves and thus a divine call to self-esteem. It's further taught that the reason we cannot love other people is that we do not adequately love ourselves, so our first duty is to learn how to value and care for ourselves. Then, presumably, we will have the inclination and the resources to love our neighbors.

Now, few of us would question the importance of self-esteem. We are learning more and more in our generation about the value of a healthy self-acceptance, but it's one thing to say that people need a clear sense of personal identity, and it's another to say that God has included that in the second great command.

Whatever our state of psychological health, most of us tend to be primarily concerned about ourselves, don't we? We're inclined to seek our own comfort, security, and advantage. When faced with the claims of a neighbor's need and our own, we are likely to pursue self-interest first. This commandment views us not as ideal selves, not as we will be when we have properly learned self-esteem, but as we are in our normal way of living. It calls us to show the same concern for another's well-being as we customarily show for our own. As a modern psychiatrist has put it, "when the satisfaction, security, and development of another person become as significant to you as your satisfaction, security and development, then love exists."[†]

How are people led to this way of living? Will healthy self-esteem automatically produce this kind of neighbor love? It hardly seems so. You and I know many who think highly of themselves, who pursue vigorously their own interests, who are brimming over with self-confidence, but who show little concern for the needs of their fellow human beings.

Will the command itself produce obedience? We know human nature and ourselves well enough to know that that doesn't happen. Simply knowing what we ought to do doesn't result in perfect performance on our part. In fact, we sometimes experience a kind of perverseness in ourselves, a tendency to rebel against norms and commands, even to move in the opposite direction.

Of what value for us then are these great commands, to us who are prone to forget God and take advantage of our neighbors? The one who voiced them, Jesus of Nazareth, is the one who keeps these commands from being a counsel of despair. His life fulfilled them. Jesus' love for God his Father was the most evident, controlling, and remarkable feature of his life. With a passionate intensity, he sought his whole life long to obey the Father's will, to accomplish his work, and to glorify his name. Wholehearted love for God was the open secret of Jesus' life.

Out of this loving relationship with the Father came his amazing compassion for people. He loved them more than he loved his own life. He spent himself on their behalf, giving himself up to die for their sins. He took all their woes on himself that he might make them truly blessed. In Christ we have the perfect pattern of what it means to love God and love one's neighbor.

But if that were the whole story, we would still be a people without hope. We would have before us only a shining ideal—impossible to accomplish—only a standard that reveals our waywardness and moral bankruptcy. Jesus does more than show us the way. He is the way. In his self-giving for our sakes, he reveals the Father's love and so bears our

[†] Harry S. Sullivan. *Conceptions of Modern Psychiatry*, Norton, 1953.

condemnation that we may find in him total forgiveness for all our sins and all our failures to love.

Best of all, on the first Easter morning, God raised Jesus from the dead. Jesus is alive, exalted, and reigning on the throne of the universe. As the risen Lord, he has sent his Holy Spirit to dwell in the lives of his people. This is the promise of the new covenant. God had declared through his prophets that a day would come when all God's people would know him, experience his gracious forgiveness, and have the law of God written on their hearts. Then the great commands to love God and love our neighbors would not be simply an external code but an inward power, not just a demand from without but an inner disposition. That's what the gift of the Holy Spirit provides. When we realize in Jesus Christ, God's wonderful love and forgiveness, we are moved by his Spirit to love God with an answering love and to love others more and more as the Lord has loved us.

So when you listen to Jesus' teaching about what the greatest commandment is, you need to not only heed what he said but also remember who he is, the life he lived, the death he died. You need to trust him as the living one who provides forgiveness for all your sins and who gives a new dynamic to make you more and more a genuinely loving person.

Study Questions

1. Evaluate this statement: "Love cannot be commanded."
2. What makes it possible for people to love God? Explain.
3. How are the two great commands related?
4. How does God's law come to be "written on our hearts"?

42

Listening to Jesus: Giving

♦

And he sat down opposite the treasury, and watched the multitude putting money into the treasury. Many rich people put in large sums. And a poor widow came, and put in two copper coins, which make a penny. And he called his disciples to him, and said to them, "Truly, I say to you, this poor widow has put in more than all those who are contributing to the treasury. For they all contributed out of their abundance; but she out of her poverty has put in everything she had, her whole living."

[Mark 12:41–44]

THIS GOSPEL ACCORDING TO MARK fairly pulses with action. Jesus seems to move swiftly from place to place. He teaches. He heals. He casts out demons. He does wonderful works. Then he hastens on. That makes it all the more striking when we come on a passage where Jesus is said to be sitting down, simply watching something.

Try to picture the scene in your mind. Jesus is in the temple precincts, sitting down in what is called the court of the women. There, against the wall, are thirteen large trumpet-shaped receptacles into which worshipers cast their offerings. Jesus watches what goes on there with keen interest. He sees the wealthy and finely robed making their large contributions. A murmur of awe passes through the crowd as they see one princely gift after another. The common people, Israel's middle class, also bring their gifts. Some of these are modest, some substantial. The people keep watching for another rich person to approach. They stand at a respectful distance but strain forward intently as another grand offering is presented.

Jesus seems strangely unimpressed by all this until a woman, obviously very poor, makes her way toward the wall. She clenches in her hand two tiny copper coins, looks at them, and tosses them into the treasury. As she's about to slip away, Jesus calls his disciples and points her out to them. He's animated now. This woman, he says, has put in more than all the rest.

This arresting little account reminds us that there are different ways of measuring what people give to God's work. First, there's a conventional, commonsense way. You see that in the crowd there in the temple courts. They are awed by the splendid contributions of the rich and dazzled by the flash of gold and silver as great wealth passes into the temple treasury.

All of us can identify to some degree with that feeling. We read in our newspapers how a wealthy benefactor has given tens of millions of dollars to her favorite charity. A prominent entertainer pays the whole cost of an expensive humanitarian project. A sports personality gives a tithe of his huge signing bonus. That's really something! we say. And it is. Who can dispute the fact that such gifts make many good things possible? What buildings can be built, what projects launched, what equipment bought, with one of these multimillion-dollar donations?

On the other hand, we tend to give scant attention to the gifts of the poor. The prospect of their giving awakens interest that is mild at best. No one will publicize what they have done. No one will praise them, cater to them, fawn over them, as is sometimes done for the rich. After all, the amount is so trifling. It's only a tiny fraction of what a person of means could do. We're inclined to see the gifts, for example, of elderly people, out of small social security pensions, as almost insignificant.

Apparently there's another way of looking at these things. It's the Lord's way. Jesus doesn't deny, of course, that the wealthy have given large sums. He would surely have acknowledged that they contributed much. What he especially wanted to say, however, was that the poor widow gave more, more than any one of those rich donors, maybe more than all of them put together. What sense can we make of that?

The wealthy have contributed, Jesus observes, out of their abundance. They made their contribution out of a large surplus. After having given, they still had plenty left. Some of them would hardly miss the large sum they had just given away.

What the woman did was quite different. Jesus says she gave out of her want, out of her lack, out of her limitation. She was a woman living on the poverty line, or perhaps far below it. Those two little copper coins (let's say they had the value of one of our pennies), were the sum total of her wealth. They were all she had. When she had given them away, there was nothing left. In the strictest sense of that word, she was then penniless. Apparently, that's what made her gift so large, so significant in the eyes of Jesus. It was given out of the depths of need.

All this must have been startling, almost incomprehensible to the disciples. Jesus had said on another occasion that it's easier for a camel to go through the eye of a needle than for a rich man to enter the kingdom of God. The disciples then were exceedingly astonished and said to him, "Then who can be saved?" They had believed that the rich in Israel surely had the best of chances for entering the kingdom. They had leisure to attend all the temple services. They could buy the finest animals for sacrifice. And, obviously, they could bring magnificent gifts. If they were ruled out, who could possibly make it? Maybe they registered some of the same astonishment when they heard how Jesus measured gifts to God's work. They couldn't understand it.

Heaven's register of great givers is apparently different than ours. Names are listed there but not in order of the size of their monetary contributions. In heaven's calculation, the value of your gift, the largeness of your generosity, is measured not by the sum you have given but by the amount you retain for yourself.

Let's try to translate that into practical terms for our lives. Suppose I want to give more to God's kingdom this year than last. It won't be a matter simply of noting my checkbook stubs so that I can be sure to contribute more dollars this year than I did last year. If I'm going to be a better giver, it will involve offering up a higher percentage of what I receive. But more important, in the eyes of Jesus, what I have left should be less than what I had left over at the end of last year.

We may estimate the growth of our giving over the years by its gradual increase, by the greater number of causes we now support and so on. Or we may do it in this radical way by measuring the increasing limitation of our remaining resources, which means that we must more and more depend on God.

When we had a fund drive in our local church some time ago, the organization helping us popularized the motto for our campaign, "Not equal gifts but equal sacrifice." I ask myself as I think about that, "Is there an element of sacrifice in my giving? Are there things I cannot do or cannot buy and places I cannot go because of it? How am I limited? How am I inconvenienced? Am I put at risk in any way? Am I forced to pray for daily provisions because of what I give?"

Now we're touching on the heart of things. Let's not misunderstand. Let's not imagine that God is a heavenly skinflint who wants to keep his children poor and delights when they are deprived. He doesn't despise the large gifts of the wealthy as though they had no significance or did no good. It is surely better that rich people share their means than keep it to themselves.

What God looks for in our giving is what it says about our relationship to him. I know a man who has struggled along on a salary that seems to us painfully small. Unfailingly, however, he gives away a tithe of what he receives. When someone asked him about that, how on such a limited income he could afford to give away a tenth, he answered with a touch of whimsy, "When you're making what I make, you can't afford not to tithe." He was saying that all his hope was in the blessing of God. All his security was in the Lord. And the most important thing for him was to honor God.

The peril of wealth for all of us is that we so quickly tend to trust in our riches and find in them our security for the future. Finding his security in his wealth was the tragic error of the man Jesus spoke about in Scripture, whom we call the rich fool.

The land of a rich man brought forth plentifully; and he thought to himself, "What shall I do, for I have nowhere to store my crops?" And he said,
"I will do this; I will pull down my barns, and build larger ones; and there
I will store all my grain and my goods. And I will say to my soul, Soul,
you have ample goods laid up for many years; take your ease, eat, drink,
be merry." But God said to him, "Fool! This night your soul is required of
you; and the things you have prepared, whose will they be?" So is he [says
Jesus] who lays up treasure for himself, and is not rich toward God.

[Luke 12:16–21]

It apparently never occurred to this man to share his growing wealth.
Instead, he would store it up for his own future use—more than he could
ever need. Instead of setting his hope in the living God who gives us all
things richly to enjoy, he depended on all that accumulated wealth to
give him a safe and happy future. He was a fool because he forgot God.
It escaped his mind that everything he called "mine" had really come as
a gift from God's fatherly hand.

When we give out of need, give beyond worldly prudence, it's a way
of saying that God is the highest good for us, that his interests come first,
and that he's the one finally who sustains our lives and in whom we place
our hope.

When we give out of abundance, we may give very little of ourselves.
To us, it's a trifle. We hardly miss it. When we give as this widow did, it's
like giving our whole lives. God looks for those who will give their hearts
and themselves. Remember those famous lines from James Russell Lowell, "The gift without the giver is bare; Who gives himself with his alms
feeds three—Himself, his hungering neighbor, and me."[†]

Apparently, some of the early Christians who heard the good news of
Christ and believed it began to give in this remarkable way. Paul writes
about some of them. "We want you to know, brethren, about the grace
of God which has been shown in the churches of Macedonia, for in a
severe test of affliction, their abundance of joy and their extreme poverty
have overflowed in a wealth of liberality on their part" (2 Cor. 8:1–2).
Notice that combination: extreme poverty, abounding joy, and gener-

---

[†] James Russell Lowell, "The Vision of Sir Launfal."

ous giving. It goes on: "For they gave according to their means, as I can testify, and beyond their means, of their own free will [out of their want and in the area of risk], begging us earnestly for the favor of taking part in the relief of the saints" (vv. 3–4). In other words, they were pleading to be allowed to give. "And this [Paul concludes], not as we expected, but first they gave themselves to the Lord and to us by the will of God" (v. 5).

That's it. They first gave themselves to the Lord. Giving that is great in God's sight arises out of a wholehearted self-offering to him, a glad and grateful commitment. Why is it, we wonder, that people give in that way, that poor people extend themselves to give beyond their ability? It's because they have caught a glimpse of God's generous heart. Paul writes, "For you know the grace of our Lord Jesus Christ, that though he was rich, yet for your sake he became poor, so that by his poverty you might become rich" (v. 9). There it is: the Lord starts out being unimaginably rich and out of a heart of great love willingly becomes poor to enrich others. People who give in that style are people who indeed know the grace of our Lord Jesus Christ.

Study Questions

1. Describe the "commonsense" view of significant giving.
2. How does this differ from the perspective expressed by Jesus?
3. Why, as you understand it, are gifts out of great need most highly valued in heaven?
4. What is the most compelling motive for Christian generosity?

43

Listening to Jesus: Endurance

◆

And you will be hated by all for my name's sake. But he who endures
to the end will be saved.

[Mark 13:13]

IT WAS DURING JESUS' LAST DAYS with his disciples, when the shadow
of the cross was already looming across his path that he gave them a
glimpse of their future. It was at once grim and glorious. His prophecy
was chilling, but his promise was full of comfort.

Notice first that the hostility his followers would experience was because
of Jesus himself. "You will be hated by all," he says, "because of my name."
There would come circumstances in the lives of his people when they
would be surrounded by hostility, when an encompassing culture would
despise them, and when they would feel themselves hated by all.

Does that sound extreme? Is it unimaginable to you that devout
believers in Jesus Christ should be so regarded, so treated by their contemporaries? However it may seem to us, it was not at all strange to the
original readers of Mark's Gospel. They were Christians who lived in the
imperial city of Rome, and many of them had experienced the reality of
which Jesus spoke. In the time of Nero, for example, persecution threatened to divide and decimate the church of Jesus Christ. Christians in
Rome were being regarded as hateful despisers of their fellow human

beings, enemies of the human race. Their allegiance to Jesus was seen as an evil superstition for which they endured the worst of punishments. Nero treated them as the vilest of criminals, for whom no ignominy or torture was too extreme. Followers of Christ have met with similar treatment in every generation of the Christian era.

It still happens today. Believers in Nepal have been harassed and driven from their churches, imprisoned, and pressured to deny their faith. There are those in northern Nigeria whose churches have been leveled and whose homes have been burned by fanatical adversaries. Missionaries on several continents have been kidnapped, beaten, imprisoned, and shot because of their loyalty to Christ.

That's the heart of it, according to Jesus. This treatment comes to Christians, he says, "because of my name"—because they are identified with him. In Acts 9 there is an account of the apostle Paul's conversion to Christ. Paul, then Saul, had been a relentless persecutor of Christians. He had arrested them, compelled them to blaspheme, sent them to prison, and voted for their execution. He had received orders to pursue them, even to far-away cities, and bring them back in bonds. When the risen Lord appeared to him on the Damascus road, Saul heard a voice saying, "Saul, Saul, why do you persecute me?" And when he answered, "Who are you, Lord?" the voice said, "I am Jesus, whom you are persecuting." Think of that. The exalted Christ describes the outrages committed against his followers as persecution of himself. They are the members of his body. Whatever is done to them is ultimately done to him.

This is what transforms persecution and suffering for the disciples of Jesus. We read of believers in the Book of Acts who actually rejoiced after they had been stoned. Why? Because they had been counted worthy, we read, to suffer shame for the name of Jesus. Paul describes that as the greatest of privileges, a wonderful kind of gift from heaven, "For it has been granted to you that for the sake of Christ you should not only believe in him but also suffer for his sake" (Phil. 1:29). He writes to the Colossians, "In my flesh I complete what is lacking in Christ's afflictions for the sake of his body, that is, the church" (Col. 1:24). When believers suffer for Christ, in other words, they suffer with him. They bear his reproach.

When speaking of his own ministry, the Lord said that the opposition of people to God descended on him. In Psalms it says about him, "The reproaches of them that reproached thee are fallen upon me" (Ps. 69:9 KJV). Hostile people expressed their rebellion against God by hating and rejecting Jesus. And now that he, the crucified one, is risen from the dead, the opposition of an unbelieving world to him is visited on his faithful followers. This is the lot of those who name the name of Jesus. They should not be surprised when hostility surrounds them. Jesus said it would be so: "In the world you have tribulation." "You will be hated . . . for my name's sake."

His great charge to his servants in the midst of the world's opposition is that they should endure. The Greek word means literally "to remain under," that is, to stand one's ground, to hold steady instead of fleeing in fear. We think of endurance sometimes as the ability to withstand hardship or persecution, without giving up or giving in. We understand it as the capacity to keep performing, keep doing what we're called to do, even under the most adverse conditions. In general, it means "hanging in there," acting with moral courage and strength when conditions are the very worst.

Jesus is the pattern for his people in this. In the letter to the Hebrews, he is described as "the pioneer and perfecter of our faith, who for the joy that was set before him endured the cross, despising the shame, and is seated at the right hand of the throne of God" (Heb. 12:2). Believers are invited to "consider him who endured from sinners such hostility against himself" (v. 3) so that they may not grow weary or fainthearted. The apostle Peter speaks of how Jesus bore the most abusive treatment in the most remarkable way. "When he was reviled, he did not revile in return; when he suffered, he did not threaten; but he trusted to him who judges justly" (1 Peter 2:23). Peter holds this up as an example for all who trust in Christ "that you should follow in his steps."

Jesus speaks here of the one who "endures to the end." The verb has no object. He doesn't say what the person must endure. Sometimes it is persecution, sometimes hostility, sometimes the most severe suffering. The one who endures to the end simply keeps on bearing it as long as there are trials to endure.

I was talking with a Russian friend not along ago. We were speaking of the different attitudes toward suffering among our countrymen. It seems that the people of his land are inclined to accept suffering as an essential part of life, whereas we Americans often tend to look on it as an unpleasant surprise, something we weren't prepared for. If we have to suffer, something must have gone terribly wrong, and frequently we feel that someone therefore ought to be sued! Perhaps this is a difference of culture and history. Or, more profoundly, it may be a difference in the seriousness with which we have taken the words of Jesus.

With him, the capacity to endure is tremendously significant. He lets his followers know that there will be plenty to bear. It seems that love and endurance are the two poles of the Christian life as Jesus understands it: doing good and bearing ill. And the two are often strangely joined. Isn't it astonishing that Jesus who was love incarnate, who went about doing good, should be treated with such extraordinary cruelty? And that some of the most humble and helpful of his servants should be hated, hounded, even martyred? It gives us a glimpse of how much we all need a savior, of how much there is in our hearts of rebellion against God. For the Lord and his followers, life in this present world definitely calls for endurance.

He cheers our hearts with a great promise, "He who endures to the end will be saved." The early Christians heard well this note in Jesus' teaching. They took it to heart. James wrote, "Blessed is the man who endures trial, for when he has stood the test he will receive the crown of life which God has promised to those who love him" (James 1:12). Paul declares, "If we endure, we shall also reign with him" (2 Tim. 2:12). The writer to the Hebrews writes to suffering Christians: "Recall the former days when, after you were enlightened, you endured a hard struggle with sufferings, sometimes being publicly exposed to abuse and affliction, and sometimes being partners with those so treated. For you had compassion on the prisoners, and you joyfully accepted the plundering of your property, since you knew that you yourselves had a better possession and an abiding one. . . . You have need of endurance," he goes on, "so that you may do the will of God and receive what is promised" (Heb. 10:32–34, 36). That's the glorious hope, which the Lord holds out before his people: first the groaning, then the glory; first the cross and then the crown.

I'm sometimes asked what Jesus means when he says that those who endure to the end will be saved. Is this, they wonder, an additional requirement for salvation? The Bible clearly teaches that for any of us to be saved we must repent and believe the good news. We must acknowledge our sins and turn from them to God. We must trust in Jesus Christ, crucified and risen, as our personal Savior. But when we have done that, the promises of God seem to assure us that we are saved. All our sins are forgiven. We are freely justified before the bar of God's justice. We are completely accepted in the beloved one, Jesus Christ. What can it mean then to be further told, "He who endures to the end will be saved"?

Does this mean that my works, my performance are, after all, the deciding factor, that even though the Bible speaks much of salvation by grace, it's only those who have the grit to hold out who can possibly make it? Does it all come down to a kind of salvation by works, or at least salvation by willingness to endure?

No, that can't be the way it is. For Jesus, salvation was completely God's work—his gift from beginning to end—impossible with men but possible with God. Salvation is a new birth, the work of God's Spirit—sovereign, unpredictable, and free. Jesus assured all who would listen that those who believed in him have, right now, eternal life.

Some kinds of believing are only apparent. Some kinds of commitment to Christ seem to be only temporary. Jesus speaks of seed that falls by the wayside and is quickly snatched away. What is sown in rocky ground immediately springs up but soon withers. Strikingly, that happens, Jesus says, when persecution comes. Then the stony-ground hearers seem to disappear.

Enduring (persevering), then, is not an additional requirement tacked on to repentance and faith. It's the sign that repentance has been real, that faith has truly received the Savior, Christ, that a person genuinely belongs to the Lord. Believers do not endure in the biblical sense simply because they are more plucky and determined than others. They are as fearful and vulnerable as anyone else, but they have the promise of the Lord, "Lo, I am with you always" (Matt. 28:20). And again, "In the world you have tribulation; but be of good cheer, I have overcome the world" (John 16:33).

Believers are strengthened with might by God's Spirit in the inner man. They endure not by sheer will power, but by watching and prayer, sustained by hope. A few more trials, a few more tears, they know, and then forever with the Lord.

Study Questions

1. According to Jesus, why does the world hate Christians? How do you understand this?
2. In your experience and observation, what kinds of things are Christians called to endure?
3. Is enduring to the end a requirement for salvation? Explain.

44

Listening to Jesus: Watchfulness

❖

Take heed, watch; for you do not know when the time will come. It is like a man going on a journey, when he leaves home and puts his servants in charge, each with his work, and commands the door-keeper to be on the watch. Watch therefore—for you do not know when the master of the house will come, in the evening, or at mid-night, or at cockcrow, or in the morning—lest he come suddenly and find you asleep. And what I say to you I say to all: Watch.

[Mark 13:33–37]

JESUS OFTEN WARNS HIS LISTENERS to be watchful. Whenever he teaches his disciples about the end of the age and his final return to earth, he calls them to be on the lookout and remain vigilant. In this text from Mark we notice the call to vigilance, to expectation, to responsibility, but the basic challenge Jesus is giving to his people in each case is to stay awake.

Why must we stay awake? He says, "because you do not know when the time will come." This is remarkable. "Of that day and hour," he says, "no one knows, not even the angels of heaven, nor the Son, but the Father only" (Matt. 24:36). No one knows the exact time of Jesus' return to earth. The angels that attend God's throne don't know. Even the blessed one, the well-beloved Son, does not know the day and the hour.

Only the Father. Since there is, then, this absolute uncertainty about the time, people are always to be on the alert.

Jesus says further, watch, because the master who has given you your task will come for a reckoning. This is the motif in many of our Lord's parables. The ruler of the household goes away for a time, leaving his servants in charge. At a moment none of them can predict, he will come back and they will need to give an account of their stewardship. The whole mood of the passage says this. Stay awake, people of the Lord! It would be tragic, if after he had appointed you to watch, he came and found you dull, drowsy, and unprepared.

Who is included in this challenge to wakefulness? Jesus tells a little one-verse parable in which apparently one person has that responsibility. He says, "It is like a man going on a journey, when he leaves home and puts his servants in charge, each with his work, and commands the doorkeeper to be on the watch." The challenge is to the doorkeeper, the one who stands by the entrance. It will be to the door that the master comes at the critical moment. The doorkeeper will need to be on the job, remaining alert and ready to welcome back his lord.

The doorkeeper is like the watchmen on the walls of a city. They are especially appointed by their fellow citizens for the task of watching. During their shift, it is of the utmost importance that they remain vigilant. The most acute and perilous failure for a watchman is that he fall asleep on the job.

These images suggest that the assignment is given to particular individuals, but Jesus goes on to widen the call. Listen to his closing words, "And what I say to you I say to all: Watch." He means, then, the four to whom he's just been speaking, Peter, James, John, and Andrew. He means the rest of the twelve. He means all the believers in Rome to whom Mark will later write. He means the whole church, throughout this present age until the final day. No believer is exempt from this assignment. Whatever our particular task and wherever we live and work, we are all called to be alert like doorkeepers, like watchmen on the wall. We all serve under the one great imperative—stay awake!

What does Jesus mean by that? How can his followers stay awake all the time? He surely doesn't expect that his servants will never sleep. In

Gethsemane he found that even his most trusted followers couldn't keep their eyes open for one hour. Not only fatigue but also sorrow and depression had made their eyelids heavy. Obviously we cannot be vigilant through all the hours of every night. We cannot stay at any post of service around the clock. Staying awake must have a deeper meaning than perpetual sleeplessness.

The Lord of love is not a tyrant, demanding of his servants the impossible. He doesn't expect us to keep our eyes open when our bodies are exhausted, our minds weary, and everything in us craves rest. Sleep is his creation, his beautiful gift. In *Macbeth* Shakespeare celebrates it as that which "knits up the ravel'd sleave of care." God does require, however, that in our waking hours, when we are not sound asleep in our beds, we are to be fully awake. In the middle of the day we may be dull and drowsy, in a fog, even while the sun is shining brightly, but we must guard against that happening in our spiritual lives. It's possible to go through life without being in touch with the realities of God and his kingdom, without being aware of what's going on around us. Jesus wants his people so wide awake, so alert to what's happening, that they'll be ready for everything that comes to them and, most of all, ready for his return. How can his followers learn to live in that way?

In Matthew 25 Jesus gives three parables that describe the dimensions of watchfulness. The first is about the ten bridesmaids who took their lamps and went out to meet the bridegroom. Five were foolish, we read, and five were wise. Five were morally and spiritually alert. We could say that the other five were walking in their sleep.

When the foolish took their lamps, they took no oil with them; but the wise took flasks of oil with their lamps. As the bridegroom was delayed, all of them became drowsy and slept. But at midnight there was a shout, "Look! Here is the bridegroom! Come out to meet him." Then all those bridesmaids got up and trimmed their lamps. The foolish said to the wise, "Give us some of your oil, for our lamps are going out." But the wise replied, "No! there will not be enough for you and for us; you had better go to the dealers and buy some for yourselves." And while they went to buy it, the bridegroom came, and those who were ready went with him into the wedding banquet; and the door was shut. Later the other bridesmaids came also, saying, "Lord, lord, open to us." But he replied, "Truly I tell you, I do not know you." Keep awake therefore, for you know neither the day nor the hour.

[Matt. 25:3–13 NRSV]

Here, watching or staying awake means making sure that our faith is not counterfeit, not an imaginary thing that at the last crisis will disappear. It has to be a faith fed by fellowship with God himself that will make us ready to meet the Lord and take our places with him. That's staying awake—being sure that you have oil in your lamp, that you are filled with the Spirit, alive with his life, and by listening and praying you stay in vital touch with the Lord.

The second parable is about the talents. Jesus says,

For it is as if a man, going on a journey, summoned his slaves and entrusted his property to them; to one he gave five talents, to another two, to another one, to each according to his ability. Then he went away. The one who had received the five talents went off at once and traded with them, and made five more talents. In the same way, the one who had the two talents made two more talents. But the one who had received the one talent went off and dug a hole in the ground and hid his master's money. After a long time the master of those slaves came and settled accounts with them. Then the one who had received the five talents came forward, bringing five more talents, saying, "Master, you handed over to me five talents; see, I have made five more talents." His master said to him, "Well done, good and trustworthy slave; you have been trustworthy in a few things, I will put you in charge of many things; enter into the joy of your master." And the one with the two talents also came forward, saying, "Master, you handed over to me two talents; see, I have made two more talents." His master said to him, "Well done, good and trustworthy slave; you have been trustworthy in a few things, I will put you in charge of many things; enter into the joy of your master." Then the one who had received the one talent also came forward, saying, "Master, I knew that you were a harsh man, reaping where you did not sow, and gathering where you did not scatter seed; so I was afraid, and I went and hid your talent in the ground. Here you have what is yours." But his master replied, "You wicked and lazy slave! You knew, did you, that I reap where I did not sow, and gather where I did not scatter? Then you ought to have invested my money with the bankers, and on my return I would have received what was my own with interest. So take the talent from him, and give it to the one with the ten talents. For to all those who have, more will be given, and they will have an abundance; but from those who have nothing, even what they have will be taken away."

[Matt 25:14–29 NRSV]

Here, staying awake or being watchful means using the time that remains before Jesus' coming in a truly profitable way. It means using the abilities we have, investing the gospel he has entrusted to us, and see-ing his kingdom grow. Staying awake means being about our Master's business and winning others to him. To stay asleep, on the other hand, is not to trust our Master, not to heed his word, and to neglect priceless opportunities in his service.

The third parable is the very familiar one about the Son of man sit-ting on the throne of his glory and all the nations gathered before him.

He will separate people one from another [says Jesus] as a shepherd sepa-rates the sheep from the goats, and he will put the sheep at his right hand and the goats at the left. Then the king will say to those at his right hand, "Come, you that are blessed by my Father, inherit the kingdom prepared for you from the foundation of the world; for I was hungry and you gave me food, I was thirsty and you gave me something to drink, I was a stranger and you welcomed me, I was naked and you gave me clothing, I was sick and you took care of me, I was in prison and you visited me." Then the right-eous will answer him, "Lord, when was it that we saw you hungry and gave you food, or thirsty and gave you something to drink? And when was it that we saw you a stranger and welcomed you, or naked and gave you clothing? And when was it that we saw you sick or in prison and visited you?" And the king will answer them, "Truly I tell you, just as you did it to one of the least of these who are members of my family, you did it to me."

[Matt. 25:32–40 NRSV]

Those on the left, on the other hand, are those who saw Jesus' brethren in all their extremities of need and did not minister to them. The King will say to them:

"You that are accursed, depart from me into the eternal fire prepared for the devil and his angels; for I was hungry and you gave me no food, I was thirsty and you gave me nothing to drink, I was a stranger and you did not welcome me, naked and you did not give me clothing, sick and in prison and you did not visit me." Then they also will answer, "Lord, when was it that we saw you hungry or thirsty or a stranger or naked or sick or in prison, and did not take care of you?" Then he will answer them, "Truly I tell you, just as you did not do it to one of the least of these, you did not do it to me."

[Matt. 25:41–45 NRSV]

The first parable speaks about alertness in our relationship to God when we live in conscious dependence on him and are filled with his Spirit. The second speaks about a keen awareness of our stewardship, our responsibility to the Lord for everything we have and all the opportunities he gives us. This third one speaks of a readiness to recognize Jesus in the little people, in the least of those who belong to his family. Staying awake, then, means more than expecting Jesus to come back at the end of the age. It means a sensitivity to his intermediate comings—when he presents himself to us in the people who are the least of his brethren.

It's possible, when we see people in anguish and need, to view them only as statistics and feel no empathy with them. Jesus wants us to feel their wants and hurts in our own hearts, to know our kinship with their humanness and their suffering, and to see in their faces glimpses of the Lord of glory. That to Jesus is what it means to stay awake.

In order to be ready when the Lord comes, we must renew our fellowship with Christ each day so that our lamps stay full of oil. We must use the time, the contacts, and the opportunities of our everyday lives to serve him, bear witness to his name, and win others to him. We must treat people, especially the struggling, suffering ones, as we would treat Jesus if we saw him in need.

Friends, if you do those things, it doesn't matter how many hours you sleep at night or even whether or not you take a nap in the daytime. If you live in that way, you are really staying awake and you'll be ready to meet the Lord when he comes.

Study Questions

1. Why, according to Jesus, should we be watchful?
2. What does it mean to keep on watching?
3. What dimension of watchfulness is brought out in each of these three parables?

45

Listening to Jesus: Prayer and Testing

◆

Watch and pray that you may not enter into temptation; the spirit
indeed is willing, but the flesh is weak.

[Mark 14:38]

JESUS KNEW that the supreme test of his life was just ahead. His hour,
as he had described it, had finally arrived. He was about to be delivered
into the hands of the elders and the chief priests and scribes to be falsely
tried, condemned, and then crucified. He was about to drink the bitter
cup of our condemnation, to feel forsaken for our sake. In the Garden
of Gethsemane on that last night, facing the horror of his death on the
cross, he began to be greatly distressed and troubled. He said to his followers, "My soul is very sorrowful, even to death."

How would he deal with the frightful darkness descending on him?
He would cope with this final test just as he had with every other. He
drew apart to pray. He invoked God as Father with a word of affection
and childlike confidence, "Abba." He confessed his faith, "All things are
possible to thee." He made known his feelings and desire, "Remove this
cup from me." Deeper than all, however, was his commitment to the

Father's purpose. "Yet not what I will, but what thou wilt." He was wide awake and praying with such intensity that sweat ran down from his brow in what seemed like great drops of blood. That's how he prepared for the final test.

He had warned his disciples that testing was ahead for them also. "You will all fall away; for it is written, 'I will strike the shepherd, and the sheep will be scattered.'" They would be under pressure to forsake him in his hour of need, to give in to fear and run away. Peter rejected the warning, at least for himself. "Even though they all fall away, I will not." The Lord replied, "Truly, I say to you, this very night, before the cock crows twice, you will deny me three times." Now it was explicit, direct, personal. Peter protested again. "If I must die with you, I will not deny you." And all the other disciples said the same thing.

Later, in Gethsemane, each man fell asleep. None of them remembered to pray. That's when Jesus gave them this remarkable charge. He came and found them sleeping, and said to Peter, "Simon, are you asleep? Could you not watch [stay awake] one hour? Watch and pray that you may not enter into temptation; the spirit indeed is willing, but the flesh is weak."

The danger was that they would enter into temptation. Sometimes the word *temptation* simply means testing. That would surely come to their Master and to them. The circumstances of Jesus' betrayal, arrest, and crucifixion would try them sorely, and there would be no escape from that. They would be weighed in the balances, their faith and loyalty severely called into question. The peril was that in the midst of all that, they would come under temptation's power. The pressures to deny their Lord and abandon his cause would become fearfully strong, and they might capitulate, fall shamefully, and prove untrue to Jesus.

Now, that's a gloomy, unsettling prospect. It must have been hard to take. How would you have felt if you had been one of those disciples? After all, you had left everything to follow Jesus. You had thrown in your lot with him, heard his teaching, beheld his mighty works. You were in the inner circle of his friends. How could you, a devoted disciple of Jesus, come under the power of temptation, and end up denying him? It didn't seem possible. The disciples couldn't imagine themselves doing that. To a man, they protested that it would never happen.

Imagine that you are Simon Peter. You have confessed your faith in Jesus as the Christ, the Messiah, the Son of the living God. He has given you a new name, the Rock. He promised to build his church on you and your bold confession. You have committed yourself to him for life. Imagine being told now that you, along with the rest, will abandon Jesus and run for your life.

You object, oh, no, Jesus, that cannot be. Maybe that could be true for some of these others but you know me, Lord. I won't let you down. And then imagine Jesus responding to you personally: Listen, before the cock crows twice tonight, you will three times deny that you ever knew me. Then you become even more vehement, "If I must die with you, Lord, I will not deny you." You can't conceive of that possibility, and you are determined that it will never happen to you, but according to Jesus, it is always a possibility that you will come under temptation's power. He later explains why this is the case. "The spirit indeed is willing, but the flesh is weak." The Lord isn't saying here that we are inwardly divided, that part of us is strong and part of us is weak, or that one aspect of our nature is willing and another is wayward. Here *spirit* stands for God and his work in our lives. *Flesh* stands for us.

There came a time in the life of God's people Israel when they were trusting in Egypt for help rather than in the living God. The prophet chides them for that: "Woe to those who go down to Egypt for help and rely on horses, who trust in chariots because they are many and in horsemen because they are very strong, but do not look to the Holy One of Israel or consult the LORD!" (Isa. 31:1). Now here is God's verdict on that situation: "The Egyptians are men, and not God; and their horses are flesh, and not spirit" (v. 3). Men and flesh are on one plane of reality, spirit and God on the other. Flesh, no matter how impressive and powerful it seems, is weak. Only the Holy One is strong.

In Psalm 51 David wrote a great prayer of repentance. "Create in me a clean heart, O God, and put a new and right spirit within me. Cast me not away from thy presence, and take not thy holy Spirit from me. Restore to me the joy of thy salvation, and uphold me with a willing spirit" (vv. 10–12). That willing spirit is always God's gift, for which a penitent people look to him and call upon him. The Spirit who makes us willing, nerves our wills and strengthens our hearts is God's own Spirit, the Holy Spirit. He is the Spirit of power, of love, and of a disciplined mind.

The flesh, on the other hand, is weak. Flesh is not just our physical bodies but our total humanness. We are physically frail and vulnerable to disease and finally to death, and the verdict pronounced over the whole of our life is that we are weak.

The point here is that God and humankind, spirit and flesh, are being spoken of as rival objects of trust. We set our hopes on the Spirit or on the flesh. We trust in God or in ourselves. When we trust in the flesh, we will be sadly disappointed. We will be leaning on a broken reed that cannot support our weight. We'll be going for refreshment to a broken cistern that can hold no water.

Do you see what Simon Peter was doing in this situation? He was trusting in his own resources. He refused to believe that he was in danger of falling because he thought himself a bigger, better man than that. What was Emerson's line in his essay, "Self Reliance"? "Trust thyself, every heart vibrates to that iron string." Something in Peter heartily agreed with that. Others might give way under pressure but not the man they called the Rock. He would take care of himself, thank you. Whatever anyone else did, he would surely be courageous.

When we have this kind of confidence, we forget God's Word, even oppose ourselves to it. Whatever Jesus had said, Peter felt he knew better. He would stand. The writer of Proverbs speaks about leaning to one's own understanding, that is, depending on our own wit and wisdom (Prov. 3:5). It's the very opposite, he says, of trusting in the Lord with all our hearts. The Christians in Laodicea did not see themselves as weak. As a church they said, "I am rich, and increased with goods, and have need of nothing." There was complacency and presumption—the very opposite of trust in God. We can set our hopes, says Paul, on uncertain riches or we can hope in the living God. We think we can withstand what defeats others because we are more spiritual, more loyal, and more courageous than they. Confident in our ability to stand, we sometimes carelessly put ourselves in temptation's way, perhaps by the books and magazines we read, by the movies we watch, by the places we frequent, by the people we let ourselves be alone with, by the dares we accept, or the forbidden things we sample from time to time. That's the kind of pride that goes before destruction, the haughty spirit that precedes a fall. We haven't paid attention to the Lord's verdict about us and our whole human makeup: vulnerable and weak.

The great need of these disciples and our great need is that we watch and pray. To watch means simply to stay awake, to remain alert, to keep vigilant. That's what we do when we recognize our vulnerability and acknowledge our weakness. That's how we walk when we know we are in enemy-occupied territory, when we know we can come under the power of temptation, and when we know it's possible for us to have a moral and spiritual collapse, even to make a shipwreck of our faith. Those who are prone to fall asleep are those who have convinced themselves there's no danger, who believe that, like Samson, they can always rouse themselves and defeat their foes. Those who stay awake, on the other hand, are those who put no confidence in the flesh, no trust in their own unaided abilities. They know they have to be on guard. They know that when the testing comes they could fall away miserably and deny their Lord.

Here's the most important part of all. Jesus calls his followers not only to keep awake but to keep on praying. When the apostle Paul describes the whole armor of God needed to stand against the wiles of the evil one, the crowning part of the equipment is the weapon of prayer. "Pray at all times in the Spirit, with all prayer and supplication" (Eph. 6:18). Prayer is the means by which we don all the other pieces of spiritual armor.

Saint John of the Ladder imagines the voice of one of the deadly sins saying this:

> They who summon me are many. Sometimes it is dullness and senseless-ness of soul that bids me come. Sometimes it is forgetfulness of things above. Aye, and there are times when it is excessive toil. My adversaries [that is, the adversaries of this deadly sin] are the singing of psalms and the labor of the hands. The thought of death is my enemy, but that which kills me outright is prayer.

Prayer is our refuge, our great defense, our mighty weapon against the foe because prayer brings us into living contact with the Lord and brings the power of his Spirit to our aid.

Was Jesus' warning just for those first disciples because they would be there at the time of his arrest? No. Mark included it in this Gospel for those Christians in Rome to whom he was writing and for us today. We all face the same peril, all labor under the same weakness, and all have the same great need.

It's not only in the major crises of life that we need to heed this word. We never know when those are coming anyway. Walking with God in the little things of life prepares us for the large ones. I love this prayer of the psalmist,

> Who can discern his errors? Clear thou me from hidden faults.
> Keep back thy servant also from presumptuous sins;
>   let them not have dominion over me!
> Then I shall be blameless, and innocent of great transgression.
>   [Ps. 19:12–13]

He's praying that God will cleanse him from those secret faults of which he isn't even aware and will keep him back from brazen, conscious willfulness. Then, living moment by moment in God's forgiveness and appealing to him for strength and refuge, he'll be innocent of the great transgression. He won't go down in any kind of final apostasy.

This word of Jesus is a word for every day. We must remain alert, conscious of our weakness and vulnerability, and appeal to God in prayer to fill us and empower us with his Spirit. Then the promise is radiant and reliable for us: We won't come under temptation's power. We can be more than conquerors through him who loved us.

Study Questions

1. What was significant about the way in which Jesus prepared for testing?
2. What does it mean to "enter into temptation"? Explain how this is different from the experience of simply being tempted.
3. What does Jesus mean when he says "the flesh is weak"?
4. How does prayer get us ready for whatever we must face?

46

Listening to Jesus: The New Covenant

◆

And as they were eating, he took bread, and blessed, and broke it, and gave it to them, and said, "Take; this is my body." And he took a cup, and when he had given thanks he gave it to them, and they all drank of it. And he said to them, "This is my blood of the covenant, which is poured out for many."

[Mark 14:22–24]

COVENANT is not a word we use every day. A covenant is a kind of agreement, a formal, solemn, official sort of bond, intended to be binding always. Both parties to a covenant commit themselves with promises. They pledge that they will be faithful to the terms of the agreement and sometimes exchange gifts as signs of the covenant between them.

The covenant we are probably most familiar with in everyday life is the marriage covenant. In marriage a man and a woman commit themselves to each other. "I, John, take you, Mary, to be my wedded wife. I, Mary, take you, John, to be my wedded husband."

Then follow the vows. "And I do promise and covenant before God and these witnesses to be your loving and faithful husband . . . your loving and faithful wife." Sometimes the partners spell out the obligations they are assuming—to love, to cherish, to honor, to keep—and in token and pledge of that covenant they often exchange rings. That seals the agreement. They sometimes even say, "till death us do part." A marriage is both a happy occasion and a solemn covenant.

Friends sometimes covenant together also, as young David did with his friend Jonathan. Nations make solemn agreements to respect one another's borders or defend mutual interests. All kinds of official transactions involve commitments, promises, and pledges. Much of the fabric of human society depends on people making and keeping such covenants.

In the Bible, covenant is one of the central themes: God making agreements with his people. One of these was formed at Mt. Sinai after God had delivered Israel from their bondage in Egypt. Through Moses, he gave them his Law on tablets of stone—what we call the Ten Commandments. He pledged himself to be their God, their Guide, their Keeper, their Portion. He would be with them always as their loving, faithful Savior.

Their part was to recognize and honor him as their God, to love him, and to keep his commands. This they pledged themselves at Sinai to do. We read about this in the book of Exodus, chapter 24. "All the words which the LORD has spoken we will do," they promised (v. 3). They offered burnt offerings and sacrificed peace offerings of oxen to God. When Moses read to them from the book of the covenant, God's revealed law, they said again, "All that the LORD has spoken we will do, and we will be obedient" (v. 7).

Then, to seal the covenant, Moses took part of the blood of the offerings and sprinkled it on the altar of worship. The rest he sprinkled on the people. This was a covenant by animal sacrifices, a solemn agreement ratified by blood. God the Redeemer and his redeemed people had pledged themselves to each other. He had shown his love for them in choosing, calling, and delivering Israel and in making himself known to them. They had responded to that love in grateful trust and obedience. God and his people were henceforth covenant partners.

The Old Testament is the record of how God kept faith with Israel and how the Israelites proved unfaithful to him. They went aside to other gods. They broke his commandments, forgot his mercies, and turned their backs on him. When he called them to repent and return, they would not listen. Strangely, tragically, they hardened their hearts against his love. Finally, God let them eat the fruit of their own way. Forsaking his protection, they were overwhelmed by their enemies. They suffered terribly, were taken captive, and languished in bitter exile. They had broken covenant with their God. What was left for them then?

One of God's faithful prophets during the exile, Jeremiah, sounded a note of hope in the midst of the darkness.

> Behold, the days are coming, says the LORD, when I will make a new covenant with the house of Israel and the house of Judah, not like the covenant which I made with their fathers when I took them by the hand to bring them out of the land of Egypt, my covenant which they broke, though I was their husband, says the LORD. But this is the covenant which I will make with the house of Israel after those days, says the LORD: I will put my law within them, and I will write it upon their hearts; and I will be their God, and they shall be my people. And no longer shall each man teach his neighbor and each his brother, saying, "Know the LORD," for they shall all know me, from the least of them to the greatest, says the LORD; for I will forgive their iniquity, and I will remember their sin no more.
>
> [Jer. 31:31–34]

Think of that! God would make a new covenant with his people. He would renew the old one which they had broken so dismally. This new covenant would be based on free forgiveness for those who sinned. It would involve also an inner transformation of the people. God's law would no longer be for them an external code written on tables of stone. It would be an inward disposition. God would inscribe it on their hearts; and they would have a new willingness to walk in his ways. Best of all, in the new covenant, God would reveal himself to his people more fully than ever before. From the least of them to the greatest, they would all know him in a rich, personal way.

Now all of that is in the background when the Lord Jesus has the Last Supper with his disciples and when he talks about covenant.

And as they were eating, he [Jesus] took bread, and blessed, and broke it, and gave it to them, and said, "Take; this is my body." And he took a cup, and when he had given thanks he gave it to them, and they all drank of it. And he said to them, "This is my blood of the covenant, which is poured out for many."

[Mark 14:22–24]

We need to understand this in the setting of a Passover meal. Jesus was presiding over the feast as a father would with the members of his family. Step by step he interpreted the elements of the meal. The food had already been served but not yet eaten. As Jesus lifted the platter of unleavened bread, he probably recited the Aramaic formula prescribed in the liturgy, "This is the bread of affliction which our fathers ate in the land of Egypt. Let everyone who hungers come and eat. Let everyone who is needy, come and eat the Passover meal."

Then each of the other elements was also explained in the light of Israel's experience in bondage. The bitter herbs reminded them of their galling slavery. The stewed fruit, which had the consistency and color of clay, recalled their making bricks as slaves. The lamb provided a reminder of God's gracious passing over of Israel when the plague of death came to Egypt.

Just before the meal came the blessing of God for the gift of bread. The head of the family would sit up from his reclining position, take a cake of the bread and recite a blessing over it in the name of all. Those around the table would identify themselves with the blessing by saying their amen. The family head broke a piece for each person present, the bread passing from hand to hand until it reached all the guests.

Then Jesus parted with tradition. While the bread was being distributed, he said, "Take; this is my body." They knew that he was soon to go away. The gift of the bread was a pledge of his continuing presence with them all the days. Even as Jesus prepared for death, this word anticipated his resurrection and his real presence with them later at the Lord's Supper.

After the meal, he took the cup and when he had given thanks, he gave it to them and they all drank. And he said, "This is my blood of the covenant, which is poured out for many."

Do you see how the new covenant became reality? It was to be based, as we saw, on God's free forgiveness. The old covenant had been an agreement by sacrifice, but that involved the blood of animals, which only hinted at God's purpose to deal with sin. The cup at the Last Supper pointed to the outpoured life of Jesus himself. He would suffer for the sins of his people. He would stand in their place, bear their sins, and give his life so that they could be forgiven. Then he would rise from the dead, triumphant over the grave. He would appear to his followers and be received up into heaven. There as the reigning Lord, he would send forth his Spirit to his people. The Holy Spirit would enter the hearts of all who believe in Jesus, bringing to them his risen presence. Christ by the Holy Spirit would transform them within, putting his law into their minds, writing it upon their hearts, and creating in them a new power to obey and love.

And so the heart of the promise would be fulfilled: From the least of them to the greatest, God's people would know him. They would see him more clearly than ever before as revealed in the face of Jesus Christ. They would enjoy the miracle of communion with him. They would experience his presence with them all the days. They would celebrate the crowning miracle of the new covenant.

We live in a world where covenants are often broken. That's one of the saddest realities in our human experience. Nations break their solemn treaties with one another and go to war on a pretext. Business partners renege on their promises to pursue selfish advantage. Husbands and wives break their promises to each other, leaving behind them a trail of broken hearts and scarred lives. What could be sadder than that?

There's something in all of us of the covenant-breaker. In so doing we also break covenant with God. It was before him that we promised that spouse of ours to be faithful unto death. We swore before God to tell the truth when we gave testimony in court or signed an official agreement. Maybe there was a time when we made confession of our faith in Christ and promised to be his faithful disciples throughout our lives, but now we have drifted away and forgotten those vows of ours. We pledged ourselves to bring up our children in the nurture and admonition of the Lord, but perhaps we haven't given much attention to their spiritual welfare, haven't taught them the Word of God, haven't prayed for their hearts to be open to the Lord, and haven't sought to live before them a godly example. All of us have been unfaithful to God in many ways.

Isn't it great to know that there is a new covenant, that into this world of infidelity and broken promises has come a faithful Savior? We sing about that in the first question of the Heidelberg Catechism, "My only comfort in life and death is that I belong, body and soul, not to myself but to my faithful Savior, Jesus Christ." He is the covenant-keeper who stood in our place and fulfilled all righteousness on our behalf. He drank to its bitter dregs the cup of judgment we deserved. Now he's alive, loving us still, mighty to save.

This means that there is a new beginning for everyone in spite of all the sin, all the broken promises and all the wanderings from God. Because Jesus died and rose again, there is forgiveness for you and for me. Because he's alive and sending forth his Holy Spirit, we can be transformed on the inside. God can write his law on our hearts. We can know him as his redeemed children. We can begin to do his will from the heart. Because of the doing and dying, the rising and reigning of Jesus Christ, we can be partners with God in the new covenant and can find in him the power to be faithful to death.

Study Questions

1. What is a covenant?
2. With what kinds of covenants are you familiar?
3. How did God's new covenant differ from the old?
4. How is Jesus central to the new covenant?

47

Listening to Jesus: Being Rejected

◆

A man planted a vineyard, and set a hedge around it, and dug a pit
for the wine press, and built a tower, and let it out to tenants, and
went into another country. When the time came, he sent a servant
to the tenants, to get from them some of the fruit of the vineyard.
And they took him and beat him, and sent him away empty-handed.
Again he sent to them another servant, and they wounded him in
the head, and treated him shamefully. And he sent another, and
him they killed; and so with many others, some they beat and some
they killed. He had still one other, a beloved son; finally he sent
him to them, saying, "They will respect my son." But those tenants
said to one another, "This is the heir; come, let us kill him, and the
inheritance will be ours." And they took him and killed him, and
cast him out of the vineyard. What will the owner of the vineyard
do? [asked Jesus.] He will come and destroy the tenants, and give
the vineyard to others. Have you not read this scripture: "The very
stone which the builders rejected has become the head of the corner; this was the Lord's doing, and it is marvelous in our eyes"?

[Mark 12:1–11]

MOST OF US KNOW how it feels to be rejected. You applied to a certain
college or trade school and were turned down. You tried for a coveted

job and went for an interview, but they hired someone else. You submitted a manuscript you had worked on for a long time, but the publisher somehow wasn't interested. Rejection.

Sometimes it's more painful still. Perhaps your mother and father divorced when you were young and neither wanted to keep you. You were desolate. Or you were in love, wanting more than anything to marry someone, but your dearest said no to you and married another. You were crushed. Rejection again.

There is someone who feels that pain with you and really understands. Jesus Christ the risen Lord shares your sorrow and knows your pain. When he came among us to share our human lot, he tasted rejection. It was more than a taste. He drank that bitter cup right down to the dregs. His whole life seemed to witness one rejection after another. The world to which he came did not welcome him. His own people didn't want him around. There was no room at the inn. Wily King Herod tried to kill Jesus while he was still a baby. When he began his public ministry, the townspeople in his village tried to push him off a cliff (see Luke 4:16–30). He was rejected by his own.

The super-religious of his day couldn't stand him. The clever scholars tried to trip him up in argument. The rulers of his nation plotted against him. They finally arrested him, flogged him, spat on him, and derided his claims. Finally the mighty Roman empire pronounced him unfit to live. He died on the cruelest instrument of torture ever devised while his enemies looked on, taunting and jeering. Yes. He was despised and rejected of men, a man of sorrows and acquainted with grief.

Jesus seemed to realize all through his ministry that this kind of treatment awaited him. His parable about the owner of the vineyard made it piercingly plain. Here, if ever, is a story of rejection. Three things about it amaze me and leave me shaking my head. The first is the terrible heartlessness of the tenants in the story who treated so badly the innocent messengers from the faraway landlord. Simply doing their job, these emissaries were there to receive what rightfully belonged to their master, but they were treated with the most savage hatred. The first was beaten and sent off with nothing. The second was publicly disgraced and gravely wounded. The third was actually killed. There followed a long succession of other messengers, each one meeting with abuse and violence. None escaped harm, and many died. Finally the master's son appeared and the tenants poured out their most brutal hostility on him. They threw his lifeless body out of the vineyard as though it were the carcass of a beast.

How could they act in that way? Surely the story is exaggerated. How could they possibly hate the lord of the vineyard that much? We read of no harm he has done them. They express no grievance, yet they treat him with implacable hatred and bitter contempt. They insult and reject him and his messengers. Not content with that, they murder the son who means more to him than his own life. The venom of their hostility is frightening, repulsive, unimaginable.

Jesus is telling here the story of his own people and how they rejected God's prophets. God is the Lord of the vineyard. Israel is the vine of his planting. The prophets are the servants who call the people to faithful stewardship. Can we believe what happened to them? Isaiah, the herald of faith, sawn asunder. Jeremiah tortured, thrown into a well, and finally slain by his countrymen. Elijah driven into hiding. Zacharias stoned to death. John the Baptist beheaded. God's spokesmen are despised and destroyed by the very ones who claim God's name.

When God sends his son, their malice bursts all bounds. They try him on false charges. Though he has never wronged anyone, they treat him like a vicious criminal. They subject him to every kind of indignity and finally torture him to death. This story Jesus told would have been incredible if it hadn't happened just that way in his own experience.

Is it so much different in modern times? Recall the names of those in this century who have spoken for God, struggled for justice, or pled for peace. How many of them have been gunned down in the streets for their trouble! So great is our passion to see the inheritance as ours, to treat God's gifts as our possessions, and to rule over what is only entrusted to us, that we seem to hate every suggestion that we and what we have could belong to someone else. So we discover to our horror that this tense, bitter story is somehow our story. We are there.

The second feature in the parable that amazes me is the patience of the owner. Imagine a powerful landowner bearing with even the first insult from such tenants. Wouldn't he march quickly with men at arms to put down this rebellion? This landlord keeps on sending messengers, and when they are ignored, abused, even killed, his response is to send still others. When these meet the same fate, he sends still more. Amazingly, they are all envoys of peace and unarmed—like lambs being sent to the slaughter.

Again, we couldn't take all that seriously if it hadn't happened that way in Israel's history. God sent one prophet after another to remind the people of their covenant responsibility, of what they owed to the God who had given them everything, but they shut their ears, stiffened their necks, hardened their hearts, and rejected one ambassador after another. God kept sending more. He described that process more than once as "rising up early and sending" them. It almost seemed as though he couldn't wait to provide another victim when the people had just banished or slaughtered one of his servants.

Now comes the part that seems most absurd. The master in the parable has exhausted his corps of messengers. There's scarcely anyone left to send. Whom can he throw to these wolves now? The cynical answer would be hire someone you have a grudge against and send him! But there's another plan. The master has a son, one son. This boy is the joy of his life, the bearer of all his hopes. He loves him as his own life. He decides to send him. Surely, he says to himself, they will reverence my boy.

What's our reaction to that? How foolish! How naïve can you be? Haven't you learned anything from what's already happened? Isn't it enough to lose your faithful servants? Are you going to put your own boy at the mercy of these killers? How will his mother feel about that? But he sent him, and quite predictably the son never had a chance. The killers made short work of him.

Would a landlord really act that way? Of course not! But God did. When we deserved the worst, he gave his best. When the world was ripe for judgment day, God sent Christmas instead. By all human logic, he played the fool. He walked right into it, gave his Son to be crucified, put his heart out there to be broken. Stranger than the wildest fiction is this longsuffering love of God.

One more thing that startles me here is the place Jesus gave to himself in the story. It's all too plain to see who the characters represent. The tenants are the chosen people, especially their leaders, those to whom God has entrusted his vineyard. God himself is the owner. The servant-messengers are his prophets. And the only son, this beloved of the father—there's no mystery there either—Jesus is describing himself.

Can you imagine any man anywhere, anytime, claiming to be the only Son of God? The prophets were men like Moses, Elijah, and Isaiah, who tower as giants among their fellows. They've known few peers in the long history of our race, but to Jesus, they are simply among the servants. He alone is the beloved Son.

Would you take something like that seriously if it came from anyone else? Wouldn't you smile indulgently or dismiss such a claim with contempt? Wouldn't you write it off as egomania, self-deception, or sheer rubbish? Somehow on the lips of Jesus it rings true. We could never have believed that a life like his were possible if it hadn't been lived out there in Galilee in Judea. How can such opposites be blended—meekness and majesty, lordship and lowly service, pity and awesome power?

Study the life of Jesus. Watch him as he walks through every day. Hear the things he said. There's not a false note anywhere. Can anyone seriously consider that the awesome personage who emerges from the Gospels could be deranged or a fraud? Yet hear how he said it straight out: I am the unique Son of the Father whom you are about to reject and crucify.

Why do you suppose Jesus told the parable? You remember the end of the story. The vinedressers are punished, the vineyard turned over to others. The climax is rejection, loss, doom. Why did he tell about that? It was surely to expose what his enemies were about to do: to lift up the persistent love of God and to reveal him as the only Son. It was never meant to be only a declaration of what is or a prophecy of what would be. Jesus must have told it with anguish, maybe even with tears. It was a wake-up call, an urgent word of warning, a summons to repent.

And why did the Gospel writers include it in their narratives? Again, it was not simply to explain what had happened on Golgotha. This became part of the gospel. Even the crucifixion couldn't destroy that invincible, seeking love of God. Christ is risen. Now in the light of all this, in spite of all this, there is mercy and hope for guilty rebels, for selfish vinedressers, even for those whose sins caused God's Son to die.

Now listen to the words with which Jesus concluded: "The very stone which the builders rejected has become the head of the corner; this was the Lord's doing, and it is marvelous in our eyes." The gospel is a story of rejection, yes, but also of triumph and restoration. God turned the tables. God raised his crucified Son from the dead. Christ's resurrection spells redemption for the most guilty and rebellious of us and is the sign that the Lord is among us still, here to claim afresh what rightly belongs to him.

Study Questions

1. What experiences of rejection have you gone through?
2. How do you explain the extreme heartlessness of these tenants?
3. What is extraordinary about the conduct of the landlord?
4. Why do you think this parable is included in the Gospel?

48

Listening to Jesus: His Return

◆

But he was silent and made no answer. Again the high priest asked him, "Are you the Christ, the Son of the Blessed?" And Jesus said, "I am; and you will see the Son of man seated at the right hand of Power, and coming with the clouds of heaven."

[Mark 14:61–62]

THERE ARE TIMES when speaking the truth may be costly, even dangerous. Suppose, for example, that you're called to be a witness at the trial of some Mafia figure. You receive anonymous phone calls that hint grimly at what may happen to you if you testify. Or suppose you know about questionable practices and cover-up attempts in an organization of which you are a part. What do you say when someone asks about this? The truth may be explosive. Or imagine that you have to confront a lifelong friend with some serious charge. In each case it's hard to tell the truth.

One of the titles that the early Christians gave to Jesus Christ was "the faithful witness." They saw him as one who spoke for God with integrity and unswerving loyalty. In saying that, they were affirming his own words about the mission on which he came, "For this was I born," he said, "and for this I have come into the world, to bear witness to the truth" (John 18:37).

This book has dealt with Jesus' teaching on a number of subjects. Finally we look at Jesus' teaching in the form of personal testimony. One of the most remarkable instances of his witnessing faithfulness came in Jesus' trial before the Sanhedrin. It was when the high priest demanded of him, "Are you the Christ, the Son of the Blessed?" As we think about this crisis and Jesus' response to it, we learn a great deal about what it means to tell the truth, to be a faithful witness.

First, quite evidently, it calls for considerable courage. Jesus knew well what was at stake in this trial. The fact that he had been arrested under cover of darkness had ominous overtones. He knew the bitter envy of the religious officials and their fury at what he had been teaching and claiming. When on trial, he had heard already the accusations of several false witnesses, obviously hired to charge him with serious crimes. It was plain that malice more than justice was at work in these proceedings. And when the question was asked, "Are you the Christ, the Son of the Blessed?" Jesus saw clearly how an affirmative answer would be received. It was the occasion his enemies had been hungrily seeking. Who but the brave would speak the truth then?

Anyone can be honest when among supportive, sympathetic friends. It's easy to expound to people a doctrine they already believe and are ready to hear with delight, but truth-speaking is a challenge when our hearers dread and hate what we are about to say. Then fear leaps up to strike us dumb or make us equivocate. We fear retaliation from those whom we may have to expose. We shrink from the loss of face, the ostracism we may meet among those who disapprove of our stand or who criticize us for making trouble. We dread the prospect that no one will stand by us and we'll be left completely alone.

The more richly favored we are and more highly placed, the more frightening it becomes for us to risk everything in the name of truth. Blaise Pascal put it piercingly in his *Pensées*: "Hence each degree of good fortune that raises us in the world takes us further from the truth, because we fear to wound those whose affection is most useful and whose dislike is most dangerous."

In our time Alexander Solzhenitsyn has displayed a rare brand of courage. Few in this generation have known the pressures to which this man was once exposed. All the might of a totalitarian state and all the cunning of its official propaganda were deployed against this one man. Yet as a *Time* article reported in its February 11, 1974, issue.

> After a massive three-week campaign against him, Alexander Solzhenitsyn last week raised his voice in counterattack. The besieged writer defied the Kremlin to refute the charges made in his book *The Gulag Archipelago.* He accused the Soviets of damning Gulag's description of Leninist and Stalinist terror out of an animal fear of disclosure. To his critics, he said, "You liars!" It was an unprecedented moment of confrontation between the state and a lone heroic man.

We are stunned and humbled at such courage, such electrifying witness to the truth.

Solzhenitsyn, of course, had some hopes that he would be spared. The Soviet Union, even in those days, had to deal with a watching world that much admired this author's heroism. He was too well-known to squelch, too symbolic a figure to be put in prison. They finally did to him all they felt they could. They deported him, declaring him a non-person.

For Jesus at his trial, there were no hopes of deliverance. No international press would herald his words. No friendly free world would be prepared to welcome him. The only ones who would hear his response that night would be men bent on destroying him. Not only were the leaders of his people against him, but behind them stood the might of imperial Rome. If he claimed before the Sanhedrin to be the Messiah, his death would surely follow as the night the day. That is precisely what he did. "I am," he said, "and you will see the Son of man seated at the right hand of Power, and coming with the clouds of heaven" (Mark 14:62). He dared to give his accusers exactly what they were looking for. Jesus above all others deserves John Bunyan's famous title: "Valiant for Truth."

Courage in Jesus' case was closely linked to something else. He was certain of the truth he proclaimed. His courage grew in part out of his unshakable personal conviction that what he said was true.

Anyone who reads straight through the Gospel according to Mark is likely to be startled when he comes to this self-witness of Jesus before

Caiaphas because up to this point Mark portrays Jesus as quite reticent in making any claims about himself. For that reason this Gospel has sometimes been called "the gospel of the secret." Jesus seems reluctant to reveal that he is the Messiah. "And he healed many who were sick with various diseases, and cast out many demons; and he would not permit the demons to speak, because they knew him" (Mark 1:34). Jesus said to a leper whom he had cleansed, "See that you say nothing to any one." When afflicted people fell before him and cried out, "You are the Son of God," he strictly ordered them "not to make him known." After he raised from death the daughter of Jairus, he strictly charged the people who had witnessed it that no one should know this. And you can imagine Simon Peter's surprise when after he had made his great confession, "You are the Christ," he heard Jesus' charge not to tell anyone.

Why did Jesus labor in this way to avoid publicity? Why did he shrink from having the crowds know that he was the Messiah? Their notions of what that meant were very different from his and he didn't want to encourage nationalistic hopes or revolutionary expectations. His reserve surely did not mean any doubt on his part that he was God's Son and Israel's Messiah. That became abundantly plain in the drama of this trial.

During the trial Jesus' life was at stake, but he was also under a solemn oath. He had been ordered by the high priest to swear before God that his testimony was true. His character and his credibility were on the line. "Tell us now," fumed the high priest. "Are you the Christ, the Son of the Blessed?" "I am," he answered. No equivocating, no qualifying, no hedging in the slightest. In the most solemnly binding circumstances imaginable, Jesus testified that he was the Son of God, the hope of Israel, the Savior of the world.

Now that, of course, doesn't constitute proof that he is all of that. Many people under extreme pressures have made claims about themselves that weren't founded in fact. What cannot be questioned, however, is that Jesus himself believed what he said. Is it imaginable that anyone so transparently genuine would perjure himself, especially when giving any other answer could have saved his life?

It could also be said that those early Christians who preached the resurrection of Jesus were mistaken or mad. We may contrive ingenious explanations for how they became so deluded, but does it make sense to say that these first-century martyrs were deliberately hoodwinking people? There are all sorts of fanatics in the world, but where are those who joyfully die for what they know to be a lie?

Jesus was so sure that he was the Lord from heaven and the world's one hope that he swore to it and sealed that testimony with his life's blood. It all comes down finally to this: either Caiaphas and the rest were right in charging him with blasphemy, or else Jesus is all that he claims to be.

One more trait of this faithful witness is that Jesus is confident that the truth will finally prevail. Jesus was not content with answering the high priest's question in the affirmative. He went on to predict the consummation of this age and his return to earth. "I am; and you will see the Son of man seated at the right hand of Power, and coming with the clouds of heaven." To the Jewish leaders, Jesus' claim to be the Messiah seemed blasphemous because they saw no evidence to support it. If this were God's own anointed one, then surely he would vindicate him, they thought. This Jesus, on the contrary, was no conqueror, no champion against the heathen nations. He had only a few fickle followers. The really important people in Israel were all against him. What foolish sacrilege to suggest that this forlorn figure, on trial for his life, could be God's mighty Messiah!

The Lord, of course, had been giving evidence of a different kind all through his ministry. The blind had received their sight from his touch. The lame had begun to walk again. Lepers had been cleansed. The oppressed and afflicted had been delivered. Even the dead had been raised to life. The religious leaders chose to overlook all that. Now they wanted him to tell them he was the Messiah. Yes, I am, he said, in effect, and this shall be your evidence. The day will come when you will see with your own eyes that God has exalted his Son as Lord over all. You will look on the one whom you have pierced. You will see him coming in the clouds of heaven with power and glory. In other words Jesus is saying that God himself will attest to this claim on the last day.

For any who follow Christ in our time, faithful witness arises not only from courage and certainty about the truth but also from the sure hope that this truth of God will triumph. Jesus looked death full in the face but knew that God would be his vindicator beyond death—and that all the world would some day know it. When we believe that beyond struggle and suffering is the Lord's "well done," that on the other side of death is sure resurrection, and that God's holy purpose cannot fail, then we, too, have fresh heart to bear our testimony.

Solzhenitsyn describes his arrest and removal to prison in these words:

> The circular upper hall is bathed in electric light, and from the depths of the railway station along two parallel escalators Muscovites rise to meet us in serried ranks. They all seemed to look at me as if expecting me to shout at least one word of truth. Why am I silent? Because these Muscovites standing on the elevator stairs are not numerous enough. My cry would be heard by 200, perhaps 400 people. What about my 200 million compatriots? I have a vague premonition that one day I will scream out for all those 200 million. Once the truth seemed doomed die. It was beaten. It was drowned. It had turned to ashes. But now the truth has come alive. No one will be able to destroy it.[†]

Today this brave man's hopes are being realized in what was formerly the Soviet Union. One day—perhaps soon—the truth of Jesus' words will be confirmed. Those who know the gospel dare to believe that the secret of all history will be revealed when the earth sees the glory of the Lord, when every knee bows to Jesus, and every tongue confesses that he is Lord. At the consummation of all things, we shall meet Jesus.

Study Questions

1. Why was it so dangerous at Jesus' trial for him to answer truthfully?
2. What "safety net" available to Solzhenitsyn was not there for Jesus?
3. Why does the Lord's forthright self-witness seem especially startling in Mark's Gospel?
4. On what can be based the hope that Jesus will indeed return in power and glory to this earth?

[†] *Time*, February 25, 1974.